The New Pioneers

The Men and Women Who Are Transforming
the Workplace and Marketplace

THOMAS PETZINGER, Jr.

SIMON & SCHUSTER

SIMON & SCHUSTER
Rockefeller Center
1230 Avenue of the Americas
New York, NY 10020

Designed by Pagesetters

Manufactured in the United States of America

10 9 8 7 6 5 4 3 2

Library of Congress Cataloging-in-Publication Data
Petzinger, Thomas.
The new pioneers : the men and women who are transforming the
workplace and marketplace / Thomas Petzinger, Jr.
p.   cm.
Includes bibliographical references (p.   ).
1. Industrial management. 2. Corporate culture. 3. Creative ability
in business. 4. Employee motivation. 5. Customer relations. 6. Suggestion systems.
7. Industrial sociology.
I. Title.
HD31.P394   1999
658—dc21   98-5013   CIP
ISBN 0-684-84636-5

To Paulette
And to Beatrice, Eva, and Janis

A door like this has cracked open five or six times since we got up on our hind legs. It's the best possible time to be alive, when almost everything you thought you knew is wrong.

TOM STOPPARD, ARCADIA

Contents

The Age of Adaptation

Lehigh Avenue in Philadelphia could be the main drag of inner-city America. Listless vagrants have the look of drugs in their eyes. Graffiti is painted over graffiti, layered like epochs of urban archaeology. Street-corner vendors display porno alongside the morning papers. Clouds of truck exhaust waft over the avenue. It was here, waiting for a crossing light to change on a bracing late-winter morning in 1995, that I awoke to the existence of an altogether new economy in America.

A giant city bus slowly roared away from the stop across the street, revealing a tiny storefront called Philadelphia Pharmacy. Walking through the door was like entering another world. The store employees radiated hospitality. The narrow aisles were jumping with customers—schoolgirls endlessly studying the makeup choices, mothers selecting household staples, old people filling Medicaid prescriptions—while the unstinting attention of the staff kept the crowd gliding easily through the store. Mostly Hispanic and African-American, mostly unmarried mothers, everyone working in this buoyant place, I soon learned, came from the depressing neighborhood surrounding it.

Everyone, that is, except the owner and head pharmacist, Richard Ost, standing behind the prescription counter in the team jacket of a suburban grade-school hockey team, "a white boy from northeast Philadelphia," as he described himself.

Like so many of his generation he had started out in corporate America, joining Thrift Drug following his graduation from pharmacy school. Almost immediately he was fed up with the frustration and sheer waste of corporate bureaucracy and politics. "I was never made to work for someone else anyway," he told me, echoing a comment I hear time and again from people of his generation. His options as a pharmacist were limited by his $10,000 in available capital, so he purchased an apothecary counter in the only place he could afford—here, in the economically depressed Lehigh Avenue area.

Ost was keen to new technology (new for the time, anyway). With a minimal investment he installed a rudimentary system to churn out prescription labels from a personal computer, printing any of about one thousand common dosages and regimens with the stroke of a key. One day he noticed an assistant, Elizabeth Leon, laboriously preparing a label by hand. "Why are you doing that?" he asked. Leon explained that her customer spoke no English and was refusing to take her medicine because she couldn't understand the label. Ost inquired further. In this largely Hispanic neighborhood, it turned out, many of his customers had the same problem, confusing quantity and frequency, putting eye drops in their mouths, or more likely missing dosages altogether until they could find someone to translate, if they ever did. So occasionally, when she had the time, Leon wrote out the label by hand, in Spanish, instead of hitting the print button on the computer.

Ost was thunderstruck. Of course! Why hadn't he always done it that way? Why didn't every pharmacy do it that way? Soon he and Elizabeth Leon were translating his one thousand standard regimens into Spanish so he and his aides could instantly create a label in either language, a single keystroke choosing between "one tablet twice a day" and "*una tableta 2 veces al dia.*"

From the simple acts of listening to his employee, caring about his customers, and adapting his technology, Ost's business positively exploded. Before long, he expanded into the rehabilitated remains of a torched-out auto parts store, adding a few aisles of general household merchandise. The display space was limited, but employees constantly restocked the shelves, going through half a truckload of merchandise a week. Staffing this expansion was not easy. When Ost found a reliable, committed employee—usually a woman, usually a mother—he locked in her loyalty with family medical benefits, almost unheard of among inner-city employers. He added profit sharing, giving his employees a stake in the sale of every item and the control of every expenditure. He conducted a fortnightly staff meeting to share up-to-the-minute financial results so employees could follow the outcome of their combined actions and figure out where they needed to improve. When a Vietnamese influx swept the Lehigh Avenue area Ost added a third language to his labeling system, as in *"Uong ngay 2 lan, moi lan 1 vien."*

As success begat success Ost could no longer handle the merchandising, ordering, and scheduling alone, so he trained his employees to handle all that themselves. He sent them to merchandising conferences; for some it was their first trip out of town. He issued them business cards so repeat customers could ask for an employee by name rather than language fluency. In the rush of closing time Ost would turn to his janitor and ask, "What do you want *me* to do?"

Ost's actions soon put him on good terms with the community's leadership as well as its rank and file. He became the first Anglo chosen as Hispanic citizen of the year, bringing priceless recognition to Philadelphia Pharmacy. When the nearby Episcopal Hospital needed someone to take over the gift shop and pharmacy concession, it turned to him, giving Ost yet another small location with high volume. Employees at his hospital store distributed a complimentary Spanish-language television guide in the patient wards upstairs with advertisements promoting the specials at his other neighborhood pharmacies. He priced his TastyKakes in the hospital store to return the correct change from a dollar bill for a cup of coffee from the vending machine. It reduced his profit margin a bit, but his snack shelf turned over eight times a day.

By the time of my visit, from his three tiny locations, Ost was doing $5 million worth of business a year—four times more business, square foot by square foot, than the average American drugstore. His prescription volume had grown so large (and his payment record so impeccable) that he began receiving discounts from Merck and other major suppliers on a par with the prices paid by national chains.

From a flagship location spanning less than one thousand square feet, Richard Ost succeeded in his challenging surroundings because he responded smoothly to everything that surrounded him. He did not contrive his way to success; there isn't a five-year plan in the world that would have identified the variety of opportunities Ost created on the fly. He grew his business not by planning but by adapting, not with business-school knowledge but with real-life experience. His employment policies, his use of technology, and even his pricing wove his business into the fabric of the surrounding community. He leaped to an even more stunning level of success because he used that community as a medium through which to unite the interests of employees, customers, civic leaders, and pharmaceutical companies alike.

Ost's celebrity eventually drew the attention of the pharmaceutical giant AmGen, which hired him to share his success secrets in a video intended for distribution to ten thousand drugstores nationwide. Soon he was traveling coast-to-coast, helping druggists get closer to their employees and customers alike. Three years following my visit to Philadelphia Pharmacy, Ost the consultant was having more impact than Ost the pharmacist. So he sold his three little pharmacies to Rite-Aid.

It was, as they say, an offer he couldn't refuse. Wall Street was in the midst of a spectacular bull market, and the pressure to sustain year upon year of earnings growth was causing big companies to pay top dollar for innovative smaller businesses. Moreover the pharmacy business was becoming a commodity business, and Ost was happy to let the big retailers slug it out over ever-shrinking margins. And although it was melancholy to see the logo of a national chain hoisted over Ost's shops, he knew he was leaving behind a better neighborhood. After closing on his sale, Ost gave his former employees nearly a quarter-million dollars in bonuses and other payments. Many of them received promotion opportunities in the big chain that Ost himself could never have provided.

From day one in business, Ost knew he was part of something bigger than himself. Like an organism in its environment, he allowed his business to change with the community and simultaneously to cause change *in* the community; he, and everyone around him, benefited by his doing so. Flush with the proceeds of his sale, he began plotting his next move as an entrepreneur.

I learned something important the morning I first entered Philadelphia Pharmacy. I had spent nearly twenty years analyzing business for the *Wall Street Journal*. I had covered some of the biggest takeovers, labor strikes, bankruptcies, and bust-ups in history. I had interviewed CEOs in penthouse suites and coal miners half a mile underground. I had supervised the *Journal*'s economics coverage from Washington and had written two books about major industries, oil and airlines. But driving away from Lehigh Avenue I realized that my career had been devoted almost entirely to the study of conflict. I had written about people and institutions locked in struggle not over the creation of wealth but over its control. After devoting exactly half my lifetime to writing about business, I knew little about how business actually *worked*.

A short time later I launched a new weekly column called "The Front Lines." Instead of rounding up the usual sources and subjects—the officers and analysts who mostly did a lot of officiating and analyzing—I resolved to write about the anonymous people who actually invented the products, sold them to customers, and came face-to-face with competitors. And with each successful person I came across it grew obvious that a revolution was under way in business, for the most part invisible in the headlines and the boardrooms, but dizzying in its effects on the front lines.

Factories, I once thought, were supposed to run with clocklike precision. Then I met Charlene Pedrolie, who managed a cinder-block furniture plant in rural Virginia. Pedrolie had ripped out the assembly line, setting gluers, staplers, and seamstresses madly scurrying to assemble sofas as they saw fit. Amid the pandemonium of the shop floor, productivity and quality were going through the roof.

Products, I always believed, were priced according to cost, with a margin for profit. Then I met Paul Graziani in King of Prussia, Pennsylvania. He was selling a disk of software called the Satellite Tool Kit, a product he developed while working as a General Electric engineer. GE sold the Satellite Tool Kit for $3 million a copy. When I first met him in 1995, Graziani was happily selling the same thing for $9,999. When I visited him again in 1997, the price had dropped to zero—yet by redefining his market his company was making more money than ever.

I used to think that only managers could make the hard decisions. Then I went to Mercedes-Benz Credit Corporation in Norwalk, Connecticut. There, employees were busily investigating ways to eliminate their own jobs. Why? Because those who succeeded were rewarded with new jobs helping the company to grow.

At one time I believed that going into business required a ransom of risk capital. Then I met a debt-ridden artist in Minneapolis who went from homelessness to a Horatio Alger story by selling lettertype designs over the World Wide Web.

Corporate America, in my experience, was fearful of regulators and wary of local activists. Then I discovered how a plant manager for DuPont had dissolved the boundary between factory and community while causing profitability to soar.

I always believed that major corporations jealously tracked every dollar, guarded every asset, and tracked the actions of every employee. Then I visited the family-owned Koch Industries of Wichita, Kansas, which had grown bigger than Boeing, Intel, or Motorola with no budgets, no central planning, and no job descriptions.

Pundits have been writing for years about a revolution in business, of course. Yet nothing had quite prepared me for such disorienting reporting experiences. I heard leaders confessing their urge to "lose control" of their organizations. I watched brick and mortar become symbols of obsolescence. People who once did business on a handshake were starting to do it on a hug, for Pete's sake!

Was I witnessing a change in the ethos of business or just a switch to some new fads? A new dawn or some new Dilbert fodder? These questions forced me to consider business on a level more fundamental than anything I'd attempted as a business editor and reporter. What were the deepest, most fundamental forces guiding business? Why did it exist at all? Could capitalism co-exist with humanism? What was leadership? Where did creativity come from?

"Reality is getting your feet wet," the British biologist Steve Jones remarked. "The only way to approach the truth in snails, or in anything else, is to go out and do the work."[1] My three-year search for answers propelled me to more than one hundred cities in thirty-two states, where I probed industries dealing in everything from microcircuitry to restaurant grease. Along the way I won access to some of today's boldest thinkers about management and economics. I also ranged into the laboratories and lecture halls of scientists whose recent discoveries in the physical world were challenging much of what we've long held true about the commercial world. The answers I found await you in these pages.

This book is a kind of debutante party for the ingenues of the new economy. I offer their stories as proof that business is undergoing a transformation as fundamental yet sudden as water shifting from liquid

to gas on the addition of a single degree. It's my aim to trace the origins of these trends, to establish their authenticity, to inform you of the details, and perhaps to inspire your enrollment—whether as entrepreneur or adviser, manager or employee, builder or trader—as a pioneer in the new economy.

More than a century ago an eminent scholar of American history, Frederick Jackson Turner, presented his fabled address "The Significance of the Frontier in American History." The frontier expansion, he declared, was "a history of evolution and adaptation," the story of "organs in response to a changed environment." Amid such possibilities, he said, "freedom of opportunity is opened, the cake of custom is broken, and new activities, new lines of growth, new institutions, and new ideals are brought into existence."

Today's pioneers have embarked on a new frontier, some in search of riches, others in search of freedom, all in search of the new. Unlike the West of old this frontier is not one of place. It is a frontier of technologies, ideas, and values. The new pioneers celebrate individuality over conformity among their employees and customers alike. They deploy technology to distribute rather than consolidate authority and creativity. They compete through resilience instead of resistance, through adaptation instead of control.[2] In a time of dizzying complexity and change, they realize that tightly drawn strategies become brittle while shared purpose endures. Capitalism, in short, is merging with humanism.

I don't lightly suggest a connection between business and life or, as Frederick Jackson Turner dared to suggest, between evolution and economics. Indeed when you look deeply enough into a growing organization or spend enough time with thriving entrepreneurs, business begins to look very much like pure biological evolution, propelled into real time on the fuel of human intelligence. Evolution's arrow has endowed us with the skills to take the measure of our surroundings, to collaborate with our colleagues, and, through countless parallel acts, to cause our organizations to adapt, all without central planning or control. Firms acting in parallel create the same patterns of change and order in an economy. And with freedom and deregulation sweeping other nations, the same dynamics are becoming evident around the globe.

We'll take some detours through biology in the pages ahead, and though the side trips will be occasional and brief, they're vital nonetheless. The connection between business and biology is beginning to per-

meate our culture, with scholars and consultants invoking ecosystems and evolution as metaphors from which business should learn. And in fact the living world is an exemplary design model for business. One is tempted to say that business isn't like nature, business *is* nature.[3]

Such mental models have awesome power in shaping our institutions. (As Einstein said, "Our theories determine what we measure."[4]) For the proof in business we need look no further than the model that held sway over business for three centuries, one that still persists among many businesspeople, perhaps most. Though the details are a bit daunting— they were to me, anyway—a brief reconstruction of this hoary framework is vital to understanding the past from which business is escaping and the future toward which it is racing.

It's a story that begins with the apple—not Eve's, but Isaac's.

ை

Sir Isaac Newton was the new Moses, presenting a few simple equations—the "laws of nature"—that never failed in predicting the tides, the orbits, or the movement of any object that could be seen or felt. Output was exactly proportional to input. Every action begat a reaction. Everything was equal to the sum of its parts. The entire universe was seen as a clockworks that could be understood by analyzing the individual parts. Newton's mechanics seemed so universal they became the organizing principle of postfeudal society itself, "the best model of government," as one authority said in 1720.[5] The principles of mechanics inspired Frederick the Great to structure the Prussian army as an assemblage of standardized parts, equipment, and command language.[6]

The very equations of economics, including those in use today, were built explicitly on the principles of mechanics and thermodyanmics, right down to the terms and symbols.[7] The economy was said to have "momentum," or was "gaining steam." A successful company ran like a "well-oiled" or "fine-tuned" machine, a poorly performing company was "off track" or "stuck in low gear." Looms, lathes, engines, presses, and ultimately assembly lines became the metronomes of the human condition.

Most damaging of all, biology itself was corrupted to fit the mechanistic view of economic man. In reality, as scientists now recognize, evolution favors cooperative traits over competitive ones in selecting for fitness. Yet "survival of the fittest"—the coinage of sociologist Herbert

Spencer, erroneously attributed to Darwin—was commandeered as cover for social domination and capitalist abandon. "The growth of a large business is merely survival of the fittest," a pious John D. Rockefeller once told a Sunday school class. "It is merely the working-out of a law of nature and a law of God."[8]

The Newtonian worldview was appropriate for its time, a reflection of the best in science. It laid the undergirdings of the industrial revolution, creating steam engines, autos, airplanes, and an allied victory in World War II (just as surely as a defeat in Vietnam). The problem with Newtonianism was that upon closer inspection the science turned out to be—well, wrong, or at best correct only within the tolerances of Newton's instruments. In deep space, as Einstein's general relativity showed, the laws of motion utterly broke down. At the subatomic level, as quantum physics showed, time sometimes went backwards and the same object could be seen in two places at once. Scientists came to terms with the sobering truth that Newton's calculus, their most powerful tool, was only a method of approximation—and that however useful in smooth, linear problems, the calculus was of no use in studying the preponderance of nature: the motion of currents, the growth of plants, the structure of economies.[9] Classical math and science could explain why the apple fell, as the physicist Per Bak once quipped, but not why the apple existed (much less why Newton was thinking about it).

With Newtonianism crumbling as a mental model, thinkers began looking elsewhere. Across the sciences researchers discovered a world of kaleidoscopic complexity and unpredictability, triggering fundamental revisions. The story of the physical sciences in the twentieth century, no differently than the story of art, literature, and music, is one of qualities taking their place alongside quantities, relationships taking their place with objects, ambiguity taking its place with order.

Except in business. Business (and government, the business of state) slept through every minute of the postmodern awakening. Even as it was toppled from unassailability in science, Newtonian mechanics remained firmly lodged as the mental model of management, from the first stirrings of the industrial revolution right through the advent of modern-day M.B.A. studies. Jobs were divided ever more narrowly, turning workers into so many tiny objects performing mindless, repetitive tasks; the whole, after all, was always equal to the sum of its parts. Management remained an act of calibration and control: input equals output, action equals reaction. History's first management consultant, Frederick Taylor, argued that "all possible brain work should be removed from the shop and placed in the planning or layout department," telling workers, "You are not supposed to think. . . . There are other people paid for thinking around here."[10] To be fair, Taylor was motivated by a wish to improve wages through higher productivity, an effort that union leaders readily supported.[11]

Command-and-control leadership prevailed to the end of the century. Government policy resided safely in the hands of "the best and the brightest." Leaders skilled at control became the leaders of modernity: GM's Alfred Sloan, the United Mine Workers' John L. Lewis, the Pentagon's Robert McNamara, ITT's Harold Geneen. The mainframe computer, housed in its off-limits and tightly sealed glass house, accelerated the centralization of information. Economics departments and MBA programs taught quantitative methods that continued to treat the workplace and marketplace as clockwork: Pay a seamstress another penny and she will produce five more pieces per hour . . . Each $1 million in national advertising buys you access to so many households. Management's job was assembling the right pieces, pointing them toward the optimum, and then making sure the system never wavered.

Perfectly kind and decent human beings (and some less kind and decent) were blinded to any purpose of organization life other than the optimization of the organization itself. "We are not in business to conduct moral activity. We are not in business to conduct socially responsible activity," IBM chairman John Akers proclaimed in 1986. "We are in business to conduct business."[12] There was, says the humorist Michael Lewis, "*noblesse* without the slightest trace of *oblige*."[13] Into the moral void came numbers, only numbers. Optimization demanded intense measurement; all measurements could be abstractly converted to dollars; and profit thus became the principal ethos of business. Indeed, by the end of the 1980s business stood on only two foundations: "re-engineering" (the application of Newtonianism to repair problems created by earlier Newtonianism) and the compulsive search for "shareholder value"—a valid pursuit except that it came to overwhelm all other expressions of value. "Greed is all right," the Wall Street titan Ivan Boesky famously decreed in a commencement address at Berkeley, a short time before his arrest for insider trading. "I think greed is healthy."[14]

That was then. We can't yet see it everywhere, but a great awakening is now under way in business. In this book we'll explore where and why it's happening, how well it works, and what we can learn from it.

᠃

Though their numbers have been slowly building for decades, the new pioneers began appearing in force after the U.S went to war in the Persian Gulf in 1991. It was a time of economic crisis. Business activity worldwide screeched to a halt, first as everyone glued his eyeballs to CNN and then as everyone realized no one else was spending a dime. A deep recession followed, but this recession was different. Instead of furloughing workers until the good times returned, this time business jettisoned workers for good. Just as economic pressures had once created larger and larger organizations, a new set of pressures began pushing business in the opposite direction. The Gulf War recession solidified a new concept in business and a new word in the vernacular: downsizing

In addition, this time the victims, to an unprecedented degree, were managers, people who had occupied the precincts of ambition. And this time, many of those shown the door found their pockets bulging with severance pay. Like a dandelion gone to seed, the corporate world released these energetic and well-capitalized progeny to the wind. In lobby directories and Yellow Pages, a teeming census of small companies began filling niches of ever-narrowing size. At nearly every level of scale—across product lines, industries, indeed entire nations—the small became more numerous and more specialized. Many big corporations became even bigger through consolidation, of course, but they also became less numerous as a result, accounting for a shrinking proportion of total economic activity. The headline-grabbing mega-mergers of the 1990s were mostly a sideshow compared to the splintering of economic power, which not only widened the access to opportunity but reduced the odds that any single failure would bring down others.

The heartbreak of downsizing was undeniable, but so was the thrill of new growth: For every job wiped out at a major company in the mid-1990s, 1.5 jobs sprang up in its place, mostly in small firms.[15] The atomization of industry also stimulated innovation, since it is well established that small firms innovate at roughly twice the rate of large ones.[16] And when the 1990s witnessed the rebirth of American leadership in world markets, it was not the mega-multinationals leading the way. Instead, small and medium-sized businesses accounted for four out of every five new dollars in export sales chalked up in the 1990s. Freed of the bloat, bureaucracy, and other baggage that weigh down their massive counterparts, these smaller businesses have become the avant-garde of the economy and the exemplars of adaptation.

Their example was not wasted on the leviathans of the corporate world. The agility, creativity, and commitment necessary to compete in the 1990s required the minds and emotions of everyone in an enterprise. Major companies in technology and entertainment industries realized their official financial reports were mostly meaningless because, however precise in measuring plant and equipment or revenue and prof-its, they didn't begin to reflect the "intellectual capital" of the organization or the value added by it. Many companies faddishly embraced the idea of "knowledge management" as if the mind could be made to behave like another piece of gear: Toss in more investment, earn a predicted return. But some others, including a few of the biggest companies in the world, took a more thoughtful approach, questioning their most fundamental precepts of learning and human relations in ways we'll explore in the chapters ahead.

Meanwhile, long-building demographic changes worked in parallel with the new economic forces. Baby boomers—the best-educated and most independent generation in world history, reared on Dr. Spock, demand feeding, and Jefferson Airplane—attained the ranks of middle and senior management in great numbers in the early 1990s. Encouraged to "question authority," as a popular bumper sticker once urged, the boomers continued this practice even after the authority was theirs. (As the social commentator Brent Staples has noted, all those kids who danced naked at Woodstock didn't vanish from the planet when they grew up.[17]) Many of these new leaders also had an inkling that happiness and fulfillment in the workplace might actually devolve to the benefit of the organization itself; indeed, in surveying their employees, MCI, Sears, and other giants found a significant link between morale and revenue.[18] What a concept: Treating people individually and with dignity—the tenant of virtually every religion in the history of the planet—turns out to be good for business!

Gender compounded the effects of generation: In the early 1990s women became part of the membership and leadership of business, helping to re-emphasize the commercial value of relationships. The ascendancy of minorities in leadership, though halting, broadened the diversity of viewpoints. And in came the so-called Generation X, whose upbringing via day care and divorce created a new kind of wariness toward institutions.

Meanwhile, an intellectual movement called "systems thinking" took a few modest steps toward validating the retreat from Newtonianism. If Newtonianism sought understanding by taking things apart (the process called "analysis"), systems thinking sought understanding things by putting them together ("synthesis"). Traditional mechanistic thinking emphasized one-way causality: how a parent affects a child, for instance. Systems thinking resists the distinction between cause and effect: parent and child affect one another mutually, and their relationship, in turn, affects other relationships. Systems thinking—seeing "the big picture," you might say—entered public consciousness through the ecology movement of the late 1960s, which emphasized the interconnectedness of all living things, and through advances in medicine and psychology, which emphasized family as well as individual wellness. By the early 1990s, this movement had put down roots in the business world as well.

Also right around 1991, the new economic and cultural forces combined with technological forces through the widespread acceptance of Windows. Yes, Windows, a disk full of code that endowed the kludgey personal computer with the liberating simplicity of a kitchen appliance (at least when it wasn't crashing). Just as all those downsized executives were thrown into their spare bedrooms to pioneer in the new economy, an easy-to-use tool met them there, a back-office-in-a-box as well as a medium for looking out on the rest of the world. Nineteen ninety-one was also a threshold year for technology inside large organizations, which for the first time spent more money on computing than every other kind of equipment put together.[19] This signaled the breakup of the mainframe computer, once accessible only to its anointed brotherhood, into millions of desktop units, turning every cubicle and every household into the equivalent of a world headquarters.

Which brings up the last of the forces converging in the early 1990s: the growth of a new global infrastructure, a universal common-carrier network providing small economic players with access to every other player. There was overnight package delivery, toll-free numbers, faxes, pagers, satellite phones, international direct-dial service, real-time desktop video conferencing, and, when nothing but a handshake would do, supersaver fares that put you anywhere in the U.S. for $199. This explained how Jake Albright and his son-in-law Bill Dudleston, working from a garage in the shadow of a grain elevator in central Illinois, could sell stereo speakers at $10,000 a pair to customers in Japan, or why a fellow like John Allen, commuting from an office overlooking the C&O Canal in Washington, D.C., could manufacture children's chewable vitamins in a former chemical-weapons plant in Siberia. In many industries time zones became a bigger factor than distance itself: In Sunnyvale, California, I watched the engineers at Amdahl Corporation programming a prototype computer that was sitting in a development lab in Tokyo; after 12 hours their partners at Hitachi picked up where they left off. A new business magazine called *Fast Company* sprang up with a motto that described the new age succinctly: "Work is personal. Computing is social. Knowledge is power."

It is a governing theme in this book: Today, everyone in every organization is an entrepreneur, while every entrepreneur belongs to an organization (probably many). In the old days, when geographical boundaries mattered, the mantra of selling strategy was "location, location, location." The new mantra, for everyone and everything in business, is "connection, connection, connection."

It would be ludicrous to imply that all companies or business people, or even most, have abandoned the old command, control, and count-it-up ethos. Conformity and compliance remain the unwritten rule at many major corporations, perhaps most. Many small business people cannot shake their self-image as the prey in an economy full of predators. For every issue of *Fast Company* hitting the newsstands, a dozen other publications perpetuate the old stereotypes. "Killer Instinct: Get It Now!" blared the cover of a recent business magazine. Rolf-Ernst Breuer, the chairman of Deutsche Bank, left little doubt of the persistence of command-and-control culture in connection with the December 1988 acquisition of Bankers Trust. "We don't believe in autonomy as an instrument of management and leadership," he told reporters. "As far as it goes, we want a centralized management of the business."[20]

Even worse, much of what passes for a new way of doing business is actually the same old model updated with fresh jargon. What good is "open-book management" when the books tell the wrong story? Why rush to "knowledge management" when the last thing organizations need is more management? "Empowerment," the most patronizing business buzzword to come along in years, perpetuates the harmful notion that an all-knowing management anoints workers with purpose and initiative.

But while the old order persists, the new order is rising alongside it—haltingly in some places, unevenly in others, but inexorably in every corner of the economy. How can I be so sure of this? Two reasons.

First, the marketplace leaves companies with little choice. In an era when change arrives without warning and threatens to eradicate the foundations of entire companies and entire industries overnight, organizations can survive only by becoming more human. Businesses that fail to engage the eyes, ears, minds, and emotions of every individual in the organization will find themselves overrun by obsolescence or crushed by competition.

Second, the new, more enlightened way of business will persist because it hews more closely to what we are as humans. One of the many economic paradoxes we'll explore in the pages ahead is that the advancing ethos of business is returning us to what business has sometimes been in the past, and what it was meant to be.

∽

In exploring the frontier of the new pioneers, I have set myself a number of tasks. Chapter 1, "Being in Business," explores the evolution of trade and technology and their origins in the nature of economic man. Chapter 2, "Everyone a Middleman," shows how every entrepreneur finds his role in the new economy and how the changing rules of the game once again favor the small. Chapter 3, " 'Have It Your Way,' " illustrates the extraordinary lengths to which pioneering companies go in the service of their customers, while Chapter 4, "What Am I Bid?," explores how the new compact with customers is revolutionizing the most fundamental concepts of pricing.

The book then moves inside the organization. In Chapter 5, "From Planning to Playing," I will show how pioneering companies continually reinvent themselves instead of attempting to control an uncontrollable future. Chapter 6, "Nobody's as Smart as Everybody," explores the nature of collective learning, its link to self-organization, and the creative dynamics of a place called "the edge of chaos." Chapter 7, "All Together Now," shows how today's diverse and often conflict-prone organizations succeed through shared vision, whose creation has become the new mission of leadership. Chapter 8, "Money and

Motivation," suggests that while people may take a job because of what it pays, they remain loyal to it, and give their best to it, for reasons other than what it puts in their pockets.

Lastly the book turns to the wider place of business in society. Chapter 9, "At Home in the Economy," shows how economic pressures are dissolving the artificial cleavage between work life and family life. Chapter 10, " 'All My Sons,' " explores how today's economic pressures have transformed social missions from acts of charity into commercial imperatives.

Aldous Huxley, whose *Brave New World* inspired a generation of fear, later advanced an alternate vision of the future that seemed outlandishly utopian for the time. The engineers of tomorrow, he imagined, would create the tools necessary for everyone to perform "profitable and intrinsically significant work." People at last would win independence from bureaucratic bosses, working as entrepreneurs in their homes, coordinating their actions as "a self-governing, cooperative group." Careers, Huxley imagined, would at last provide "a more humanely satisfying life for people."[21]

For many, Huxley's dream is becoming a reality. Whether in multinational corporations or small home offices, job shops or big factories, people are acquiring the tools to pursue profitable and intrinsically significant work. They are pursuing and fulfilling their own concepts of themselves. These newly liberated entrepreneurs, as Huxley dared to dream, are casting themselves together as a self-directed lot and providing once unimaginable rewards to themselves and their fellow humans. And all indications suggest that these changes are just beginning. In the age of adaptation, there is no endgame, no optimum, no finale. There is only what comes next, and how we shape it.

1

Being in Business

Standing five feet tall in steel-toed boots, Charlene Pedrolie first entered the whitewashed cinder-block building in April 1995. This was the factory in which Rowe Furniture Company had been turning out sofas, love seats, and easy chairs in the Appalachian foothills of western Virginia for forty years.

Pedrolie was the plant's new manufacturing chief, and as unlikely as anyone you'd expect in such a job. She was pure Midwest—St. Louis–bred, high school cheerleader, Washington University class of '83—suddenly thrown into a town where people still displayed Confederate flag decals in the rear windshields of their pickups. She was female in an industry where the bosses had always been men, and she was young, in her early thirties, on a management team some of whose members had worked at the plant for longer than she had been alive.

Though traded on the New York Stock Exchange, Rowe Furniture, to judge by this plant, was no exemplar of futuristic management. With its windows painted over to save on cooling costs, the factory housed about five hundred workers, most robotically repeating identical motions eight hours at a stretch. It was like something out of eighteenth-century France—one person cutting, another sewing, another gluing; someone tucking, someone else stapling, others inspecting, labeling, and loading. Knocking out a simple piece of upholstered furniture spanned myriad dozens of steps, each executed to a drumbeat set in the front office. The pay was good by rural standards but the work was exquisitely boring: You punched your time card, turned off your brain, and performed exactly as the bosses required. "It was a dictatorship in here," recalled John Sisson, who helped construct the plant in the 1950s and who spent the next forty years working in it. He should know, having spent many of those years as general manager.

The low-cost and compliant nonunion workforce helped propel Rowe Furniture into showrooms across America, where the company became known for presentable products in decent fabrics—not quite to Ethan Allen specifications, perhaps, but inexpensive enough to win over the parents of the postwar era and later their children, the baby boomers. Meanwhile a second generation moved into the factory as well, taking over the jobs in which their parents had retired, died, or simply burnt out on account of drudgery.

But by the mid-1990s Rowe was undergoing a revolution in the marketplace, which is why Charlene Pedrolie found herself on the threshold of the depressing plant.

Rowe's market research showed that furniture buyers had grown impatient and impulsive. They wanted custom-designed products—the choice from a much wider selection than any showroom could display—yet they rejected the idea of waiting the standard three or more months for delivery. According to Rowe's studies, customers were deferring and even abandoning furniture-buying decisions simply because they couldn't have precisely what they wanted right now. Ingeniously, Rowe's marketing people responded by installing a network of showroom computer terminals, enabling customers to match fabrics and furniture models to their individual tastes. With a click of the mouse the order would be dispatched to tiny Salem, Virginia, where the Rowe plant would knock out a plaid chair for the Greenes, followed by a striped sofa for the Rhagavans, and so on. And best of all, the marketing people promised delivery within a month.

To which the people in the factory had two words: Yeah. Right.

Creating a new, hyper-efficient assembly process was the job for which Rowe had turned to Pedrolie, who despite her youth and conspicuousness was shot through with self-assuredness. Growing up she had watched her mother and grandmother build a small bridal shop into a thriving tuxedo-rental chain. Trained in chemical engineering, she had managed a soap line for Lever Brothers and later a lighting plant for General Electric, a factory twice voted under her leadership as the best plant among twenty-six contenders in the GE Lighting Division.

But the most telling measure of Pedrolie's self-confidence was her awareness coming into the job—not just her awareness, in fact, but her conviction—that the answer to Rowe's problems would never come solely from her. Nor could it come from any leader alone. As she saw it, the answer resided mainly in the collective minds of the people actually doing the work. Nobody knew this kind of sewing, after all, better than the seamstresses themselves. Anyone who made his living gluing armrests on love seats knew more about that kind of gluing than just about anybody on the planet. Pedrolie also realized that each of these workers also knew more about the adjacent specialties than anyone except the people in those jobs. And although years on an assembly line had blinded them individually to the entire operation, the odds were pretty good that with the right information in their hands the people who had been doing it for so long were the best ones to figure out how to put the pieces together for greater speed and efficiency.

So Pedrolie began dismantling. Most supervisory positions were eliminated. In fact, entire departments were eliminated. Everyone in the plant received a crash course in the skills he had previously seen at a distance: Gluers were taught to staple and staplers to glue; framers to upholster and upholsterers to frame. As a way of reinforcing the ideas that things were changing, Pedrolie ordered the paint scraped from the windows.

Before long the five hundred workers were assembling themselves into clusters—"cells," Pedrolie called them. Each group selected its own members, like kids drawing sandlot teammates. Each group received responsibility for a particular line of product and began creating its own processes, schedules, and routines, all varying according to the mix of workers and products in each group. With the assembly line about to become a thing of the past, the teams figured out the most sensible arrangements for clustering their power tools, which were hung from the ceiling on electrical cords, color-coded by cell. "Every cell started with a blank sheet of paper," Pedrolie would recall. "They figured out the process from beginning to end." If anyone on the production floor wanted to explore making special arrangements with an outside vendor, that worker simply picked up the phone and made the call.

The teams did not conduct this work in a vacuum; there were engineers, administrative specialists, and Pedrolie herself pitching in throughout the process. But the managers acted mainly as backups—as consultants, of a sort—leaving the employees to develop the new system on their own. "They were inventing the process," Pedrolie says. "They would think through the intricacies of each step and map it out. Then we'd massage it together."

Finally the new structure was in place, and one Monday morning everyone arrived to find the factory as they had proposed to redesign it. After years of standing in a single spot and having the furniture come to them, the workers were suddenly walking from one partly assembled piece to another, feeling their way, bumping into each other, making mistakes. Production turned helter-skelter. Some people couldn't tolerate the ambiguity of their assignments and walked out without returning. Others who failed to make the adjustment were eventually let go.

For Pedrolie herself, it was a time of sweaty palms and sleepless nights. As the workers struggled to iron out the kinks in the system a surge in orders hit, throwing the factory even more deeply behind. Overtime ran into the stratosphere; tempers grew short; one worker had a nervous breakdown on the job. The naysayers in the corporate offices shook their heads and clucked their tongues. The college girl from GE, it seemed, was about to fall flat on her face. Sisson, the longtime general manager, looked on with dismay. "It was really touch and go," he would recall. "We really didn't know if it would work out or not."

More than a few factories, alas, get stuck at this point. People become so preoccupied with shifting blame they lose all interest in finding solutions. Workers who never wanted accountability say they won't be made the scapegoats and disengage further; managers who never wanted to give up control smugly say we told you so. The factory reverts to the old ways, or fails altogether. The pages of the business press, including my own newspaper, contain many accounts of such "failed experiments."

Had it been anyone else in charge of Rowe's effort, it, too, might have slipped into ignominy. But Pedrolie held firm. The assembly line was gone for good, she said; it could not be reinstalled. By refusing to let anyone out—by forcing workers and managers to stay in the game and by cheering them on at every opportunity, which came naturally to her—she forced everyone to realize that self-organization was the only path to a sane workday and a secure future. Instead of letting the plant fail, everyone began pitching in.

Even more important, Pedrolie had installed a "safety net," as she called it, and the safety net was information. Every member of every team at every moment had instant access to up-to-date information—about order flows, order output, productivity, and quality. Data once closely guarded by top management became the common property of the shop floor. People had the instantaneous opportunity to see which of their actions worked and which didn't—and they reacted! And adjusted! This wasn't as easy as I probably make it sound. Rowe still had computers locked in the hands of a few professionals who dallied over her requests to generate new reports and information. Using her sharpest political skills, she engineered the ouster of the firm's computer chief and brought in one of her pals from GE.

At Pedrolie's urging, people unaccustomed to talking with anyone other than the folks at the adjacent stations began coursing the four corners of the factory, chatting up anyone who might offer the glimmer of a solution to the problem of the moment. In time, representatives from each of the teams, acting entirely on their own, began holding impromptu meetings over the course of a shift to check on each other's progress. An informal process of give-and-take emerged between teams as well as within teams.

After several weeks of plant-wide pandemonium, the pieces at last fell into place, causing productivity and quality to shoot through the roof. Before long the factory was delivering custom-made goods to the consumer within thirty days; several months later the lead time had reached merely ten days, a stunning accomplishment in an industry accustomed to working on lead times of as long as six months. A culture of speed permeated the plant. When a technology specialist named Ken Potter wanted to install a state-of-the-art frame-cutting tool, he was stunned to win management's instant approval. "It's exciting to feel like you're on the cutting edge," he said as the new computer-controlled machine buzzed behind him. "In the past we were told to wait until someone else in the industry got one."

Best of all, the sense of personal control—"this is my job and I'll figure out how to do it"—bred a culture of innovation in every corner of the plant. A group came together to form a "down-pillow task force" to invent a better stuffing process. (The workers could easily absent themselves from their regular jobs because cross-training had created so much bench strength behind every position.) A group of workers increased the capacity of the drying kilns by feeding in sawdust as a fuel; as the efficiency of the kilns grew they began selling the excess drying capacity to outside lumber treaters through their own marketing program, creating an altogether new business (with an 80 percent profit margin).

The Rowe Furniture turnaround is meaningful on many levels. It dramatizes the range of initiative that people display when freed to do their best work. It reveals the creative power of human interaction. It suggests that efficiency is intrinsic; that people are naturally productive; that when inspired with vision, equipped with the right tools, and guided by information about their own performance, people will build on each other's actions to a more efficient result than any single brain could design. In fact it's rather like saying that being good in business calls on being good at being human.

᠕

The history of business won't tell us much about the future, but it certainly reveals why business was born and why it has persisted so long. These are facts we're wise to consider in choosing what we expect of business today and what we hope of it tomorrow.

"The market is not an invention of capitalism," Mikhail Gorbachev once told the *Wall Street Journal*. "It is an invention of civilization."[1] He could have gone further: Civilization is an invention of business, and business is an invention of life. Business consists of technology and trade, both of which predate our species. *Homo erectus* mined quarries for stone tools as many as 1.4 million years ago. Language itself may be a by-product of technology: Some researchers believe toolmaking helped to create the neural connections necessary for speech. Trade in ax parts dates at least to 200,000 B.C., long before humans left Africa for Europe and Asia.[2]

Our economic identity is stamped all over our language and culture. The earliest known examples of cuneiform writing involved business transactions almost exclusively—ledgers and inventories accounting for everything from livestock to olive oil.[3] In many ancient languages the word equivalent of "business" shares the same roots as "life"; in old Sanskrit, "man" was derived from a word meaning to weigh, value,

count out, or share. The words "commerce" and "market," (as well as the French *merci,* for gratitude) share their origins in Mercury, the god of trade and information.[4]

Trade predates agriculture, government, religion, art, law, and symbolic communication, indeed every organizing social force except the family. Why should this be so? The answer is evolution. Samuel Butler once remarked that a chicken was an egg's way of making another egg. No differently do genes program every living thing to strive for efficiency, because efficiency, after all, allows genes to live on.[5] With sufficient information, any living thing will find the shortest distance to food, which makes the food go further; those who succeed bear more progeny with the same traits. "Evolution," as one of Darwin's biographers wrote, "thus blindly follows the route of maximum resources use."[6] To put it another way, efficiency is evolution in action. Whether we are born free, born to be wild, born in the U.S.A., or born to lose, we are all, as living things, born to economize.

Nobody has thought more deeply about the origins of business than William C. Frederick, who did his Ph.D. work in both anthropology and economics. Frederick served as dean of the University of Pittsburgh business school, studied business systems across Europe in nearly a decade of work with the Ford Foundation, and became one of the world's leading authorities on business ethics. His decades of research ultimately persuaded him that all living things harbor an impulse to economize as a bulwark against the universal propensity toward the loss of energy and form, a force called entropy. "This economizing process is the only way to survive, grow, develop, and flourish," he wrote in a landmark 1995 study. "Overall, life on earth has been a roaring economizing success story."[7] In the case of us humans, business is the tool we use to lighten our loads, "the main economizing vehicle on which organized human life depends," Frederick says. The corporation thus is "as Darwinian as a frog."[8]

Once evolution created the impulse to economize, there was nothing to stop it. We economize through the division of labor (because people vary in their skills) and the exchange of resources (because regions vary as well). Add those together and you get technology, the specialized artifacts of business; widen the boundaries of contact and you get trade; throw it all together and you get economic progress from nothing more than the clump of rock, the tub of water, and the daily dose of sunlight that compose the planet earth.

There is a word that describes how life creates unlimited possibilities from such finite resources, a term, though rooted in nineteenth-century biology, that is getting some use in economics today. The word is "emergence." When systems become sufficiently complex and interconnected, the interaction self-assembles into a new, higher order: molecules into cells, cells into organs, organs into organisms, organisms into societies. This is economizing, life creating more from less, something from nothing—"order for free," as the molecular biologist Stuart Kauffman puts it.[9] At each level emergence creates more than the sum of its parts, as in one plus one equals three. The strength of an alloy may exceed the combined strength of the metals that compose it. A jazz ensemble creates a sound that no one could imagine by listening to the instruments individually.

Emergence creates new qualities as well as greater quantities: What appears chaotic at one level (the undirected motions of furniture workers, the bustle of a million computer users) may generate stunningly ordered behavior at the next level (a more efficient factory, a new medium called the Internet). The science writer James Gleick, whose 1987 book *Chaos* helped inspire the popularization of so-called complexity theory, described it this way: "Simple systems give rise to complex behaviors. Complex systems give rise to simple behavior. And most important, the laws of complexity hold universally, caring not at all for the details of a system's constituent atoms."[10]

Although Newtonianism long blinded people to the idea, economizing is pure emergence. Some business leaders began realizing this in the 1970s when they began using the word "synergy" (a term taken from anthropology) to describe the corporate equivalent of one-plus-one-equals-three. Says the biologist Tyler Volk of New York University, "Very little of importance is ever just the sum of its parts, except money."[11]

⟡

Before returning to the real world it's worth acknowledging two deep laws about economizing.

The first is that economizing occurs through learning and that every living thing, at bottom, learns in the identical way: through the elegantly simple and constantly recurring process of action, feedback, and synthesis. Feedback exists in every system, since "a system," to quote the science writer Kevin Kelly, "is anything that talks to itself."[12]

Feedback is information that constantly travels the same route (hence, "feedback loop") but never exactly repeats itself because it changes the thing that produces it. When feedback persists in regular waves it magnifies—feeds on itself, so to speak—ultimately running out of control: the familiar screech that Jimi Hendrix created by waving his guitar pickups in front of his speakers. Most living systems, however, such as jungles and stock markets, maintain a rough balance thanks to negative feedback, which dampens changes instead of magnifying them.

When feedback causes a living thing to change behavior, that's learning, whether a bacterium gravitating toward a sugar gradient or a child reckoning blocks. Learning, it's true, is full of spectacular nuance and complexity, but there's no getting away from that feedback cycle of action, reaction, and synthesis, not on any scale of life. Human creativity, says the Nobel chemistry laureate Ilya Prigogine, is "part of a fundamental trend present at all levels of nature."[13] Or, as Stuart Kauffman quips, "We may find that *E. coli* and IBM do indeed know their worlds in much the same way."[14]

I know a business consultant named Fritz Dressler, who during the Cold War conducted psychological profiles of foreign leaders for the State Department. He also immersed himself in the 1950s fighter-pilot studies that identified the fabled OODA cycle—observe, orient, do, act. In later years Dressler conducted a full-time investigation of every well-established theory of human knowledge—such familiar and unfamiliar theories as the "cognitive cycle," the Delphi Process, and on and on. Every one of them, Dressler realized, was stricken through with the identical arrow: the cycle of action, feedback, and synthesis. "The process we call creativity is in fact nature's evolutionary process running in real time," Dressler says.[15] It is "evolution on the fly."[16]

The second deep law about economizing is that it occurs best in groups. A solitary inventor laboring in his lab is every bit as important to human development as the solitary mutation is to the evolution of a bacterium, but in either case it takes a village (so to speak) to propagate the outcome. When nutrients run low, certain bacteria self-organize into slime molds that consume less than the bugs would otherwise. African termites, who are nearly blind and quite stupid individually, create ventilated structures fifteen feet high, full of chambers, overpasses, ventilation tunnels, and fungus gardens—ten-ton masterpieces that may stand for more than three hundred years—without ever consulting a set of plans.[17]

Self-organization is a universal property of life, creating order in everything from zebra stripes to human brains.[18] Dee Hock, then a bank executive in Seattle, laid out the basic elements of the global VISA credit-card system in 1970—then watched the network emerge all by itself, with no planning or control at the center. "The organization had to be based on biological concepts to evolve—in effect, to invent and organize itself," he explained.[19] This should come as no surprise, Hock has often said, since any living system organized around a valid purpose will find its way to an efficient result. "Who is the president of your immune system?" Hock once asked me. "Where is the CEO of the jungle?" We know the capacity to self-organize is inborn in humans because it is a skill we display when forced to act on instinct: during an emergency, as when rivers overflow or hurricanes approach.

Humans, let's admit, differ from termites (and corporations from termite mounds) in quite a few ways, but in only two that need concern us here: in the speed and range at which they apply the laws of economizing. Cells may spend millions of generations evolving a more efficient trait, but organisms with neurons can learn on the spot. And with the onslaught of real-time communication, each human brain becomes like a single cell in a huge social brain—a "team mind," as Fritz Dressler calls it—which itself is evolving.

The other big difference: A cell acts within a very small environment; humans, by contrast, have evolved eyesight, language, money, telegraphs, modems, and wireless pagers, all for taking soundings from a wide environment (locating the nearest mammoth herd, or receiving stock quotes from the floor of the Big Board) and, in turn, for causing change over that vast expanse (attacking the mammoths, selling IBM). Somewhere between mammoth hunting and real-time stock trading our bodies quit adapting to the environment because our minds created technologies through which we could adapt instead. Everything evolves, including the nature of evolution itself.

But each advance in our economizing takes us one step beyond our ability to regulate its *diseconomizing* effects. We attain astonishing new efficiencies by forming tribes and inventing spears until one day there are no mammoths left to breed new ones. Japan creates sleek "just-in-time" supply chains to eliminate factory inventories, only to substitute them with an armada of trucks that clog the highways and pollute the air. We create amazingly clean, efficient, and inexpensive electricity from uranium until—darn!—we remember to account for nuclear disposal, and the cost increases a thousandfold. Employers and insurance companies create bureaucracies to control medical costs only to find that the bureaucracy engulfs the entire system, driving costs higher. Through the growing use of systems thinking, scientists came to recognize that "we can never do merely one thing," as one commentator noted in the 1960s. "Wishing to kill insects, we may put an end to the singing of birds."[20]

Though it sometimes works slowly, reason invariably breaks through these blinders and discovers the unintended effects of our actions, since every new advance in human understanding at some point widens the boundaries in which we can see our systems operating. To the extent that business remains blind to the damage caused by economizing, it ought to be forgiven. To the extent it ignores or shifts harm to someone else—by exporting deplorable working conditions, for instance, or by knowingly pushing the cost of toxic accumulation into future generations—then we are acting unethically. "Business *can* provide meaning for workers and customers," says the author and entrepreneur Paul Hawken, "but not until it understands that the trust it undertakes and the growth it assumes are part of a larger covenant."[21]

❧

Growing up near a factory called Lordstown, I could see the effects on the workplace itself of business's resistance to that covenant. The Lordstown plant, in Lordstown, Ohio, is a fabled General Motors factory a few miles from the gritty old steel town of Youngstown. I remember touring the plant as a grade-school student when it opened in 1966. Stretching one mile, the tour guide said, it ranked among the biggest factories in the world; you could clock it yourself on the odometer of your GM car. Staffing the plant with returning Vietnam veterans, Lordstown established the high-water mark in the trade-off between mindless work and high pay. Job specialization was so extreme and individual duties so rote that some people could do them half-asleep—or drunk, or high. For when the whistle sounded for a lunch break you could see people sprinting across the expanse of plant and parking lot to their cars, peeling away to one of the liquor stores or taverns outside the plant gate, guzzling beer and inhaling joints every minute of the return trip, the buzz taking hold just as the assembly line shuddered back into motion.

This was economizing, 1970s-style—and it *was* economical if all you measured was how many Chevy Novas rolled out by the hour. But the economics were not so good once General Motors began widening the boundaries of the analysis—the warranty expense of all those defects, the alienation of loyal customers, the cost of absenteeism, medical benefits, turnover, family strife, theft, union militancy, and government regulation. Lordstown was a monument to the Newtonian fallacy that input equals output, that if a big plant was good then a bigger plant was better. In the giantism of the postwar era, institutions of all kinds outgrew their ability to control their own complexity—from GM to IBM, from a social system in the Deep South to a campus in Berkeley, from Nixon's White House to Brezhnev's Kremlin.

Why? Because they were not paying attention to the feedback in their systems. They dismissed it as a false signal. They could no longer hear the effects of their own actions—and nothing long survives without listening to its own effects and answering back with change.

The first person to recognize this in the corporate world—and whose actions would ultimately save Western industry from itself—was a rather curmudgeonly physicist named W. Edwards Deming, who, while not exactly a household name, has become a demigod to leaders of the product-quality movement. Deming grew up in Wyoming surrounded by farming, a vocation that demands the long view and in which everything is connected to everything. Deming, to quote one of his biographers, "also possessed a deeply religious belief in human potential."[22] In his work as an industrial statistician Deming could see that even infinitesimal variations tend to compound in large mechanical systems. Unlike a living system, with its dynamic balance of positive and negative feedback, an unregulated mechanical system experiences variations that produce larger variations in the same direction, eliminating consistency and ultimately causing failure. The solution, Deming found, was tracking not just the output of a machine but also its tiny variations in performance, and the variations between machines, and variations across entire factories, and making constant adjustments accordingly. Deming had discovered nothing other than a new application for the timeless idea of action, feedback, synthesis—evolution itself brought to the factory floor.

These practices came to be called "quality control," and they helped an unskilled and hastily assembled Allied workforce turn out better weapons in World War II. But in peacetime, when Deming approached the chieftains of corporate America to suggest that their mighty and victorious operations could continue to benefit from his ideas, he was laughed out of every boardroom he entered. So Deming looked for receptive ears elsewhere. He found them in Japan.

Japan was not only eager to rebuild its crushed economy, it was also more attuned than the West to nonlinear thinking—the principle holding that systems do not always behave in smooth, continuous, or perfectly predictable ways. Deming became a powerful force at many Japanese companies—no-name outfits like Toyota, Mitsubishi, and Matsushita, for instance—helping them to turn the once-derided phrase "Made in Japan" into a synonym for quality and efficiency. He expanded the concept of tracking machine feedback by listening not just to the machines but to the *workers* operating those machines, and not only listening to those workers but allowing them to take corrective action of their own accord; experience, after all, creates tacit knowledge that no one can articulate.[23] Deming did not stop there. He counseled his Japanese clients to listen also to the customers purchasing the worker's products, and ultimately to the entire economic society in which those customers operated—in short, to widen the boundaries by which managers studied the effects of their economizing. He told the Japanese that instead of locking into a theoretic optimum they should allow evolution to persist, a concept the Japanese called *kaizen,* meaning "continuous improvement." Although Japan created a number of the world's biggest corporations thanks in large part to Deming's aid, their size was the result of their success, not its cause.

Once Japan had cleaned the Newtonian clocks of American industry, Deming's ideas began taking hold in the West, but with a difference. In the U.S. and Europe a bustling industry of consultants packaged his methods into user-friendly "programs" and "methodologies" with names like Quality Circles, Total Quality Management, and "empowerment." These initiatives often brought about significant improvements, but managers invariably cut short the progress when they realized they could not simply put the program in place and walk away. They failed to realize that adaptation is a way of living—better yet, a way of changing—that never stops. While many managers abandoned Deming's ideas in the 1980s in search of the next fad, some continued practicing them into the 1990s. Those that did so were rewarded with a leadership sensibility that harmonized with the radical changes sweeping the business world—intense and unpredictable competition, fast-changing technology, and a newly diverse and demanding workforce. Even many automotive industry managers benefited from their persistent if unfashionable embrace of Deming's concepts. One such manager was Mark Schmink.

By the summer of 1997 Schmink had spent more than twenty years with a Toledo-based company called Dana Corporation—not exactly a small company at nearly $7 billion a year in sales, but a flyspeck by the standards of the auto industry. Dana made big, heavy parts for the Big Three automakers—axles, brakes, chassis, and other contraptions full of welding. A lanky, white-haired, and soft-spoken engineer of forty-eight, Schmink had spent much of his time with Dana studying management methods in Japan.

In 1993 Dana awarded Schmink an extraordinary assignment: building, then operating, a factory in Stockton, California, to make a single product for a single customer: truck undercarriages for Toyota. By then the biggest auto company on earth, Toyota would ship unassembled steel parts—more than 130 different beams, braces, corners, caps, and the like for each chassis—all the way from Japan to the Dana plant in Stockton. There, Dana would put the pieces together and dispatch them on a continuous truck convoy to a Toyota plant sixty-three miles away.[24] As Toyota's truck-production schedules changed, so would Dana's, instantaneously, through a real-time computer link.

But this was the stunning part: Dana agreed to provide Toyota a price *cut* once a year beginning in 1997. Not an inflation-adjusted price cut but an actual, hard-dollar price cut, a promise that left the chassis plant with no choice but to economize relentlessly and never let up.

This was a truly startling concession on Dana's part. The plant was designed for staggering efficiency to begin with—not with any uniformity of methods, as favored in the Industrial Age, but with a diversity of them. For instance Toyota had long favored the quality and consistency of robotic welders, while Dana strongly favored the nuance and intuitive "feel" that human welders possess. So this particular plant was built as a hybrid, with a dozen robots, like twitchy spider legs, applying long welds to the sides of each chassis. Then a half-dozen human welders took over, snapping down their masks in unison, closing in on all sides and applying dozens of spot welds, turning the air ablaze with crackling blue sparks.

Just as vexing, Dana knew it could never finance the price cuts by reducing the wages it paid to its workers; on the contrary, reducing wages is almost always a poor choice when the objective is economizing. Neither could Dana finance the price cut by substituting cheaper raw materials, because Toyota was providing all of those. The only way Dana could fulfill its commitment was to find ways of improving on its assembly process—and then find ways of improving on the improvements, without end. "You can only work and sweat so much; it's finite," Schmink told me. "That leaves you with finding better ways to do things. To my knowledge, that's not finite at all."

Schmink began by choosing welders with zero experience, reasoning that unconditioned hands would be freer to explore new ways of welding. He insisted that everyone learn every job in the plant so people knew how each task fit into the whole, and that no one lodge himself in a permanent assignment, thereby maintaining a supply of fresh perspectives. Schmink had no choice but to engage the complete intellectual involvement of every man and woman in the plant. It was as if Schmink were trying to undo nearly a century of Frederick Taylor's job specialization—"you are not paid to think"—in a single stroke.

The Stockton area—largely agricultural, though drawing more industry all the time—is an ethnic melting pot, which both facilitated and complicated Schmink's efforts. In the interests of generating a constant stream of new ideas he wanted the greatest diversity of backgrounds possible, and he got it, with nineteen different nationalities represented among the first three hundred people he hired. But the Stockton community was also riven with ethnic conflict and occasional outbursts of violence, and there was no way to keep these tensions from breaching the plant gate. At one point, through a sheer administrative error, the company newsletter neglected to print a notice about an employee-organized Cinco de Mayo celebration. An Hispanic group felt deeply slighted—disaffection that the economic mission of the plant could ill afford. Schmink called a plant-wide meeting to explain the benign circumstances of the oversight and to apologize, preventing the hot feelings from boiling over.

Schmink created a plant library stocked not only with research materials but bestsellers on tape to get people's minds moving in their cars on the way to work. He fostered the culture of continuous improvement by telling stories of his upbringing as the son of a Methodist minister: "The churchgoer does not become a truly devoted and learned Christian his first Sunday in a pew," he told the plant at one point. "His dedication to his religion grows as he learns more and as he practices those new beliefs." Worker teams met regularly to question every routine of the plant, right down to the sequencing of individual welds.

Schmink also required that every employee submit two productivity ideas in writing each month, an organized attempt to foster and capture feedback from the people closest to the process. Many of the suggestions involved working conditions—smoke control, better ergonomics, break schedules—none of which would seem immediately to benefit the productivity of the plant, except that by taking the widest view possible Schmink recognized that the effect of the work on people's minds and bodies deeply influenced how they performed that work. In 1996 alone, with the first annual price cut approaching at year-end, a maintenance apprentice named Matt Johnson came up with 180 ideas—the installation of an electronic eye to assist in placing a cross-member, for instance, and the purchase of backup welding guns—thanks partly to his having worked in so many different assignments. "After moving all over," he said, "I could see problems up and down the line." As time passed, ideas begat ideas. As welder Ray Smith explained it, "I have my impact on somebody else's impact on somebody else's impact"—as clear an expression of systems thinking you'll ever hear.

While hungrily gobbling up the ideas, Schmink sent feedback in the other direction as well. Personally responding to every written suggestion (his most time-consuming duty) was itself an act of positive feedback that motivated even more ideas to come in. He reported minute-by-minute productivity figures on electronic displays that looked like gymnasium scoreboards. He celebrated the conquest of every milestone with an event—a rib eye lunch, a family barbecue, a day of free sodas, anything to sustain the conviction that even small improvements were vital.

Finally, at the beginning of 1997, Dana cut Toyota's price 0.84 percent—a meaningful step, though well short of its 2 percent target. "Our vision is not a reality yet," Schmink acknowledged when I visited. His candor was admirable, but there was no disputing that such incremental changes, when taken together, were beginning to have a national economic effect. For it was in the late 1990s that the major automotive companies, thanks almost entirely to the elevated role of feedback in their affairs, provoked a new kind of sticker shock: the first price reductions that most auto buyers had seen in their lifetimes, the dividend paid by economizing.

ᔑ

Every act of economizing involves some combination of five ingredients—labor, energy, material, space, and time; information can substitute or even eliminate much of each.[25] The economist Brian Arthur observed that the old economy was based on materials (lumber, for instance) held together with information (blueprints), while the new economy is based on information (lines of computer code) held together by material (a floppy disk).[26] Until recently Sprint equipped each of two thousand installers with 125 pounds of maps and other documents. Now the installers carry the same information in a two-pound computer provided by a small Florida company called Wave Corporation.

But where does information come from? Consider the lowly binary, nothing but a pair of anything. A binary is the simplest form of complexity.[27] The most complex technology known to the mind—consciousness itself—is reducible to nothing more complex than two states, a few billion neurons alternating between charged and discharged. (Talk about emergence!) Those neurons themselves are the products of binary devices called genes, which function no differently than so many tiny toggle switches. Now, our computers operate the identical principle of on and off, yes and no, 1 and 0. "Technology's taproot," says William Frederick of Pitt, "extends far down into genetic systems of very ancient lineage."[28]

The economizing power of information is accelerating through additional trends, each compounding the others. First, we now have more *information about information,* applications that can help researchers sort through billions of organic molecules in the search of new drugs, for instance, or that help businesspeople sort through millions of files in the search for new customers. Second, and more important, we have distributed this heightened computing power to vastly more people—more brains connected to more ever-more-powerful tools, each in pursuit of a more productive and pleasurable way of living (a network, as Marshall McLuhan forecast in 1962, that would become the global equivalent of the human nervous system.[29])

Third, and most important of all, the number and diversity of these information-handling tools is multiplying because people can invent them, produce them, and in some cases even distribute them acting as organizations of one. Software development, the fastest growing industry in the world, is also among the most democratic. The only barrier to entry is the creativity of the mind. There are no economies of scale in software development—in fact, software development suffers from reverse economies of scale, which is why big projects are typically broken down into teams of about seven to a dozen. Microsoft's size confers advantage only because it is mainly a marketing company that happens to produce software (much of it simply acquired from small companies.) These days a kid in a dorm room can invent a technology so powerful it makes Bill Gates shiver, as occurred when Mark Andreessen of the University of Illinois created the Web browser that ultimately became Netscape Communications Corporation.

Because anyone can now create a powerful economizing tool, we have more people applying more different ideas and making more progress, as I learned during a snowy winter weekend in Idaho Falls with an entrepreneur named Gary Schneider.

Schneider grew up around cultivation as well as contraption, the grandson of a farmer and the son of a union railroader. Coming out of high school he followed his father into railroading until he had shoveled enough rock under enough track to realize he could never spend his life doing it. He enrolled in the University of Arizona, where he studied agriculture as well as operations research, the science by which major organizations used high-tech tools to utilize resources more efficiently. It was a combination of which he would make profitable use.

At the time, major agribusiness companies used mainframe computers to help in their planting strategies, but there was nothing like that for the family farm. In a class on entrepreneurship Schneider wrote a business plan around an imaginary software tool by which farmers could analyze crop prices and growing costs. Working on the assignment convinced Schneider that driving the guesswork out of field planning and crop selection could revolutionize farming, vastly reducing the use of seed, fuel, fertilizer, and human labor while increasing profits. But the year was 1986 and the personal computer had just come on the scene. It lacked both the power and the ease of use to put such power at the fingertips of farmers. Schneider could only dream about the potential of his tool, and get on with the rest of his life.

Before long he wound up on a government scholarship in graduate school at Massachusetts Institute of Technology, the citadel of "systems thinking." He was electrified studying the laws and properties of interconnectedness, a way of thinking that helped him see the connections among agriculture, engineering, entrepreneurialism, and government policy. (He also noticed that some of the challenging concepts in systems thinking came more easily to students with backgrounds in engineering or biology—integrative disciplines, after all—and less easily to those more practiced at taking things apart, such as the finance and accounting students.) Systems thinking also gave Schneider new insights into the design, use, and commercialization of the farming tool of which he was still dreaming. Before long he again threw himself into the project, but it was the early 1990s, and desktop power was still insufficient to crunch the kind of numbers Schneider had in mind. He also owed the U.S. government a three-year tour of duty in exchange for its having underwritten his master's degree. He sustained his interest in agriculture by taking an Energy Department job in the farm state of Idaho, where, upon discharging his obligations to the government, he left to form a new company called AgDecisions Research.

By that time he had been living with his dream for a decade, during which he not only continued upgrading the algorithms in his program but also revived his old undergraduate business plan. With $100,000 in venture capital and the help of his wife, Maudi Gomez, and a single programmer named Blake Schwendiman, he had the product within a year. He shipped the code to a husband-and-wife company that copied the program onto CD-ROMs, produced the printed materials, and shrink-wrapped the whole thing for sale to small farms.

Ultimately, farm equipment dealers began acquiring rights to the program so they could help customers plan their plantings. I remarked to him that after ten years, his old jalopy had at last become a hot rod. Betraying just a trace of offense, he answered, "I tend to think of it as a bean seed, just below the surface—dormant, although inside the seed there's biological development. Once the seed sprouts, it takes off fast."

Again and again, when I bore deeply into the affairs of an interesting and effective entrepreneur or organization, particularly into the use of technology, a link to the natural order of life begins to reveal itself.

In Cambridge, Massachusetts, for instance, I spent some time at a robotics company called Intelligent Automation Systems, whose founder, Steve Gordon, began his career at the intersection of biology and mechanics, as a prostheses engineer. Frustrated at his inability to match the perfection of nature's designs, he switched into manufacturing, specializing in "machine vision"—systems that allow robots to watch what they are doing and to make instant adjustments, almost like Deming's quality control conducted in real time. At the time of my visit in late 1997 Gordon and his team were building a machine that a major sportswear manufacturer hoped to use for repatriating manufacturing from the sewing sweatshops of Asia. Even though people there worked for pennies an hour, Gordon's machine would make them uneconomical. Gordon's reputation as a machine builder also drew him back into biology, designing machines to synthesize the raw material of tomorrow: DNA, the information of life.

Genetics also lurked in the background when I showed up at a factory in Moline, Illinois, where Deere & Company assembled farm equipment. The problem afflicting the plant was similar to the one that Charlene Pedrolie had inherited at Rowe Furniture: The marketing department was offering customers the opportunity to order custom-made equipment, causing havoc on the assembly line. Deere's schedulers had spent months trying to optimize the sequence of the orders so that the line would run smoothly, but to no avail.

Deere turned over the problem to a staff analyst named Bill Fulkerson, a slightly rumpled, bespectacled grandfather and former math professor who had spent several years toiling anonymously on technical issues. Fulkerson found out about computer programs called "genetic algorithms," which could randomly "breed" schedules, comparing one against another and keeping the better of two, on and on through millions of iterations—a system inspired explicitly by the feedback loop of genetic natural selection. Operating overnight on a desktop PC, Deere's genetic algorithms turned the Deere factory into a model of industrial economizing—truck trailers delivering parts precisely when needed; self-organizing worker teams building custom equipment, no two alike; each product rolling off the end of the assembly line into an idling truck awaiting the delivery of precisely that machine for Farmer Jones. Notably, Deere began referring to the Moline facility as a "living factory."[30]

Perhaps most amazing, the greatest leaps are yet to come. "Technologies are feeding back on themselves; we're taking off," says Danny Hillis, the founder of Thinking Machines Corporation. "We're at that point analogous to when single-cell organisms were turning into multicelled organisms."[31] It is to this labyrinth of ever richer and more robust connections that we now turn.

CHAPTER
2

Everyone a Middleman

It ranks among the most famous soundbites in all of economic history: "It is not from the benevolence of the butcher, the brewer, or the baker that we expect our dinner, but from regard to their own self-interest."[1] Like many soundbites, however, this one loses most of its meaning outside of context.

Contrary to widespread impressions, Adam Smith, the inventor of economics, celebrated the individual not solely as an end in himself but as the member of a community, one whose purpose was a better society. He hailed the power of "connexions and dependencies" in promoting the greater good. He spoke of the entrepreneur as "a single cell in a larger organism."[2] He said technological progress came from "combining together the powers of the most distant and dissimilar objects."[3] In the very paragraph of *The Wealth of Nations* containing his oft-quoted axiom of self-interest, Smith also makes the following claim: "In civilized society, [man] stands at all times in need of the cooperation and assistance of great multitudes." One telling fact: When Smith died his estate was negligible. He had given it all away.[4]

After a century of hiding, Smith's values are reemerging through the pressures of a complex and interdependent world. Until recently most business owners saw themselves as lone battlers eking out their claim in a hostile environment; many, perhaps most, still do. But the kind of spectacular success possible in today's economy is accessible not at arm's length but through a full embrace. As the economy splinters into ever-smaller pieces, those pieces come together in more and different ways. So while the economy prospers through expressions of individuality, those very individuals prosper principally through expressions of solidarity. Where business is concerned, the personal and the social are two halves of the identical dynamic, no differently, as it happens, than elsewhere in nature.

As we'll explore in this chapter, every act of innovation occurs through synthesis: a combination of differing people, varying technologies, or far-flung business practices. That was as true of General Motors in its heyday as it is today. But now accelerating communications make it less useful to organize this action under a single roof; today's technology, in other words, is diluting the value of the monolithic corporation as an economizing force. Best of all, this new, decentralized economy creates opportunities for anyone to establish new combinations—to create value as a middleman—as I learned from a fellow named Joe Morabito.

He grew up in a gritty, slushy Ohio steel town near Youngstown (by sheer coincidence a few miles from where I grew up). His grandfather, an uneducated immigrant from Italy, started out slinging cans of olive oil over his shoulder and peddling them from door to door. The old man eventually acquired a cart to carry the cans. Soon he was selling fruit as well as oil. Then the cart became a store, and the store became several stores, providing a living for the entire Morabito clan. Young Joe Morabito grew up with business in his blood.

As the steel mills of the region played out, Morabito followed his older brother to Los Angeles, putting himself through junior college and later through Cal State by selling shoes in Beverly Hills. That was when Beverly Hills still mattered, and the glib, bombastic Morabito counted the likes of Tina Turner and Priscilla Presley among his customers. He practiced the classic art of "selling wide, selling deep," always encouraging the customer to step into a better shoe or a second pair and above all leaving her with such a fine feeling that she would scarcely think of ever buying from someone else. But the smooth-talking sales guy had another side. After finally graduating from college he taught in the public schools of impoverished East Los Angeles, a job in which nothing worked unless you connected with people at an intensely personal level. At age twenty-nine, after six years in education, he was approaching burnout when a personnel official phoned him about taking a top administrator's post in the school district. "To be honest with you, we're really looking for a Mexican," the recruiter said. "But we understand you're Italian, you have a mustache, and you speak Spanish. So maybe you'll do." Morabito quit in disgust.

His brother, by then a vice-chancellor at UCLA, urged him to join the business world and passed along a job tip: Merrill Lynch, the brokerage firm, was building an operation called Merrill Lynch Relocation Management and was hiring staff for a West Coast operation. Helping corporate clients transfer their employees sounded halfway interesting to Joe Morabito, who before long found himself deep in the logistics of moving hundreds of Price Waterhouse employees to Orlando so they could assume the auditing chores at Disney World.

It was a heady, wild, and—as anyone who has been through a corporate relocation knows—exasperating business. In the late 1970s America was afflicted with "stagflation," the deadly combination of sluggish economic growth and high inflation. The Federal Reserve had pushed interest rates to dizzying heights. Houses sold slowly and were ridiculously expensive to maintain in inventory. Merrill Lynch capitalized on these conditions by purchasing houses directly from transferred employees (for their purported appraised value) then charging employers a fat fee for each day the property remained unsold. When a house was finally sold, Merrill Lynch also pocketed a portion of the real estate commission.

Morabito was put off by the zero-sum mind-set that the firm brought to the realty practice, which he attributed to its Wall Street culture. The company treated relocation like stock trading: Your profit was perfectly proportional to somebody else's loss. "Merrill Lynch was very much into somebody winning and somebody losing," he would recall. So Morabito took a bold step, launching a consulting practice within the company to advise corporate clients on how to *cut* their costs in a move. Doing this often involved the radical step of pulling together services from various other divisions of Merrill Lynch—business units so far-flung in those days they barely knew of one another: realty, mortgage, cash management, and others. Morabito's success in creating a single, customized product from Merrill Lynch's disparate divisions was so revolutionary that the company hailed him in a feature and photograph in its 1985 annual report.

The 1980s finally caught up with Morabito when Merrill Lynch assigned some tough guys from New York to manage the West Coast office where he worked. Morabito's boss kept a hard hat on display at the entrance to his office as a warning that underlings would be bashed if things went awry. "It was the ugliest of the ugly," Morabito says now. Before long he and several others fled the company, sending Merrill Lynch Relocation on a downhill slide from which it never fully recovered. Ultimately the parent company unloaded the relocation business. The buyer was Prudential, another hard-nosed financial services concern.

On his own and incurably entrepreneurial, Morabito in 1991 purchased a small corporate relocation agency owned by the timber giant Weyerhaeuser and reopened as a new company called Paragon Decision Resources, based in Irvine, California. Paragon lacked the capital to take unsold houses into inventory as Merrill Lynch once had. It also lacked the kind of national realty network that Prudential was putting together. But Morabito didn't view his new company merely as a way to churn fees and commissions on real estate. Instead, Morabito resolved to reorient the relocation process, treating home selling as just one of many critical links in a complex and delicate chain. He figured that by shrewdly sequencing the events—house hunting, mortgage application, cash advances, packing schedules, flight arrangements, realty closing, and the myriad steps in between—he could generate tremendous savings for the corporate client, far beyond what he had ever accomplished at Merrill Lynch. And by giving transferred employees a single point of contact, he could spare them the trauma of bouncing from department to department within a firm. The big relocation outfits worked on economies of scale; Morabito would work on economies of scope.

There were no blueprints for such a business. Making travel arrangements quicker and at lower cost required leasing his own airline computer-reservation terminals. To speed the transfer of cash advances and realty payments he hard-wired his computer systems to those of his clients, enabling Paragon to issue checks on its clients' accounts. Where he lacked capabilities he forged alliances—a partnership with Deloitte and Touche to help cope with international tax codes, another with Citibank to handle international money flows. He lined up other firms to provide language training, spouse job-hunting assistance, psychological counseling, and elder care—anything in the interests of a seamless solution. When Morabito's sales people called on potential customers, they also made a point of pitching the services of Paragon's vendors, just as those companies began pitching the services of Paragon in their sales calls.

At each step Paragon immersed itself ever more intimately in the affairs of its customers and they in Paragon's. Clients began receiving Paragon's employee newsletter while employees began receiving the client newsletter. In approaching potential clients in Silicon Valley, Morabito began offering year-by-year fee reductions—in advance, not much different from what Dana had done for Toyota. "The price of their products keeps declining," Morabito explained. "Why shouldn't ours?" The culture of service infused Morabito's entire organization, as he himself realized one day when a number of his employees showed up wearing beepers. Even at the risk of becoming twenty-four-hour-a-day workers, they wanted to be sure that relocating families were never out of touch. "I didn't tell anybody to do that," Morabito said.

One day Abbott Laboratories in suburban north Chicago invited Paragon to bid for half of its relocation business, a huge and much-prized piece of work. Most of the business was already in the hands of Morabito's old firm, now part of Prudential, tingeing the bidding contest with personal rivalry. Morabito flew to Chicago to make his pitch to Robert Beck, a top personnel executive for the medical-supply company. Beck was floored by Morabito's manner. "He wanted to find out what I needed, not what he could sell me," Beck would recall, still incredulous a few years after the event. Beck was equally stunned at how much money Morabito estimated he could save Abbott, simply by applying expert, unbiased knowledge and timing to the exigencies of a relocation. "This guy's not for real!" the Abbott executive told himself. Abbott Labs agreed to take a chance on the upstart Paragon, cutting way back on its dealings with Prudential. Joe Morabito had defeated his former employer, the number-one player in corporate relocation.

But because relocating a family is one of the most stressful events in life (ranking with death and divorce), Abbott wanted to maintain close oversight of the process it was outsourcing. When Beck asked whether Paragon could establish a branch office in Chicago to handle Abbott's business, Morabito agreed on the spot. Literally within days, the new space had been leased and the new office fully staffed. On top of that Morabito agreed to have his employees report to an Abbott executive—even to receive their performance reviews from the client—while remaining on Paragon's payroll.

Then Morabito unfurled his true collaborative colors: He began out-sourcing local realty listings to his dreaded competitor, Prudential Realty. Morabito was actually handing over business to the very firm from which he was taking business. At one point Morabito went head-to-head for the coveted Schlumberger Limited account against the giant Associates Realty Management, a unit of Ford Motor Company, at the very moment that he was *hiring* Associates to help him service some new business at Motorola. On yet another occasion Morabito lost out to Associates in a bidding contest for the Dell Computer account—and phoned congratulations to the president of Associates, who, after all, was a business partner as well as a competitor. Morabito even began inviting his competitors to the training sessions he con-ducted for clients and employees.

The net effect of putting together the best packages of services possi-ble was creating customers who dared not dream of replacing Paragon. Indeed, when Bob Beck left Abbott Labs for the computer maker Gateway 2000, he immediately turned over Gateway's relocation oper-ations to Paragon. "I didn't even bid it," Beck commented. "I just said, 'Joe, come out here.' " Abbott meanwhile switched the last of its relo-cation business from Prudential to Paragon.

By 1999 Paragon was pulling in annual revenue of $9 million and moving families worldwide at the rate of ten thousand a year for dozens of blue-chip clients. And along the way something happened that Joe Morabito himself never could have predicted: the emergence of an altogether new definition of what it meant to handle relocation. Abbott Labs put Paragon in charge of a training program that cycled executives through a series of six-month assignments. Sprint asked Paragon to handle auto leases overseas. The National Association of Electrical Distributors hired Paragon not only to move its headquarters offices but to recruit thirty-five new staff members, search for a new president, and write the job descriptions for everyone in the organiza-tion. Paragon had morphed into an entire human-resources organiza-tion. It had been years since Joe Morabito had sold a pair of ladies' shoes, but he was still selling wider and deeper.

He could have sold out or taken his company public at any moment for huge bucks. But being in the middle was Morabito's life and his love, and he had zero interest in managing to the short-term expecta-tions of Wall Street. "I'm not focused on our quarterly performance," he said. "I'm focused on getting customers for life." Neither, he said, was he interested in cashing out any of his interest. "I'm not out to milk this company," he told me. "I am a builder."

∽

I know people who would laugh at Morabito for his practice of giving business to his competition. Robert Crandall, the hyper-competitive chairman of American Airlines, was acclaimed by his board for his ability to put entire competing airlines out of business. (He once appeared before an employee meeting in war paint and bandana, a toy machine gun in his arms.) I also know executives who would belittle Morabito for treating his vendors so reverentially. Albert "Chainsaw Al" Dunlap, who won infamy for his brutal firings at Scott Paper and Sunbeam, has boasted of giving his own business partners the same rough treatment. "I'm terrific at beating up suppliers," he said.[5] Robert Odom, who spent years as chairman of U.S. Home, the nation's largest homebuilder, used to urge his executives to study Ayn Rand's *The Virtues of Selfishness*.[6] Not one of these macho males, however, built their businesses from nothing, as Morabito did.

People in business can certainly be forgiven their fixation on competition. It's practically in the water we drink: The rigid Newtonian mental model and the persistence of social Darwinism have conditioned people to see life as a struggle for finite resources. In the academic literature, discussions of competition and predation outweigh studies of cooperation by a factor of 900 percent.[7] The Discovery Channel and others fill hours of programming with internecine animal warfare. "People think they know biology and the way the natural world functions because they've seen bighorn sheep locking horns on PBS,"[8] says the organizational theorist Margaret Wheatley. Thus we get books with titles like *Looking Out for Number One* and *Mean Business*.

These worldviews are based on erroneous science. "Competition has no special status in biological dynamics," says the British biologist Brian Goodwin. "What is important is the pattern of relationships and interactions that exist and how they contribute to the system as an integrated whole."[9] In a book memorably titled *Why Big Fierce Animals Are Rare*, the biologist Paul Colinvaux remarks, "Natural selection designs different kinds of animals so they avoid competition. A fit animal is not one that fights well, but one that avoids fighting altogether."[10] This is true of no species more than man. Having traded brute strength and fanged jaws for large, delicate brains, "humans are innately disposed to avoid violent physical contact," says the Harvard biologist Edward O. Wilson.[11] That we still sometimes do proves only that our evolution has far from run its course.

I say this recognizing that the competitive stakes are higher than ever in business. Today, market share can disappear overnight, as the once-invulnerable Nike has discovered. No industry is immune from instant obsolescence, as the makers of diamond record styluses and eight-track tape heads learned. A cost structure that works one day (high-priced cell phones) crumbles the next (free cell phones). It's ludicrous to hail "the death of competition," to cite the title of an otherwise valuable best-selling book.[12] One also sees much written these days about "coopetition" among big companies—you know, firms competing in one market space while cooperating in another. But when big competitors cooperate, they're usually cutting backroom deals at the expense of their vendors or customers—the way major airline partners list each other's flights as their own, for instance, a practice, known as "code sharing," in which they use their joint marketing muscle to crowd out competitors.

In truth, business is becoming more competitive and cooperative at once, which should come as no surprise. In business as elsewhere in nature, competition is actually a form of cooperation! Competition sorts the efficient from the inefficient, the fast from the slow, no differently than in the natural world. Competition selects the better way for all to follow. Except for the immediate casualties, competition benefits everyone, in ecosystems and economies alike. "He who wrestles with us strengthens our nerves, and sharpens our skill," Edmund Burke said. "Our antagonist is our helper."[13]

This helps explain why pioneering business people see competition in a new light. Of course they must compete—but in nearly every case the number and variety of their competitive relationships is trifling compared with their cooperative relationships, their "connexions and dependencies," to recall Adam Smith's words. And it's foolish to let worry about the few overwhelm concern about the many, as a fellow named Tom Kozak taught me.

Kozak, age forty-four when I met him, won a science-fair prize for an electrical circuit when he was in the ninth grade and never quit hooking things together. After graduating from high school at age sixteen he went straight to work in computers, with no time for college.

He wound up as a techie at a company called Panduit Corporation, headquartered in the south Chicago suburb of Tinley Park. With 2,500 employees, plants worldwide and sales of $300 million a year, Panduit made an array of gewgaws for an increasingly interconnected world: wire, crimpers, connectors, strippers, and many others, a stunning 60,000 products in all.

Panduit was also one of the most secretive outfits I had ever visited. Entering the headquarters suite from the reception area I slipped my visitor badge (don't you hate those things?) into my coat pocket—until my hosts firmly requested that I clip it back on. I was not permitted to walk twenty paces down the corridor to the men's room without an escort. Product ideas, I was told, are too easily copied and too short-lived to leave any security measure unspared. All of which makes Tom Kozak's actions all the more remarkable.

For as long as anyone could remember Panduit and its competitors had shipped electrical parts to independent dealers, who stockpiled the myriad bits and pieces that cable installers and electrical contractors used on the job—a total of $60 billion worth of parts each year, industrywide. The distributors, alas, were not a happy lot. At a time when all of industry was cutting inventories to the bone, the proliferation of electrical parts was killing them. Carrying costs had climbed to an astonishing 30 percent of the inventory value. The distributors' profit margins had slipped to a paltry 1.5 percent of sales, tantamount to nothing. Even some of the most established distributors were in danger of going under. Yet Panduit (no different from any of its competitors) needed to keep the distribution channel alive and vibrant. It was the sole pipeline to the market, and improving the distributors' lot was Panduit's best hope for growth. "If you don't grow," as Kozak told me, "you die."

From all he could see, the answer was putting the suppliers and distributors on more intimate and up-to-date terms, so that parts flowed through the supply chain only as needed rather than as hedges against future shortages. This, in turn, meant a move in only one direction: to electronic data interchange. EDI, as it's commonly called, is one of the archetypal "economizing" technologies of the digital age. Synchronizing data across the supply chain saves keystrokes, cuts head counts, reduces error, and eliminates lag. It relies on suppliers to keep track of a customer's inventories, and to replenish them according to whatever sort of formula the parties have agreed upon in advance.

But Kozak had made little headway introducing such economies. The distributors were largely local firms owned by first-generation founders dating to the immediate postwar era. The distributors had scrimped for profit for so long they could scarcely imagine giving their suppliers any say-so over what was happening in their stockrooms. "No manufacturer will ever manage *my* inventory!" some of them swore. Even more vexing, each distributor had dozens or perhaps hundreds of separate suppliers. Every one of them had a slightly different ordering processes, and they had never come close to standardizing parts numbers.

Kozak realized that someone, anyone, had to overcome the inertia. So he began evangelizing—first within Panduit, where the senior management, notwithstanding its secretiveness, easily grasped the importance of his proposal, and then within the industry at large. Before long he was standing before four major competitors who had been invited to Tinley Park to hear his ideas. It was the most nervous he had been in his years at Panduit. The industry's only hope, he told them, was to begin standardizing all aspects of all transactions between factories and distributors. "Can't we agree to put the purchase order number in the same place?" he pleaded. To his astonishment, three of the four arch-competitors agreed to cooperate on the spot. "I nearly fell over," he later recalled.

Kozak then began schmoozing the distributors. After recruiting a few guinea pigs to demonstrate the economizing powers of EDI, he talked several of them into pressuring additional manufacturers to join the plan. In 1995 alone Kozak made seventy-five presentations around the industry. "We're all in this together!" he pleaded. Cynics continually asked why he—why Panduit—was taking the lead. "If the distributors don't survive, *we* don't survive!" he answered.

Today, hundreds of distributors have gone on-line. Some have integrated with suppliers so tightly that they function with the efficiency of an organism. Each morning the computers at Panduit and the other suppliers wake up, phone the distributors, take inventory, and decide how many items (if any) to ship that day. The mind-meld goes both ways; a distributor can touch a button to find out if Panduit has a particular part sitting in its own inventory ready for shipment.

Kozak's actions have radiated beyond even his own industry. An organization called the Uniform Code Council, which fixes standards for bar codes, adopted his work in worldwide guidelines for all industrial and commercial electronic data interchange, paving the way for another leap forward in electronic commerce. Kozak, for his part, having pulled together so many people and processes, wound up creating a new company, called Pan-Pro. Its mission: selling software and consulting services to help companies find competitive advantage in the cooperative marketplace he himself had helped to create.

⌇

It was people like Joe Morabito and Tom Kozak who defined the ethos of pioneer America. Notwithstanding the mythology of the "rugged individualist," it was communal roof raisings, quilting bees, granges, guilds, and cooperatives that executed the daily agenda of Manifest Destiny. Tocqueville witnessed Americans continually practicing "the art of association," which he called "the mother of all action."[14] Families plunging west from Independence, Missouri, in the 1850s organized joint companies and elected treasurers who changed terms every few weeks.[15] "The pioneer," said Frederick Jackson Turner in his 1893 essay on the West, "had boundless confidence in the future of his own community."

The corporation, however, soon followed as a vehicle for raising capital for railroads; for installing huge, central energy sources (water wheels, steam boilers); and for seizing the economies of scale through massive production runs. Where individual entrepreneurs and family firms had once self-organized around society's needs, corporations began to absorb this activity within their own walls. In the 1937 work for which he would ultimately win a Nobel Prize, the economist Ronald H. Coase argued that corporations existed to eliminate transaction costs that would otherwise exist between individual entrepreneurs.[16]

In the century following the Civil War and beyond, scale economies propelled business through an unrelenting loop of positive feedback: Longer production runs justified the creation and installation of specialized machines; these machines reduced costs; lower costs meant higher profits, which attracted more capital for expansion, which further increased the production runs. As corporations traded across larger geographical territories, they began absorbing the suppliers and distributors in their paths. Ford became a major steel manufacturer, U.S. Steel a major coal producer, Texaco a major retailer. The independent entrepreneur was left to scramble for crumbs, as Sinclair Lewis described in his 1922 novel *Babbitt*. "He made nothing in particular, neither butter nor shoes nor poetry," Lewis wrote of George Babbitt, "but he was nimble in the calling of selling homes for more than people could afford to pay."[17]

Once mass production had given way to national markets, these created mass merchandising, which gave birth to mass media. Ultimately, by the 1970s, national branding reached even more deeply into the domain of the independent entrepreneur: the service economy, including restaurants, car-repair shops, tax-preparation firms, and ultimately even barber shops and medical practices. Entrepreneurs were crowded into an ever-smaller corner of the economy, mostly to package, integrate, or otherwise make a market for someone else's product, becoming travel agents, say, or "value-added resellers" of computers and peripherals.

Now many pundits warn that the same terrible fate awaits even them. As the theory goes, information technology puts producers directly in contact with their customers, collapsing the distribution chain, wiping out all those who have made their living by taking orders or breaking big lots into smaller lots. A spooky technical term has been coined for this process: disintermediation. "Middleman functions between consumers and producers are being eliminated," the futurist Don Tapscott wrote in the influential bestseller *The Digital Economy*.[18] Patrick McGovern, chairman of International Data Group, the world's largest high-tech publisher, is even more dour. "The intermediary is doomed," he wrote in *Forbes ASAP*. "Technology strips him of effectiveness."[19]

I think the doomsayers are flat wrong. Information technology is the friend of the middleman. Technology wipes out inefficiency, it's true—and thank goodness. But that is hardly the only way it adds value. As Joe Morabito's story shows, technology makes possible the integration of services on the smallest of scales. It has created a whole category of firms called "infomediaries," turning teachers and grad students from Stanford and Carnegie Mellon into overnight millionaires. Technology explains how a single entrepreneur can create Amazon.com, the world's largest bookstore, on little more than a great idea.

Or consider Roger Dube. In fifteen years at IBM he watched the company strangulate promising business opportunities through bureaucracy and "not invented here" syndrome. Brilliant technologies and great inventions were everywhere, he realized—in the bowels of big industrial labs, in universities, in basements and garages—many holding the key to unlocking a vexing technological problem elsewhere. So with a modest investment Dube formed a company in Boca Raton, Florida, to search out existing, underused technologies through extremely aggressive database exploration and electronic networking. Large manufacturing companies that wiped out their R&D departments in the downsizing of the early '90s began engaging Dube's firm to locate new manufacturing processes or machines, many of them designed by engineers who themselves had been downsized. "Necessity is the mother of invention, and we communicate the necessity to the best of the best inventors worldwide," Dube says. His company, Gate Technologies, also began monitoring the four corners of the science world for clients who wanted to avoid getting surprised by upstart companies offering their hot new technologies to someone else. "There is no question that information technology is the necessary ingredient," Dube says. By 1998 he had five employees bringing in more than $1 million in annual revenue.

Technology also provides a marketing platform on which scale economics have no meaning. I spent some time in Minneapolis with a twenty-eight-year-old named Charles Anderson, who goes by the Web handle of Chank Diesel. Only a year earlier Chank had been "practically homeless," as he put it, living in the dreary basement headquarters of a Minneapolis punk-rock magazine called *Cake*. But he had a talent for drawing the alphabet, inspired partly by his love of Art Deco–style motel lettering that he saw plowed under by major hotel chains in his native Florida. By 1997 he was on the World Wide Web, offering free downloadable digital fonts but also special fonts in exchange for a $10 payment by credit card. ("Fonts are like water," his Web site noted. "You can get it for free, but the kind you pay for tastes much better.") Even at $10 a transaction, he was yielding more money from his Web site than General Motors or Exxon had ever harvested from theirs.

Soon Chank had built a community of regular Web-site visitors, mainly artists and designers who tuned in not just to check out his latest fonts but to read his zany (often indecorous) accounts of his punkadelic lifestyle. Before long he was seeing his designs everywhere, from the Cartoon Network to a dollar-off coupon for Nestlé Toll House Morsels to a full-page ad for Northwest Airlines in the *Wall*

Street Journal. Chank also began distributing fonts from other design-ers, some from Europe and Asia, thereby earning a small premium for himself. By the time of my visit in 1997 he had three part-time employ-ees working in a converted warehouse with striped walls and a copy of Gainsborough's *Blue Boy* hanging on the wall.

People like Roger Dube, Chank Diesel, and dozens of others I know are turning Coase's 1937 theory of the corporation entirely on its head. "In the absence of transaction costs," Coase said in a wildly hypothet-ical moment, "there is no economic basis for the existence of the firm."[20] Indeed, large organizations are now outsourcing the very func-tions they had once brought in-house—printing, training, mainte-nance, engineering, and even manufacturing itself. Microbrew International of Rochester has designed a high-tech brewery that costs less than $100,000 and fits in less than one hundred square feet. By eliminating the need for shipment from a distant factory, these tiny breweries produced customized, high-quality, local beers for less than Budweiser can deliver it—the economies of locality trumping the economies of scale, thanks to technology.

But what of all the mega-mergers? one might fairly ask. The late 1990s, after all, witnessed a record pace of corporate combinations. But look again. Usually, consolidation follows commoditization. Telecommunications, banking, media, retail—the industries caught up in the huge mergers of the 1990s were those whose products had been reduced to sheer volume economics. When entrepreneurs can no longer add value to an established industry—when gains can occur only by wringing out transaction cost or by locking out competitors—then consolidation makes economic sense. Consolidation, in other words, follows commoditization. In one measure of the declining economic influence of giant firms, the 1965 *Fortune* 500 accounted for 20 per-cent of all American jobs; by 1995 the figure had fallen to 10 percent.[21]

Large firms will always exist, of course, in industries where scale economies apply. But there are no scale economies in creativity. Microsoft prospers through size because it is less a software develop-ment company than a distribution company. The banking, media, retail, and communication industries have also devolved into com-modity distributors, just like airlines in the early '90s, oil in the 1980s, and brokerage in the 1970s.

Behind the huge, new monoliths, however, lies an ever-*increasing* number of small players who do add value and therefore earn some-thing better than commodity margins. Even as the big media companies merge, they purchase the creative services of an ever-expanding complement of freelance writers, editors, producers, designers, and the like; though the number of book publishers has plunged, the number of authors being published has soared. While telecommunication becomes like the pipeline business, more and more small companies (and, obviously, many large ones, too) create intelligent applications for use along that network, from voice-recognition to videoconferencing products. As banking turns into bookkeeping, a host of nonbank firms invent new credit and financial services.

These small firms are multiplying for much the same reason that big firms are consolidating: technology. The same communication and information technology by which Wal-Mart wiped out small-time retailers permits a small-time industrial distributor to compete with General Electric. Digital technology is the first infinitely scalable economizing tool. It is driving marginal costs toward zero. It reduces or eliminates barriers to entry, enabling middlemen to add value not just by assembling materials but by exercising their minds. Technology is taking the capital out of capitalism.

მ

Nobody I know exemplifies the bright future of the middleman better than Jerry Whitlock, the "Seal Man" of Stockton, Georgia. Whitlock sells seals and gaskets, an independent distributor working for himself—precisely the kind of intermediary the experts seem determined to disintermediate. The son of a truck driver, he grew up in rural Georgia and went to work out of high school chasing smokestacks from town to town, conducting cold calls at every factory he could find. It was the early 1970s—recession years—and he considered no order too small: a few metric O-rings here, a handful of V-rings there, grease seals, pump packing, you name it. "I did it the hard way," he told me when I visited his home near Atlanta. "No mentor, no financial support, no nothing."

In the course of tracking down so many seriously obscure parts, Whitlock amassed a mountain of catalogues and bulletins, organizing and cross-referencing them in a set of huge, black binders. Likewise his Rolodex grew and grew, listing vital contacts who could either supply any part or tell him who could. Briefly Whitlock took a tour through corporate America, but he was appalled to find himself surrounded by sleazy financial dealings and the pressure to cut corners. And he quickly burnt out on managing inventories, supervising employees, and flying as often as fifty times a year. So in 1995 he once again struck out on his own—not in his car this time, but in a spare room in the home on his wooded suburban lot.

Never was a gasket salesman so wired. He bought two cell phones, lashed a beeper to his belt, and purchased an automatic fax machine to broadcast one hundred single-page advertisements overnight to carefully targeted prospects. Whitlock's faxes boasted of his experience with "rush jobs," his access to "oddball, hard-to-find parts," and his purported standing as a "worldwide supplier to industry." He dubbed himself "the Seal Man," adding a likeness of himself to his stationery to give customers a feeling for the fellow on the other end of the fax. He also hired his sister to work part-time from her home phoning prospects who had responded to one of his faxes. Then Whitlock added e-mail, eventually installing a program that forwarded any messages containing a few promising key words (such as "quote" or "order") to his pager for instant call-back. He scanned his entire twenty-four-page catalogue into a site on the World Wide Web and notified the major searching services to include his Web address under "seals" and "gaskets."

The truth is that no amount of technology assures a profitable connection, but it surely helps to create a potential selling opportunity. As inquiries arrived by phone, fax, and e-mail, Whitlock dug into those old notebooks years in the making. Motion Industries needs a part for a Bulgarian-made press. A giant motor at Carolina Power & Light keeps catching fire because no one can replace a persistently leaky oil seal. A call from GM, another from TVA, another from Smucker's. At such moments Whitlock flipped through his golden Rolodex or reached back into his years of experience hanging out on shop floors. When he tracked down a part he arranged for its shipment by overnight express to his two-car garage. There, his wife, Rita, connected to him by two-way radio, switched the incoming product into a new box with an invoice, dropped in a "Seal Man" refrigerator magnet, and immediately sent the package out. By 1997 he was doing $1 million worth of business a year, and with costs so low his gross margins averaged about 60 percent—a sum representing the value of the know-how he brought to every order.

And his growth had only begun. Whitlock's niche expanded with the spreading World Wide Web, bringing in customers from around the globe. "Last week I had inquiries or orders from Indonesia, Dubai, Singapore, Sweden, Trinidad, Chile, Mexico, and several others," he told me at one point. Technology also expanded his reach for supply beyond his old set of black binders. By 1998 he was buying from vendors in Germany, Venezuela, Ireland, Australia, and Austria. He forged a close relationship with an Indian entrepreneur with whom he established a small, captive manufacturing operation—all via e-mail. "A guy right around the corner from me never heard of me till he saw me on the Internet," Whitlock said, sitting at his built-in plywood desk, his wife packing boxes a few yards away, the UPS truck in his driveway, his cell phone warbling.

Whitlock's success enabled him and Rita to spend a lot of time in a Florida vacation home without leaving the business behind. He scanned his Rolodex and his industrial directories into his laptop. He mounted a post over the transmission hump in his truck to keep the laptop within reach as he drove. He forwarded all his calls. And when an order could not wait for repackaging in his garage, he simply arranged a drop shipment straight from his supplier to his customer.

He was the ultimate middleman. He added value by knowing where to find the gasket equivalent of a needle in the marketplace equivalent of a haystack, creating a profitable storefront in the new village square that is the world.

೨

The Seal Man succeeded because he had a niche—but "niche" is a poorly understood word in business, corrupted by generations of people thinking of it as a hiding place from competition, or as a haven for collecting revenue to which no one else has yet laid claim. "Hit 'em where they ain't," says a highly successful "niche consultant" and best-selling author.[22] These purported experts counsel clients to "differentiate" themselves from the competition by adding a unique feature to an established product. This is empty advice in the new economy. Differentiation may provide marginal benefits for a high-volume commodity distributor—making cheeseburgers square instead of round, say, or adding engine cleaners to high-octane fuel—but merely being different no longer opens niches. When people try to define their businesses (or for that matter their careers) according to what the competition isn't, they're not filling a niche. They're simply occupying a habitat.

So what does it mean to create a niche? Consider the natural world, from which, after all, we borrow the term. A niche is a safe place, to be sure, for it's there that a species faces the least competition for resources. But it is also a place from which a single species supports other species and in turn is supported by them. Decades after they had been depleted by furriers, sea otters were reintroduced to California's coastal waters. Before long, the otters had cut back on the explosive sea-urchin population. That permitted the kelp to return, as any beach-goer along Big Sur can attest. And a flourishing new community of algae took root, drawing gray whales in from the deep.[23]

"Organizations, like organisms, are not really discrete entities," says the Canadian organizational theorist Gareth Morgan. "They do not live in isolation and are not self-sufficient. Rather, they exist as elements in a complex ecosystem."[24] Or, to paraphrase the biologist Edward O. Wilson, a niche is not merely a place but a *role*.[25] In ecosystems, just as in economies, everyone is a middleman.

But how exactly is a new niche created? The French biologist and Nobel recipient François Jacob once called nature a tinkerer, building new species from "odds and ends."[26] Entrepreneurs find niches through the same kind of *bricolage*, as I realized when discovering that there was a little bit of Cleveland—and a lot of Carol Latham—inside my laptop computer.

Growing up in the old industrial outpost of Sharon, Pennsylvania, in the mid-1950s, Carol Latham loved science but was discouraged by all social convention from studying it in college. But then the Soviet Union launched Sputnik, history's first artificial satellite. While terrifying Americans, nothing so propelled them toward technological achievement. The Sputnik panic accelerated development of the transistor, sounded the starting gun for the race to the moon, and made a chemistry major of Carol Latham.

Four years later, with a bachelor's degree and top grades in hand from Ohio Wesleyan University, she drew a job offer from Standard Oil Company of Ohio—the venerable old Sohio, which sat at the pinnacle of the Cleveland corporate establishment. Sohio gave Latham the choice of two assignments: working in the research lab, where scientists pressed the boundaries of chemistry, or in the development lab, where they conducted the prosaic but profitable work of turning known technologies into new products. A stubbornly practical person, Latham chose the less exotic assignment, plunging into the development of bendable, stretchable new hydrocarbons known in the lab as polymers. Most people came to call them "plastics."

Before long Latham was sidelined by a distraction for which Sputnik had provided no remedy: full-time motherhood. She reared three children in tree-lined suburban Lakewood, Ohio, surrounded by the proliferation of plastics she had briefly played a role in developing. But good lab skills never become obsolete, so when Latham went through a divorce in 1981 and found herself once again in need of work, she looked up her old boss. He was still there and she was soon back in her Sohio lab coat.

By this time, in the era of the oil shock, "alternative energy" had succeeded plastics as the rage in petrochemical research. And although the scientific method hadn't changed much in twenty years, the culture of the lab assuredly had. The place was filled with Ph.D.s, each desperate for success in his own narrow specialty. Jealousy was rampant. One scientist actually sabotaged one of Latham's experiments involving the use of hydrogen as a fuel.

Meanwhile, with merger mania sweeping Big Oil, Sohio suddenly wound up in the ceramics business, introducing yet another new research agenda. Now the lab was expected to create new ceramics that could conduct heat out of tightly packed electronic components. It was a daunting research challenge, but with a small, new, hot-running device called a personal computer coming to market, the payoff was potentially huge.

Carol Latham pondered the problem. Ceramics would be excellent for cooling the interior of a PC, there was no doubt of that, but they were brittle and adhered poorly to hot metal. If only ceramics were sticky . . . if only they were pliable . . .

Eureka! In a flash, past and present collided in the middle of Latham's mind. Why not combine ceramics and plastics? Plastics were bendable, moldable, pourable, stretchable, and adhesive—everything a designer might require inside the tiny spaces of a personal computer. Latham traveled to a few electronics conferences and could see that the problem of heat was big and destined to get bigger. Intel was ready to launch a new generation of computer chip, the 386, which would generate three times as much heat as the model it was replacing (just as the 486 and later the Pentium would run roughly three times hotter than each of its predecessors). Before long a newfangled PC known as a "laptop" was making strides in the marketplace, intensifying the heat problem. Carol Latham was overpowered with the conviction that the electronics world needed a new kind of heat-removing material and that she had combined precisely the right materials in the lab at Sohio.

None of the Ph.D.s and lab managers cared in the slightest, however; crossing into plastics, after all, was no way to make your name in ceramics. It didn't help that she was a woman—particularly, she thought, after Sohio had been taken over by British Petroleum, where workplace gender attitudes lagged behind those in the U.S. "I just wanted to be taken seriously," she would recall. "But there was a moat, a river, a mountain. I couldn't get anywhere. So one day I just resigned."

Her niche, her role, was staring right at her: turning low-value commodity chemicals into a high-value substance that would improve the performance of electronic equipment. Initially she set up shop on her suburban living room table. When the time came to buy equipment she leased her home to tenants and moved into a small apartment, using the difference to pay the rent on a small corner of a large commercial plant. (As part of the bargain, the owner of the building insisted she clean all the restrooms every week.) Latham's elderly mother tossed in some retirement funds. Her son's fiancée worked without pay. She called her company Thermagon Incorporated (as in "heat be gone"). Before long, Latham had hired a West Coast representative and was making sales calls herself, asking electronics companies whether they had any heat problems she could solve. To combat the skepticism of her mostly male customers, she identified herself on her business cards not as Thermagon's president but as its "technical director."

Her first order came from IBM, which asked whether she could make a molded part with heat-conducting properties; easily she did. Then a company called Aavid Engineering, a major distributor of traditional heat-control products, added some of her products to its catalogue. "She has this great willingness to listen to everybody's special nuance," recalled Henry Villaume, then the engineer chief at Aavid. "She's a good applications person." Silicon Graphics began sending various metal pieces, asking if she could make a heat-reducer stick to them. Each day she sent a new sample to Silicon Graphics by FedEx, and the next day the company asked her if she could make it a little softer; soon she had added a heat-reducing putty to her product line. And although Intel couldn't use Thermagon products in its chips, it did recommend them to companies building laptops with Pentium processors. Thermagon even began making printed circuit boards with thermal conductors built right into the surface—products that found their way into antilock braking systems and other huge applications.

When I visited Thermagon in 1997, it was immediately obvious that Carol Latham, mixer of ceramics and plastics, had an appreciation for improbable combinations. She had moved the business into a former knitting mill along a dreary stretch of industrial West 25th Street in

Cleveland, with a dreary, black water tower on the roof and a new, high-tech "clean room" on the inside. She hung hokey reproductions of American historical documents on one wall and arresting electron-microscope photos of organic molecules on the next. Two of her sons had joined the business; one was an engineer, the other a history major. With eighteen employees she was doing $10 million worth of annual business and growing at a rate of about 200 percent a year. And she had only begun.

◇

Latham's lesson is universal, though too seldom seen: Economic niches, like ecological ones, take form around innovations—and innovation most often occurs through combination. Though long forgotten in an era of extreme specialization, the power of combination is evident on every level of scale. In its brimming supply of "distant and dissimilar objects," to repeat Adam Smith's lovely phrase, the world contains infinite undiscovered combinations—atoms become molecules, words become poetry, a handful of notes becomes an endless book of song. Add gospel to blues and you get rhythm and blues; throw in a white boy from Memphis and you get rock 'n' roll. "Every act of imagination is the discovery of likenesses between two things which were thought unlike," says the mathematician Jacob Bronowski in *The Origins of Knowledge and Imagination*.[27] In a similar vein the humanist psychologist Abraham Maslow in 1964 defined invention as "a sudden integration of previously known bits of knowledge not yet suitably patterned."[28]

The proof is overwhelming. After spending two years watching research scientists conduct hundreds of experiments, Kevin Dunbar of McGill University in Montreal concluded that they "rely largely on analogy—the process of applying knowledge in one area to solve problems in another."[29] In a study based on 630,000 U.S. patents, the Israel Institute of Technology asserted, "Innovation is essentially a process of coupling."[30] The highly itinerant Quakers accelerated the industrial revolution in England by skillfully applying the practices of one industry to another. For instance, they used coke, a high-energy fuel developed for the brewing process, as a substitute for charcoal in the production of a new and stronger cast iron, without which the steam engine would never have taken off.[31] By contrast, societies that centrally managed technological development, as the emperors of ancient

China did, were highly stable but produced little material wealth.

Today humanity may be on the verge of what a brilliant financial economist named Mark White calls a "combinatorial explosion." Working from an obscure academic outpost in Mexico City, White has studied the proliferation of technologies and the abundance of communications bandwidth, conditions that make possible vastly more combinations than the world has people to discover. "Every time technologists discover a single new material," he writes—think of Carol Latham— "humanity then has the potential to make every known object in a new and potentially quite useful way. In turn, these individual objects combine with known assemblies of objects to create further new possibilities. These possibilities then radiate out into the complements and substitutes for all known objects and object assemblies, creating further possibilities. Each and every new material expands the entire scope of human technology."[32] The same is true of new processes as well.

But how does one begin to discover the valuable combinations from the infinite that await? What distinguishes a combination that creates a niche from one that merely turns a hamburger patty from round to square? The answer is a special kind of vision, the ability to see practices, materials, markets, or relationships that will change how people do things. "Entrepreneurs are in the business of changing history," says Fernando Flores, who is the most original thinker I have met on the subject of entrepreneurialism. "They give their cultures or industries new styles for dealing with people and things."[33] Entrepreneurs not only shun conventional practice but strive to create a new practice. Or, as John Dewey once said, "Ideas are worthless, except as they pass into actions which rearrange and reconstruct in some way, be it little or large, the world in which we live."[34] Today, unlike in Dewey's time, it is entrepreneurs, scientists, and medical people rather than statesmen, artists, and intellectuals who are leading this charge.

Such bold advances often arise from nothing more than a heightened awareness of everyday living. "The innovator needs a very concrete vision of the new invention that she thinks will succeed before she can go about acquiring the necessary knowledge," Flores says. This demands a sharp eye for "marginal practices," he goes on, for spotting "something that someone else is doing, which is not central to us, and could even belong to another industry. As leaders, we need to fall in love with the cultivation of marginal practices, because this is where we see the future before it happens."[35]

This explains how a former college professor named Morris Shepard built a flourishing value-added enterprise in a commodity industry. In 1995 he had just returned from a three-year academic outpost in Europe and was wondering what to do with the rest of his life. With a Starbuck's latte in his hand, he settled in under a shade tree with a copy of the *New York Times*. There, buried in the D section, he read about a new Xerox copier that could quickly and cheaply turn out entire bound books.

At that moment Shepard realized he was staring at his future. "You know nothing about publishing or printing except you read a lot," his wife scolded. That was true, but he also knew about the headaches of college professors. In years of teaching and administration he had always been maddened by the problems of pulling together far-flung articles and book chapters for students. With one of those souped-up copiers, he thought, he could serve a niche market for academics.

Recall that a niche is not a place but a role—a role between other niche players playing their own roles. Shepard knew better than to offer mere photocopying services, even in a specialized market. So he resolved also to conduct the research and negotiations necessary to secure whatever copyrights were necessary to pull together a syllabus of material, solving another huge problem for professors. He installed scanners and electronic editing systems to despeckle each article while converting it to a standard page size. Then, he would not only print the books but drop-ship them to whatever student co-op or local bookstore the customer required.

Now that's a niche.

He set up his business, called Book Tech, in a downtown storefront in Winchester, Massachusetts, where a struggling retailer photocopier had operated. Maxing out his credit cards, remortgaging his house, and sweet-talking Xerox into a lease he could live with, he opened for business. The business took off and didn't stop, doubling in its second year with two thousand customers and tripling in its third. Doesn't he worry about some big operator horning into his market space? Hardly. In 1998 Barnes & Noble outsourced much of its custom-copying business to him. Retail consolidation has spelled doom for many small booksellers, it's true—but it has apparently opened opportunities for anyone who can add value in the printing process.

As in the case of fontmeister Chank Diesel and Seal Man Jerry Whitlock, electronic communication became vital to Book Tech's success. With no particular strategy or expectation Moe Shepard opened a Web site in 1997 because every other business seemed to be doing the same. For a while orders came in that way at the rate of two or three a month. By the spring of 1998 he was getting a dozen orders a *day* via the Web. Before long he was installing an Oracle database to permit any client to design her own bound teaching materials. "We're going to be instrumental in helping teachers finally overthrow the tyranny of textbooks," he said modestly.

Of course, not all such combinations occur to people while day-dreaming over a latte. Some are discovered only through a directed process of trial and error. That much was evident in the time I spent at a New York design firm called Deskey Associates, founded by the acclaimed Donald Deskey, who created the Art Deco look of Radio City Music Hall in 1932. Through the years Deskey Associates became best known for adapting packaging to the hand, such as the squeeze-able tube for Crest toothpaste, the shapely Aqua Velva bottle, and the roll-on applicator for Ban deodorant. Deskey was the home of a young designer named Jim Warner, who, like many trained artists, harbored a fascination for the hand. Warner created a grip for the Windex spray bottle that hung easily from the thumb and the self-draining spout for liquid Tide—not merely "new and improved" differentiations but design changes that secured niches for the companies that owned them by altering how people actually handled and applied the product.

One day while prospecting for clients Warner happened to recall his summers working as a house painter. At that moment he could feel his hand clutching a paint scraper—weary, sweaty, slipping on the grip. If ever a product needed improvement, he thought, it was the lowly paint scraper. So he contacted a maker of painters' tools named Red Devil Incorporated, an old brand whose products, he learned, were being crowded out of the ascendant home-improvement megastores; because all paint scrapers were alike, only the highest-volume and lowest-cost producer had a chance, and Red Devil qualified in neither category. Warner made a sales call and soon had a contract to come up with the first new scraper design in generations.

He took many steps you might easily imagine: time and motion stud-ies, meetings with focus groups, talks with retailers. But he also began casting for a new combination. He and his colleagues conducted a "world audit" of hand tools, using their friends and business acquain-tances to pick up scrapers from inland China to urban France. This exposed them to the extremes of design, including a highly ergonomic, avant-garde scraper born in the progressive studios of Germany. Warner also assembled a menagerie of all the handles he could find—

from skillets, steak knives, ice scrapers, even shovels—and attached them to scraper blades. From this he learned that consumers (especially women, with whom Red Devil was particularly eager to position itself) favored a fatter handle than anyone had used. Combining that principle with the graceful curves inspired by the German design, Warner created, as Red Devil ultimately called it, "the first hand tool that didn't forget the hand."

Even a new grip can change a little bit of history. "I may not be saving lives," Warner said, "but if you brush your teeth or scrape a chair, you're getting something of greater value." (Warner and several of his associates ultimately joined a design firm called the Coleman Group, where they carried on such work for the likes of Pepsi and Nescafé.)

Thomas Edison's assertion that genius was 99 percent perspiration and 1 percent inspiration was great PR in a country that honored the dignity of individual effort, but it was just plain wrong. Certainly, the development of working applications often demands drudgery and persistence. But in today's marketplace, invention of a niche-producing innovation arises less often from long and precise work than from the haphazard and ambiguous work of establishing, as Adam Smith put it, new "connexions and dependencies."

The proliferation of economic players and the increasing connectedness among them is creating a kind of cocktail party economy. The next time you're invited to a party, make a point of arriving unfashionably early. You'll notice that when the guests are still few, they cluster into a single clump. Then, as a few more people arrive, you notice two groups coalescing, then three after a few more guests arrive. Though the total crowd grows larger, the individual crowds grow smaller. Often, by the end of the evening, people have simply paired off. (The identical dynamic is seen in Internet discussion groups: the larger the group, the smaller the size of the subgroups.)[36]

The reason is that diversity begets diversity.[37] Variety creates feedback that creates more variety. The more possible combinations that can exist, the more that usually will exist. In the case of the cocktail party, you'll see people's eyes beginning to dart around the room. Bores get less slack. All this describes the new world economy, in which the doorbell just keeps ringing.

We should expect no less of new technology because technology is a natural accelerator of economic diversity. Diversity in nature drives creativity; each new species creates new opportunities for new species to be created. "Niches are continually created by new technologies, and the very act of filling a niche provides new niches,"[38] says John Holland of the University of Michigan, who studies both biology and economics. Business bootstraps its own growth in the same way that ecosystems do. "Novel goods create niches for still further new goods," says the molecular biologist Stuart Kauffman.[39] Diversity is the signature of nature's constant thrust toward economizing; as species multiply, they become more efficient at using resources and make the entire ecosystem more resistant to drought, disease, and other stress (one good reason, not so incidentally, to despair the accelerating rates of species extinction).[40] A rain forest with its stunning biological diversity extracts vastly more of the available wealth from the soil and sun. In precisely the same way, notes Mark White, "a complex economy extracts a lot more of the available wealth from its human and material resources than a simple economy."[41]

In an era that rewards inventiveness, diversity permits specialists to adapt in groups to ever-changing markets—if they show skill in building relationships. In the old days of jazz, from the Big Band era through the cool years of the early 1960s, a great bandleader could churn out recordings and hold down a gig for months or even years by maintaining the optimal assemblage of musicians. Those days are gone, as I had the chance to observe in a studio in the basement of the old Public School Nine in Brooklyn (where Aaron Copland happened to attend school). An alto saxophonist named Greg Abate, well known for virtuosity in bebop circles, was recording his seventh compact disc. But Abate needed to accommodate the popularity of Latin rhythms, so he brought together a pianist, drummer, bassist, and conga player to give him precisely the sound he was seeking. Each of the musicians, coming together for only two days as the "Greg Abate Quintet," was also a bandleader in his own right. Each had issued his own CDs, some of which, in turn, featured Abate as a session musician if the recording happened to demand a top bebop specialist on sax. "Years ago, cats were in familiar units," Abate, then fifty, told me. (Early in his career Abate himself had spent two years with Ray Charles.) "Now it's all networking—e-mail, faxes, phone calls. You can't just be a musician. You've got to know how to communicate." It's by constantly combining with the diversity around them, in short, that jazz musicians now sustain their individual staying power.

Fashion is another vivid exemplar of the explosion in cultural combinations; the gifted young rock musician named Beck takes the stage in Indian garb to sing a country-and-western–style song with a rap overlay. Food styles are rapidly combining in what biologist Stuart Kauffman calls "recombinant cuisine." The cooking analogy also inspires economist Paul Romer of Stanford, who writes, "Economic growth occurs whenever people take resources and rearrange them in ways that are more valuable. . . . Human history teaches us, however, that growth springs from better recipes, not just from more cooking."[42]

Indeed as I saw one day in rural southeastern Ohio, a kitchen can literally cook up economic niches.

꙳

The Community Kitchen Incubator of Athens, Ohio, was the brainchild of June Holley, herself an interesting combination of experiences. Once a farmworker, an inner-city schoolteacher, and a back-to-nature subsistence dweller, Holley moved to Athens in 1981 to study and teach sociology at Ohio University. In so much of what she studied, from French feminism to evolutionary biology, it struck her that free-forming and constantly changing relationships seemed to provide the foundation for growth.

Outside of the local campus, Athens didn't have much of an economy and the surrounding area even less. Athens sits on the edge of Appalachia, where economic development programs had long involved massive and mostly fruitless federal interventions. Maybe, Holley thought, it was time for the region to try bootstrapping itself, making something out of whatever resources and native ingenuity were available at hand. So she formed an operation in an office over the campus bookstore called the Appalachian Center for Economic Networks, or ACEnet, to begin introducing people to one another.

Along the way she traveled to northern Italy, known throughout the world for its teeming communities of small business—thousands of tiny, family-owned enterprises continually forming new economic networks in particular industries. In a district called Castel Goffredo, for instance, she found 179 tiny firms that spun thread and wove fabrics, cutting, dyeing, stitching, and packaging them, thereby turning the region into the world's leading producer of high-fashion hosiery. She found a similar pattern in the knitwear networks of Carpi and among the two hundred tile manufacturers of Sassuolo. Small firms in Prato had come together to popularize a new fabric called washed silk. Despite its many idiosyncrasies, each region had two things in common. First, there was a central information-sharing center—some sort of trade association or service facility, usually private, often maintained by local banks. These information centers were the modern-day commercial equivalent of the bustling town squares of northern Italy in which the exchange of ideas gave rise to the Renaissance. The second common denominator among the manufacturing networks was that each involved a single end product—its own market niche, a single niche created of many smaller niches.[43]

Some time after returning from Italy, June Holley took a good look around Appalachia. Farming had never become a major industry in Appalachia because of rugged topography, yet prime weather conditions enabled many people to support themselves with small parcels of crops. Unfortunately, people sold their harvest at roadside or through farmers' markets, where prices were low. It was no way to make a living, but it *was* excellent produce. And because they worked on essentially no budget, the small mountain growers produced all-organic crops, free of costly pesticides and fertilizers. Perhaps, Holley thought, the subsistence farmers of the region could begin combining their products and their individual skills—adding value to each other's products—in a way that created an economic niche for the entire region: specialty, organically grown foods.

Of course, there are no town squares in Appalachia, so Holley set out to create the equivalent, which is how the ACEnet kitchen came into being.

With money from a few foundations and church denominations she and her staff turned an abandoned lumberyard into a sprawling complex of meeting rooms, a library full of food regulations and marketing materials, an on-line research center, a retail storefront for test-marketing new products, and, in the back, a three thousand-square-foot cooking facility. Hundreds of small farmers and small businesses regularly came and went to swap information, combine skills, and create joint products. "Put two people in a room," Holley explained, "and they'll figure out how to come out ahead together."

At the time of my visit, a local worker-owned store called Crumbs Bakery was rolling out spinach pastries, adding value to local produce. A recent Ohio University graduate named Chris Chmiel was cutting up a wild Appalachian fruit called the pawpaw; a local restaurant buys his pawpaws for a drink called a "pawpaw colada." A local garbanzo-bean grower was selling hummus through a European hearth-bread retailer in the area, which wholesaled bread to a campus sandwich-cart operator who received free time in the community kitchen in exchange for helping to maintain the equipment there.

You get the idea.

By 1998, after two years of operation, the kitchen incubator had spawned more businesses than June Holley could keep track of, the result of relationships radiating from the kitchen out into the community. "That's the sign of success," she told me. "People parlay their connections into other groups, and everyone becomes a resource for everybody."

Which brings us full circle to Adam Smith. It is not through benevolence, as he wisely pointed out, that the butcher, brewer, and baker provide our dinner—but neither is it through self-interest alone. It is through their niche-begetting dealings that we enjoy the fruit of a free economy. For more than a century this truth was largely hidden as major corporations filled the center of economic life. But now technology is devaluing the major corporation. The functions that corporations brought in-house are being automated, distributing value-creating opportunities across the landscape to be seized by millions of entrepreneurs—not by acting alone, as big companies once could, but by acting together. Every act of economizing occurs not within but between; every business exists only because, and precisely as a consequence, of its connections to other businesses.

Smith's contemporary Thomas Paine once hailed "the diversity of the talents in different men for reciprocally accommodating the wants to each other."[44] Smith himself commented, "Give me that which I want, and you shall have this which you want. It is in this manner that we obtain from one another the far greater part of those good offices which we stand in need of."[45] For a century, this process was organized largely through servility to capital. Today's pioneers organize it through service to customers, the subject to which we now turn.

CHAPTER
3

"Have It Your Way"

In an economy that connects everything to everything, where is the starting point? If everyone is a middleman, who is the prime mover?

In the Industrial Age the investor occupied this role, and nothing big occurred without his endowments. Because J. P. Morgan considered them good investments, we got railroads 150 years ago. General Electric's easy access to the corporate finance markets created a new era of household conveniences seventy years ago. Investors flocked to the airline industry fifteen years ago, fueling such a fleet expansion that flying became affordable nearly to all. As the waves of affluence washed over society, it was investors, gravitating toward the highest available return, who determined which desires would be sated and when.

We were happy to let them decide what we wanted because we were a growing nation, a culture on the make. We worked hard and we expected rewards. The main economic constraint was supply and we tolerated mass production because it put affluence within closer reach. "You can have any color you want," Henry Ford famously remarked, "as long as it's black." As the economist John Kenneth Galbraith wrote in the 1960s: "The initiative in deciding what is to be produced comes not from the sovereign consumer. . . . Rather it comes from the great producing organization, which reaches forward to control the markets that it is presumed to serve, and, beyond, to bend the consumer to its needs."[1] A popular economics dictionary of 1990 vintage, spanning more than 1,700 entries and 562 pages, does not even include the word "customer."[2]

The first tiny stirrings of change were evident in fast food. In the early 1970s an upstart chain called Burger King redesigned the burger-assembly process to offer a limited deli-style choice (a very limited choice, to be sure) on condiments. "Hold the pickle, hold the lettuce," went the cheerful jingle. "Special orders don't upset us." As rival McDonald's rolled forward its famous burger odometers—"10 billion sold" and counting—Burger King got a foot in the door partly by promising customers they could "have it your way." Raised affluent and educated, baby boomers, it seemed, did want it their way.

Then, in a nearly-forgotten event, something extraordinary happened in what was then the world's biggest industry. In 1979 Saudi Arabia, the most powerful producer of anything anywhere in those days, incredulously watched consumers in America, Japan, and Europe throttling down their consumption of oil. As preposterous as it seemed, consumers were actually driving more slowly, purchasing fuel-efficient cars, and wearing sweaters around the house. Just as horrifying to OPEC, new oil supplies were coming onstream in the North Sea and the North Slope. Desperate for revenue, choking on its absurdly high debt load, Saudi Arabia began discounting the price of a barrel of crude according to how much that barrel would fetch at the gasoline pump. "Netback pricing," they called it. And for the first time, the American motorist and the Japanese utility executive were literally dictating the price at which the most powerful cartel in history was drawing oil from the ground.

The consumer *perestroika* soon spread, causing panic among the captains of global industry.[3] In a desperate grab for market share, major corporations opened the spigots of capital wider than ever (most of it borrowed, no different than Saudi Arabia's), except that this time demand had overtaken supply as the principle economic constraint. In an orgy of overbuilding, overharvesting, and overmining, the most prosaic commodities soared in supply—oil, lumber, clothing, housing, food, toys. If there was any doubt about the abundance of product it was erased in the mid-1990s, when the major beer manufacturers increased the size of a case to thirty cans from twenty-four with no increase in price (and then increased the size of the drinking hole by 40 percent so people could pour it in faster). In many cases the cost of acquiring a customer began to exceed the cost of the product itself—roughly $50 in the case of the average direct-mail customer, for instance. To build customer loyalty the airlines introduced frequent-flier programs, thinly disguised price cuts that simply pushed costs into the future, creating value for no one.

But many other large businesses did try to compete in new and worthwhile ways—through the quality revolution, for instance, as we have previously explored, as well as in the movement toward "mass customization." These trends, like so many others we consider new, also trace their roots to pre-industrial times, when every horse received a custom-fitted shoe and every dress was made to measure—when the seller, in short, came face-to-face with the customer. The difference today is that companies can provide quality, custom-made merchandise at spectacularly lower levels of cost.

Every business, of course, is a customer in its own right. And as household customers demand more value, the same pressure cascades along the entire supply chain. In dealings between businesses, which account for the majority of economic activity, an altogether new level of intimacy is beginning to take form, as we'll explore in this chapter and next. Pioneering companies see customers not just as sources of revenue but as resources in the value-creating process. Instead of merely partnering with customers they are moving to become alter egos. In some unlikely cases they are attempting to get inside their customers' hearts as well as their heads. They recognize that the dealings of customer and supplier constitute not just an economic relationship but an ethical one. And though most don't realize it, by sharing in the deepest concerns of their customers they are emulating one of the most fundamental forces in nature, a process called co-evolution.

᧬

My high school biology teacher, Jim Lendon, used to say that whenever we were stumped for a test answer we had a fair shot at guessing correctly with "surface area." Surface area helps to explain just about everything in biology. Exchanges and interactions pass through surfaces; the greater the surface, the greater the range and volume of interaction. People exchange such vast quantities of oxygen and CO_2 with the atmosphere because their lungs pack in the surface area of a tennis court.[4]

Big companies traditionally exposed the smallest possible surface area to the outside world. This was in keeping with their fear of permitting any employee to operate outside her narrow specialty. All sales occurred through a sales department, where the special skills included a glad hand and a tolerance for martinis. Only a media relations specialist was permitted to speak with the media; it was like a trained-seal act. I recently closed a bank account because I received poor service; when I volunteered an explanation for my action, the clerk cut me off, explaining that my reason might be of use only to the customer-service department. Peter Drucker has estimated that 90 percent of the information used within a major corporation is generated inside the four walls of that corporation, amounting to naval contemplation on a grand scale.[5]

Lately a number of companies have been exposing more surface area to the outside world, both to render more service to customers and to absorb more information from them. At a Lucent Technologies plant in Mount Olive, New Jersey, assembly workers conduct plant tours and attend trade shows. At Rowe Furniture, production workers speak directly to retailers and distributors. Procter & Gamble captures data from anyone calling a toll-free information line and feeds the information back into its product-development efforts.

But the most targeted and effective customer research I've seen occurs in small companies. In Springfield, Illinois, Bill Dudleston began building stereo speakers in his father-in-law's garage in the early 1980s. Though he didn't have a lot of cash he could afford to buy classified ads in the back of various audiophile magazines. Dudleston carefully crafted the wording of his ads to see which features and specifications drew the greatest number of inquiries, then focused his design efforts accordingly; tracking ad responses rather than survey responses more clearly measured the motivation of a buying decision. When Dudleston began shipping speakers he discovered that audiophiles were notoriously finicky customers—but the frustration of selling to them was more than offset by the sophistication of their views and their eagerness to opine. Each piece of intelligence played some role in his building the next set of speakers. "We had a very tight feedback loop with every customer," he says. Ultimately his designs won spectacular reviews in the audiophile press and a cult following, particularly in Japan. With annual sales exceeding $2.5 million, Dudleston was still capturing reaction from every customer he and his staff spoke with, recording it in a database for use in future designs.

Or consider the experience of a company called Specialized Bicycle Components, located near San Jose, California. Specialized helped to create the mountain-biking craze in the 1980s by rolling out the first mass-produced bike of its kind. Founder Mike Sinyard had a fanatical interest in product design, though he did it entirely within his own head. He put together a crack sales team that pushed the product into stores, though they took little time to hear how the retailers responded. Then Schwinn and other big bike companies jumped into Sinyard's niche. With massive factories, bottomless ad budgets, and their special pricing incentives for "big box" stores like Kmart, the big companies instantly commoditized the mountain bike business.

Sinyard knew he could never play that game, so he began tapping a network of small but numerous independent bike shops. And because these dealers were themselves cycling enthusiasts with sophisticated customers, their knowledge could help Specialized race ahead of the commodity producers in product design—if he listened closely. "Customer-advisory boards" have been around for years, but usually these are excuses for salespeople and big customers to play golf and otherwise whoop it up on the vendor's tab. Sinyard wanted something different. His board of shop owners came in regularly to review not only his existing products but everything that was still on the drawing board, and to compare these designs with whatever the competition was offering. "The feedback is so powerful," Sinyard says. "It makes things so clear. It makes everything so grounded." He also began bringing individual employees into the meetings when one of their designs or product specialties was at issue—experts so wrapped up in the technicalities of design they sometimes lost sight of serving the customer. "It's one thing to hear criticism from a sales guy or the president of the company," Sinyard says. "But when you hear it from the customer, you treat it as an edict." As a consequence his products never stop changing, launching Specialized Bicycle Components on its way to $200 million in annual sales.

Responding to customers may involve nothing more complex than pure human empathy. A banker I know in Colorado, Steve Bosley, built a tiny community institution called the Bank of Boulder into a regional powerhouse by projecting himself into the position of his customers. For one, Bosley preferred conducting his own banking in front of a human teller. When other banks began cutting back on drive-through teller windows in favor of ATM machines, he went the other way, expanding drive-through service with live tellers twenty-four hours a day. The service was not profitable in itself, but it generated an image of customer service that advertisements could never buy. Bosley launched a ten-kilometer run called the Bolder Boulder, which became one of the most popular in the world, drawing thousands of contestants into his bank branches every year for entry forms. He offered an extra quarter-point of interest on certain certificates of deposit when the University of Colorado won a big game, the kind of premium that cost very little but that drew massive deposits to the bank.

Once, running just a little behind schedule, Bosley found himself banging on the door of a dry cleaner at one minute past closing as a punk clerk inside the store silently shook his head and pointed to his watch; from that moment forward the Bank of Boulder never closed a branch door earlier than 5:39 P.M. Does this stuff pay off? Always a moneymaker, the Bank of Boulder was once ranked the most profitable community bank among the thousands in America.

ᔕ

Among the insipid fads sweeping business lately is that of the "boundaryless organization," an oxymoron if ever there was one. Every organization has an edge; otherwise it wouldn't be an organization. Boundaries create identities. Boundaries hold things in. But that needn't require their keeping all things *out*. City walls and cell membranes absorb as well as protect.

Every living thing is what biologists call a "complex adaptive system." The properties of complex adaptive systems apply across scale, from a single cell to any society of them—hive, immune system, legislature, corporation. A complex adaptive system continually interacts with its environment and alters its internal state accordingly. It simultaneously alters the state of the environment that affected it, an environment that invariably includes other complex adaptive systems. Says the biologist Richard Lewontin: "The environment is not a structure imposed on living beings from the outside, but is in fact a creation of those beings."[6] This is what biologists call co-evolution. Says Stewart Brand, founder of a magazine called *CoEvolution Quarterly* and an organization called the Global Business Network, "Evolution is adapting to meet one's needs. Coevolution, the larger view, is adapting to meet each other's needs."[7]

It is the constant change caused by this interplay that allows any living thing to survive. Because they tried to rule their environments rather than co-evolve with them, most companies created during the Industrial Age also died during the Industrial Age. But I know one company that did co-evolve with its environment at every step—causing its market to change, while simultaneously changing with it—and it survives today as the oldest business operating in America: Avedis Zildjian Company, the world's largest maker of musical cymbals.

It was founded in 1623 in old Constantinople, where an alchemist named Avedis combined some copper and tin in hopes it would become gold. He failed in the gold gambit but noticed that the alloy, when pounded into a sheet and struck with a hammer, rang with extraordinary clarity. He began making musical cymbals to provide pomp for kings and inspiration for troops. He was accorded the surname Zildjian, meaning "cymbal maker."

And so it went for three hundred years until 1929, when Avedis Zildjian III brought the business to the immigrant enclave of Quincy, Massachusetts. It was, to say the least, a lousy year in which to launch new markets: Marching bands would become frivolities in the Depression era. But Avedis persisted in his mission, traveling as far west as Chicago in an effort to collect a few sales. And there, while dropping in on a few Prohibition-era speakeasies, he discovered black Americans making a new music called "swing." No musician himself, he asked the drummers he met to suggest ways of adapting the company's product for the new sound. Count Basie's drummer, Jo Jones, suggested putting a pair of cymbals on a pole, either to be crashed together with a pedal or struck with a stick; thus did Avedis create the "hi-hat" cymbal. The hottest drummer of the swing era, Gene Krupa of the Benny Goodman Orchestra, said he would love to drive the beat of the band on something brighter than a snare drum, which to that point had served as the metronome of swing. So Avedis made a big cymbal with a lot of ping and a fast decay and called the product a "ride."

Avedis's son Armand took over product development as the beboppers stormed jazz in the 1950s. The legendary Max Roach used to say that he needed only to describe a sound in his head for Armand to produce the requisite cymbal. More sizzle? Armand had rivets loosely mounted into the disk. Fewer overtones? He beat the thing with a hammer. Zildjian's reputation as the instrument of choice among the most sophisticated musicians inspired a following in the rock world as well. Ringo Starr rode his way to stardom on a Zildjian "ride."

In every case, these product innovations changed the world of drumming, which in its turn changed the product lineup at Zildjian. Cymbals developed for jazz pollinated the world of rock, which inspired new styles in jazz—all of which sent drummers to Zildjian in search of new sounds. Instead of telling the market what it needed, the company provided the market what it wanted, and never stopped prospering as a result. Not long ago Alex Acuna, late of the jazz-fusion band Weather Report, spent several days in the engineering lab at Zildjian helping to develop a cymbal that could be struck with the open hand while he was playing timbals. Acuna described the sounds he was hearing in his head while the engineers turned out one prototype after another. "They were able to discern everything I was saying," he told me. This led to a whole new product category for the hot Latin music market.

⌇

Once a rarity among such companies as Zildjian, co-evolution between supplier and marketplace are becoming far more commonplace in the postindustrial era. One executive I know, Ron Rosenzweig, has consciously moved to mimic nature's co-evolutionary dynamics.

Growing up in the Borough Park section of Brooklyn, Rosenzweig ran with the Tarpon Social Athletic Club, the benign-sounding name of a 1950s street gang; his mother once counted five knife holes in his jacket. But during his summer jobs at the shore he glimpsed longingly into a world of merriment and affluence. He wangled his way into the engineering program at City College, a hotbed of young men on the make. (One of his classmates was a kid from Hungary named Andy Grove, who would go on to build Intel.) Though singularly unsuited to corporate life, Rosenzweig gave it a shot, helping to develop transistors at RCA. He did this work from engineering diagrams and spec sheets with no idea of the purpose to which the product would be used, much less who the customer was. On the rare occasion that he expressed curiosity about RCA's customers, Rosenzweig was told to quit meddling. That was the sales department's concern.

Ultimately, after launching and later selling a successful high-tech startup, Rosenzweig and some partners formed a company called

Anadigics Incorporated to make microchips on an exotic substance called gallium arsenide, which handles high-frequency radio signals much better than silicon chips. His timing, it first seemed, was propitious. The Reagan-era Strategic Defense Initiative—"Star Wars," as it became known in the headlines—was going to be a high-frequency affair, tailor-made for gallium arsenide chips. But Rosenzweig had guessed wrong. The Star Wars escapade went bust and Anadigics very nearly with it. By the end of the 1980s, Rosenzweig would glumly recall, "we were a failure." The company's only survival hope was selling its exotic chips in the commercial marketplace.

In one vital way, Rosenzweig's experience as a government contractor helped out. When the government is your only customer—when every application is unique and when cost is no object—you tend to listen carefully to the customer's specifications. So with ears wide open Rosenzweig approached companies in the telecommunications business: cell phone, cable television, direct broadcasting, and fiber-optic transmission, all applications in which wider bandwidth and shorter frequencies seemed to cry out for gallium arsenide. Of course, cell-phone and cable companies, unlike the government, are not bottomless pits of money. Anadigics would have to design customized chips and produce them at a price that lowered the customer's cost of doing business.

So Rosenzweig took a bold step. He put his engineers in charge of his sales effort, all but dissolving the shell of marketing people surrounding the technicians. He literally turned his company inside out, allowing direct lines of communication to emerge between his once-anonymous techies and the world of potential customers that lay outside. Selling and engineering, in short, become indistinguishable, part and parcel of one process. "People with a fundamental engineering skill set are best suited to solving the customer's problem," Rosenzweig would explain. "We give them this responsibility and tell them, 'It's your job to satisfy the customer in the time he wants. You are not limited by any budget or travel allowance. Just do what you have to do.' "

Thus an engineer named Ron Michaels, for one, flew at every opportunity to a trade show, a convention, a customer site, or even a retail store—anywhere he could lay his hands on a set-top converter or any other type of cable-TV switching gear. He would then drag the box back to his cubicle, a thoroughly unremarkable workplace except for the electrical hieroglyphics hanging on the partitions and the nice view of the New Jersey woods along one side. He would poke inside the box to stare at the maze of circuitry and componentry, exploring whether any number of the individual parts (fifty of them, perhaps, or even more) could be combined into a single chip, thereby reducing not only the size of the box but the cost of making it. He would then pop the question to the potential purchaser: "How much would it be worth to you to substitute all these parts for a single chip?" The customer would name a figure.

Ron Michaels would then race back to New Jersey and begin designing, working with his colleagues at the workbench to create a prototype. They would test it and send it to their would-be customer. They would refine it further, based on the customer's feedback. Then Michaels would move to make a deal with the customer—no golf, no steak dinners, just a freewheeling discussion of physics and economics.

Ron Rosenzweig, Ron Michaels, and everyone else at Anadigics had exposed the very heart of its operation to the marketplace, drawing the customer, in turn, back into itself. "In what we do," Michaels says, "if you have the solution, it sells itself."

It sells itself. When buyer and seller design a product together, the sales process begins to evaporate. An intelligent exchange between engineers—creating precisely what the customer needs, instead of what one party wishes for the other—makes an anachronism of the well-practiced sales pitch. But this is the magical part: Anadigics wins not only a sale, but it walks away with a new chip design that it can attempt to sell elsewhere. Anadigics has customized a product for one customer, yes—but the knowledge gleaned from that customer helps Anadigics win more customers. While being shaped by the marketplace, Anadigics, in turn is shaping the marketplace, the same kind of co-evolutionary process exhibited by all living systems.

∽

In a mercantilist world of fixed wealth, buyers and sellers were adversaries. But wealth is not fixed. Wealth is emergent when buyers and sellers become partners instead of adversaries in economizing. Indeed, companies like Anadigics are beginning to blur the distinction of buyer and seller, slowly pushing the very concept of the customer toward obsolescence. Many companies, says David Stephenson, a business consultant in Boston, are moving to "a seamless cycle in which the customer and the producer become inseparable." In this respect, too, business grows close to the ways of nature, where everything acts simultaneously as customer and producer.

Small companies are well suited to such tight integration. A company in Baltimore called United States Aluminate converts great piles of white, powdery aluminum trihydrite into alum, which, in turn, it ships to many customers. Occupying a massive, seventy-year-old brick plant south of the docks, U.S. Aluminate operates in a much larger factory than its manufacturing process requires. So it invites its major supplier, Alcan, to store a heaping pile of raw material, as many as a million pounds, in one great, cavernous wing of the plant. Alcan serves many other customers in the Baltimore area from that pile, but U.S. Aluminate provides the storage space at no charge. Why? Because Alcan, in exchange, bills U.S. Aluminate for its own purchases of the material only as it's being consumed. In this arrangement, who is the customer and who is the vendor? It's a meaningless question. "Everybody is each other's customer," says Tim Askew, the president of U.S. Aluminate.

This is not barter, which periodically shows flashes of faddism in business. Bartering is an even, one-for-one exchange, rigorously accounted for, little different from a straightforward financial transaction except that one party pays in goods or services instead of cash. In the symbiotic biological model, businesses instead exchange resources that fulfill a higher purpose in the hands of other businesses without regard to balancing the interests. To cite another example at U.S. Aluminate, the company encourages one of its major trucking vendors to park idle trailers in a spare lot outside the U.S. Aluminate plant; in turn, the drivers from the trucking company load their own trucks with finished products rather than sitting around watching U.S. Aluminate's employees do it. Nobody bothers figuring out who comes out ahead in financial terms; why bother when less wasted space and less wasted time means more economizing—the emergence of more wealth—for all? "What we're doing for them costs us no money," says Tim Askew. "What they're doing for us costs no money. A big chemical company can't break down barriers like that."

⌒

While many companies are getting better at customer service, one industry has gotten a lot worse lately. That industry is medicine. The onslaught of managed care has commoditized what was once among the most delicate relationships in all of commerce, that of doctor and patient. The practice of "capitation" creates the risk of a doctor visit becoming a cattle call. Accounting for the payment of services has overwhelmed the rendering of the services themselves. Yet a few islands of great service exist even in medicine, mainly, it seems, in places where people have thrown off their Newtonian blinders and recognized that putting the customer first can redound to the benefit of the provider as well. With so many competing claims on every dollar, every process, and every hour of time and attention, the interests of the customer—the patient—serve as a common ground for making the entire system more efficient.

LDS Hospital in Salt Lake City is such a place. LDS (as in Latter-day Saints) is a 520-bed teaching hospital and so-called trauma-one center with a stellar clinical reputation. Within the hospital, LDS long ago opened an outpatient surgery clinic, in which an ever-larger percentage of procedures were being conducted. And although the surgical staff was acclaimed, management recognized that the overall patient experience left something to be desired.

The main problem was delay. The surgery line was jam-packed as early as 5:30 every morning. Some patients spent the entire day lurching from check-in to pre-op to anesthesia to surgery to recovery to post-op, with too much of the time spent simply waiting. As much as some people may wish to convalesce at length as admitted hospital patients, no one wants to turn a four-hour outpatient experience into a nine-hour ordeal. If LDS wanted to maintain (much less extend) its position in the marketplace, it had to figure out how to get patients through faster without degrading clinical results.

The job of facilitating the planning process went to Diane Kelly, who had worked for fifteen years as a registered nurse, mostly in neonatal intensive care, before earning her M.B.A. and becoming an internal "quality consultant." In her years in intensive care Kelly was often perplexed by the priorities that families exhibited in even the most dire medical situations. "I'm working like crazy to save a baby, but the parents get upset because the grandparents didn't get to see the baby!" she recalls. In time she could see that medicine was only part of health care. "Health care providers hold people's lives in their hands at a very vulnerable time," she says. "Health care is about a personal encounter." Most of the people on the business side of health care have little intellectual grasp and even less emotional grasp of this concept. Indeed, after moving to the business side herself Kelly became convinced that some of the most intractable problems of the industry could be solved only by people who, like her, combined far-flung disciplines. "Innovation will come from people who have crossed the boundaries from other disciplines," she says—from business to medicine, from medicine to law, and so on.

In the reengineering study of the surgery clinic, Kelly insisted on involving the maximum number of nurses—people, in her experience, who knew the whole patient as well as the individual surgeries they variously received. She also insisted that the members of the reengineering committee visit as many other hospitals as possible to explore which of their outpatient-surgical practices could be employed at LDS. And throughout the study process she continually harped on the "vision statement" of the initiative, which put as its first priority "to provide a patient/family focused quality culture."

Kelly was grateful to discover a powerful ally in the process: a new chief administrator in the surgery line named Joan Lelis, herself a nurse. Under previous leadership, the policy for change was simply "give the surgeons whatever they wanted," as Kelly put it. Lelis, for her part, acknowledged that the surgeon must call the shots on procedures—but not necessarily on process. In that respect she, too, insisted on using the patient as the point of departure. "If you're guided by only one phrase—what is best for the patient—you will always come up with the right answer," Lelis insists. (Hearing Lelis and Kelly say this over and over began to remind me of the best editors I have worked for. When in doubt, they would often say, do only what's right for the reader. Everything else will fall into place.)

Studying the surgery line from the patients' point of view was disturbingly illuminating. Surgeons showing up late for the first round of surgeries at 7:30 A.M. threw off the schedule for the entire day. The various hospital departments—admitting, financing, lab, surgery—all conducted their own separate interaction with the patient on each of their individual schedules. A poor physical layout, including a long corridor separating the operating rooms from pre-op, compounded the inefficiencies: Once a patient was called to surgery he spent forty minutes waiting for an orderly to arrive with a wheelchair or gurney. And because this was an outpatient surgery center located inside a hospital, the anesthesiologists were accustomed to administering heavy sedation, often slowing the patient's recovery from otherwise minor surgery and further clogging the entire line. *The operation was a success, but the patient is pissed.*

In talking to patients the researchers discovered a subtext in the complaints about delays: resentment over the loss of personal control. Patients spent the day in God-awful gauze gowns, stripped of their underwear, their backsides exposed to the world. Partly this reflected a medical culture that considered the procedure, not the patient, as the customer. As Joan Lelis put it to me, "If you're naked on a stretcher on your back, you're pretty subservient." Family members, meanwhile, had to roam the hospital in search of change so they could coax a cup of coffee from a vending machine. Lelis marveled at the arrogance of it. "You're spending $3,000 on a loved one, but you'd better bring correct change."

Fortunately, Lelis had the political standing to push through big changes, and although the staff surgeons effectively had veto power, most were too busy to get very deeply involved in the reengineering process. Because few patients enjoy getting stuck with needles, the nurses created a process for capturing the blood from the insertion of each patient's intravenous needle and sending it to the lab for whatever tests were necessary. This cut down not only on discomfort but on time, money, and scheduling complexity. The unremitting bureaucratic questions and paperwork were all replaced with a single registration packet that patients picked up in their doctors' offices and completed days before ever setting foot in the hospital; last-minute administrative details were attended to in a single phone call the day before surgery. The nurses set up a check-in system for the coats and valuables of patients and family members, which eliminated the need for every family to encamp with their belongings in a pre-op room for the entire day. A family-friendly waiting area was created, stocked with free snacks and drinks. There would be no more desperate searches for correct change.

That was only the beginning. Patients had always resented having to purchase their post-op medications from the hospital pharmacy; simply freeing them to use their neighborhood drugstore got them out of the surgery line sooner, further relieving the congestion. Also in the interests of saving time, the nurses made a heretical proposal to allow healthy outpatients to *walk into surgery* under their own power, accompanied by their family members, rather than waiting forty minutes for a wheelchair or a gurney. That idea got the attention of the surgeons, who after years of paying ghastly malpractice premiums vowed that Joan Lelis, not they, would suffer the personal liability on that one. The risk-management department also went "eek" at the idea. Yet as the reengineering committee pointed out, the hospital permitted out-patients to traverse any other distance in the building by foot. Why should the march into surgery be any different?

In a similar vein, the nurses suggested allowing patients to wear underwear beneath their hospital gowns. The administrators could scarcely believe their ears: "Show me one place in the literature where patients wear underwear to surgery!" one top administrator demanded. (The nurses noted that restricting change to what had been attempted elsewhere would automatically eliminate the possibility of any break-through in performance.) And why stop at underwear, the nurses asked? The hospital was conducting more and more outpatient cataract opera-tions; why not let these patients wear their clothes into surgery? Contamination! the purists cried. But clothing is no dirtier than the skin beneath it, the nurses answered. This change eliminated a major post-op bottleneck caused by elderly patients who could not dress themselves or tie their shoes with their heads clouded by anesthesia and their depth perception altered by the removal of their cataracts.

As the changes took effect the nurses observed another unintended effect. Patients were actually reducing their recovery times! People were no longer looking at ceiling tiles on their way into surgery like characters in an episode of *Dr. Kildare*. They went into surgery feeling better and came out of it feeling better. In case after case they were ready to leave the joint faster, which in turn freed up even more space for other patients. Because they had studied practices at a number of stand-alone clinics, the nurses even presumed to tell the physicians that the outpatients would be better off with less anesthesia, hastening their recoveries, speeding their exit, and freeing up still more capacity.

By 1997, volume at the LDS surgery line had surged 50 percent with no increase in square footage and no increase in staff. Customer-service surveys were positive and costs were under control. And it dawned on Diane Kelly that the nurses' intuitive conviction that the patient should come first benefited the surgery line itself at every single step. Everyone and everything connected with the process—surgeon, staff, insurers, time, cost, and quality—seemed to come out ahead when the patients' interests came first.

What was really happening, of course, was that the change teams simply put common sense first. In a complex process of many players, the interest of the patient was the one unifying characteristic—the best baseline for calibration—because the patient was the only person touched by every step.

ᔕ

Is there a limit to empathy? Adopting the customers' point of view may be fine in banking, chip-making, and medical care—but what about when the customer is downright irrational? In a fast-changing world, sometimes even the customer doesn't know the customer's point of view.

Take the concrete business. Delivering concrete is a tough business anywhere, but imagine doing it in a major city in Mexico. The weather is wild, the traffic unpredictable. Labor disruptions erupt spontaneously and government inspections hit construction sites capriciously. Yet every load of concrete is never more than ninety minutes from spoiling in the rotating cylinder on the back of a truck.[8]

Pandemonium, as you would expect, long ruled the central operations center of Cementos Mexicanos—swearing, screaming, occasionally fisticuffs, and the oft-told lie that the truck was "on its way." In the second-floor office overlooking a lot full of trucks, dispatchers took orders for any of eight thousand grades of concrete, dispatching them to a half-dozen regional mixing plants, each with its own large fleet of trucks. This complexity was exacerbated by the astonishing fact that more than half of all orders were changed by customers, many repeatedly, some at the last minute. Cemex, as the company is known, tried to train its customers into sticking with their orders by imposing financial penalties and by demanding longer lead times, but no such rules could conquer the natural disarray of the marketplace. Cemex could promise a delivery in nothing less than a three-hour window, pinning down entire construction crews as if they were waiting for the cable guy.

In their study of the problem, two internal consultants, Kenneth Massey and Homero Resendez, came to respect the customer chaos as an immovable force. In searching for coping measures their thoughts turned to another perishable product with highly unpredictable customer actions: pizza delivery. They attempted to schedule a fact-finding mission to Domino's Pizza in the U.S., but Domino's declined to host the visit, informing them its methods were secret.[9] So instead the team traveled to Memphis to watch the miracle of Federal Express, another operation built entirely around perishable products submitted on a moment's notice from any and all locations. The visitors were awed at the stunning efficiency and the brilliant use of information systems at the FedEx hub in Memphis, but nothing dazzled them quite so much as the FedEx marketing guarantee: It's on time or it's on us. It seemed an impossible dream to imagine making the same offer with cement deliveries in Mexico.

The Cemex team began to question the company's entire approach to the market. Rather than punishing the customer with penalties and lead times, perhaps it should make last-minute changes routine. That, after all, was the unwavering culture of the marketplace. "Living with chaos," the team members began to call it. So they scheduled another field trip, this one to the 911 dispatch center at the Houston Fire Department. The visitors sat rapt in the darkened room, incredulous at the utter poise with which the dispatchers fielded heart attacks, fires, false alarms, and emergencies of an unknown nature. There were just enough ambulances and paramedics in just the right parts of town, it seemed. And it hit the visitors from Mexico: Though individually unpredictable, emergencies occurred in sufficient number that a pattern could be discerned and planned for. "It was a revelation," a team member named Paul de la Fuenta later recalled.

So Cemex resolved to embrace the complexity of the marketplace rather than resist it, doing business on the customer's terms, however zany. They called the project Sincronizacion Dinamica de Operaciones—the dynamic synchronization of operations. And it would be the customer setting the tempo. Delivery trucks were cut loose from their zone assignments and set free to roam the city as part of one big pool, with an artificial intelligence system triangulating them against order destinations and mixing plants, all while taking account of traffic patterns. Trucks were outfitted with transmitters and receivers connected to the Global Positioning Satellite System, giving the computer real-time data about the location, direction, and speed of every vehicle in the city to within a tenth of a mile.

But in the same way that information is meaningless without action, technology alone is powerless to create a new culture, a fact that millions of businesses in the U.S. and elsewhere still fail to grasp. "Technology," as Homero Resendez told me, "is the great enabler. But in the end the central concern is the customer call." So Cemex drivers, with an average schooling of six years, were enrolled in weekly customer-service classes spanning two years. Onerous work rules had to be gutted so that nothing got in the way of getting the order through on time; the unions assented on the promise that greater efficiency would lead to higher pay. "Instead of delivering concrete they are delivering a service," explained operations manager Francisco Perez. "They used to think of themselves as drivers. But concrete can be delivered by anyone. Now they know they're delivering a service the competition cannot deliver."

By the time of my visit, same-day service and free, unlimited order changes were standard. The company had just introduced the kind of guarantee that Resendez and Massey had been dreaming of since their trip to Memphis: If the load fails to arrive within twenty minutes of schedule, the buyer gets back twenty pesos per cubic meter—*"20 minutos o 20 pesos,"* as the company's advertising put it—representing a discount of about 5 percent. With reliability exceeding 98 percent and vehicle efficiency exceeding the U.S. benchmark by nearly 50 percent, Cemex could afford a much more generous guarantee, but even twenty pesos was shocking enough to swamp the competition, while leaving room open for an even steeper discount once the competition caught up.

If it ever does. Few companies manage to absorb the culture of the marketplace so thoroughly as Cemex. "My main concern used to be equipment efficiency," said Perez, the operations manager. "Now my concern is satisfying the customer." Or as Resendez put it, "We are selling a promise."

⌇

Selling a promise. "Capitalism is promises," the libertarian columnist John Chamberlain wrote years ago. "The promises are everywhere, and it is rarely that one is ever broken."[10] Language itself is based on the expectation of reliance. "When people communicate, they don't simply pass information back and forth. They get things done," says Fernando Flores. "The fundamental unit of communication is not the particular words or propositions, but the underlying *commitment* expressed by them."[11]

Long before there were contracts or even laws, trade occurred on word alone. Those who kept their word were rewarded by others keeping their word. It was through trade that humans discovered trust— "the conviction of things not seen,"[12] in one biblical definition; "the residue of promises fulfilled,"[13] in a modern definition. The ethics of trust, like every other basic human value, evolved because those who possessed it left behind more progeny than those who didn't. "Human social existence, unlike animal sociality, is based on the genetic propensity to form long-term contracts that evolve by culture into moral precepts and law," says biologist Edward O. Wilson. "Over the eons, humans have discovered which covenants are necessary for survival, and we accepted the necessity of securing them by sacred oath."[14] What people now call the Golden Rule formed the foundation of every major religion on the planet, in some estimations becoming the most fundamental more of human society. "We live," as the philosopher Martin Buber wrote, "in currents of universal reciprocity."[15]

Failing to deliver has always been a cheat. Whether through neglect, incompetence, or because somebody else offered a better deal, turning one's back on a commercial commitment is every bit as wrong as underweighing, overcharging, or scrimping on quality. Fraud gets the headlines, but the simple failure to perform extracts many times the toll. And although the reckoning is sometimes slow in coming, service breakdowns in commerce and trade are seldom forgotten. The back-office crisis on Wall Street in the 1960s, in which investment houses accepted orders they could not process, helped drive the individual investor out of the market, fostering the mutual-fund boom. People Express airline, which in its early days was known for consistent if simple service, accelerated its demise with notorious rates of passenger overbooking. Reliability is the *sine qua non* of commerce, the most critical crossbeam undergirding integrity in business.

In recent times, integrity came to have a much narrower meaning. People began to mistake integrity for "compliance," making it synonymous with ass-covering. Bribe no foreign officials, dump no dioxin, tolerate no sexual harassment—ta-da, you have shown integrity. This kind of integrity not only kept you out of jail but in the good graces of liberals, aldermen, and anyone else who might harass your business. But the real meaning of integrity goes much further: Like "integrate" and "entire," with which it shares its root, integrity means serving the whole, "the quality or state of being undivided." Similarly does ethics, the study of right and wrong, share meaning with "ethos," which is the sum of the characteristics that define a whole. Ethics and integrity are about knowing the effects of your actions on a wider circle—and caring about those effects.

It is not a coincidence that the new economy—a more tightly *integrated* economy—demands integrity on the part of every participant. Yet if the new economy has a dark side, it is the toleration of imperfect performance. Technology, alas, has become today's all-purpose cover for the failure to deliver, exemplified by the maddeningly familiar statement that "the computers are down." More than fifty years after a couple of professors fired up ENIAC in the basement of the engineering school at the University of Pennsylvania, people still think of computers as fragile miracle machines. Consumers persist in allowing the software industry to label its product defects with the benign term "bugs." In the past fifteen years, as automakers and other industrial manufacturers used technology to help restore quality and reliability to their products, major high-tech vendors themselves allowed theirs to go the other way. Products regularly go to market with known defects, a shrug of the shoulders, and the resignation that "the customer never uses that feature anyway."

To a degree—a very limited degree—computing and allied technologies deserve some slack. Computing, as I have argued, is evolution incarnate, the hyper-speed mechanical embodiment of the action-feedback-synthesis process by which all learning and progress occur. Every new technology requires a shakedown period, and computing is perpetually new. But that doesn't forgive technology its notoriously poor record. The pharmacy and aerospace industries are also constantly innovating, but we brook no breakdowns by them. Good restaurateurs are continually innovating, but a single bad meal drives away a customer forever. In addition, the computing industry, just like the networked economy it has created, is itself a giant community of contingency, causing even small breakdowns to have system-wide repercussions—as when a single bad line of code causes phone service to vanish in an entire region, causing thousands of businesses there to fail their own customers.

That was the case during one of the great service debacles of the on-line age: the breakdown at America Online in 1996 and 1997. Intent on locking in AOL's place as the leading on-line service, AOL founder Steve Case, a former Pizza Hut and Procter & Gamble marketeer, flooded America with arresting come-ons and free sign-up software—"gunning for growth," as he put it in an interview with *Wired* magazine.[16] Entrepreneurs and telecommuters, lured by AOL's excellent e-mail interface and a bit of proprietary, business-oriented content, threw themselves irretrievably into on-line invoicing and promotion, printing AOL addresses on their letterheads and calling cards. Literally millions of business people came to rely on AOL as a utility. I was one of them, printing my AOL e-mail address at the end of my weekly column in the *Wall Street Journal* to solicit reader feedback. And AOL went out of its way to assure us we could count on it. As the free disks brought in more and more subscribers, tell-tale service interruptions began to occur, but Steve Case assured customers of the company's "single-minded focus" on customers and its "obsession" with good service. "We will make whatever changes—do whatever we need to—to keep that commitment to you," he declared in a letter to members.[17]

But meanwhile, rival services were also coming on line, not just from hundreds of small, local providers but from the behemoth AT&T and from Microsoft as well. Wall Street clamored for AOL to take drastic action against the loss of market share. So Case rolled out a flat-rate pricing plan that gave users every incentive to connect ad infinitum to a network that was painfully finite. What's more, he did so, by his own public acknowledgment, fully aware that AOL had too little capacity to serve the onslaught. The company was suddenly generating the busy signal heard 'round the world, turning America On-Line into America On-Hold (or AOHell, as a wag in Philadelphia quipped). Even more appalling, AOL continued signing up new customers. Once, at the very moment I was encountering the unstinting busy signal, I could hear a pitch for the toll-free registration line over the Nickelodeon network, which my kids were watching. You could get through to sign up, but not to log on.

AOL's breakdowns were soon visited on the customers of its customers. Small businesses, having found e-mail instantly addictive, found themselves unable to send and receive orders and reports. AOL became a symbol of bad service in America, low-tech and high-tech alike. A trade magazine called *Air Conditioning, Heating & Refrigeration News* reflected on the lesson for its industry. "Don't sell what you can't support," the magazine warned. "Selling one more unit than you can support is a violation of trust."[18] Attorneys general in more than half the states brought suit. Ultimately AOL agreed to provide refunds or free time to some eight million people, as well as promising to accelerate more than one-third of a billion dollars in system upgrades. And indeed AOL, this time, proved to be as good as its word, improving its service reliability to a degree befitting a company of its size and importance in the digital economy.

"Coordination of complex activities requires redundancy," the planning guru Aaron Wildavsky wrote years ago. "The larger the number of participants in an enterprise, the greater the need for redundancy."[19] Here, too, nature provides the best design model, with massively parallel, fault-tolerant systems operating at every level of scale, from communities of cells, all of which harbor the identical DNA code, to ecological communities, which develop multiple food and energy resources. Some authorities are convinced that most of the software running in the world will be involved in making sure *other* software is running okay. "Too much of the economy and too many people's lives will depend on billion-line programs to let them go down for even an instant," writes Kevin Kelly of *Wired*.[20]

The service breakdown at AOL was a failure of management, to be sure, but also a failure of trust and ethics. In my frustration I switched to Microsoft's MSN, which turned out to be very nearly as bad. Despite having billions of dollars in cash lying around, Microsoft was nearly as guilty as AOL of insufficient capacity. And, unlike AOL, Microsoft did little to upgrade the quality and reliability of its service. In the end, the joke was on me.

In time, though, I began to see that delivery failures by the giants of technology were not representative of the whole industry. A young Ph.D. student at Carnegie Mellon named Ken Lang had invented a new kind of "intelligent" on-line search tool that drew intense customer interest and lots of venture capital—but he spent months resisting the pressure to put the product out to market until he knew it would operate flawlessly. (A few short years after Lang had introduced his product, called WiseWire, it was purchased by Lycos, operator of a major Internet search engine, for nearly $40 million.) While AOL and Microsoft often said "don't blame us" for busy signals when local phone companies were to blame, an upstart outfit in Atlanta called MindSpring Corporation worked actively with local telcos to identify capacity problems in *their* networks—and refused to take on new customers in cities where the phone companies were slow to respond.

Contrary to all the "slacker" stereotypes, the high-tech entrepreneurs of Generation X, not their middle-aged counterparts like Bill Gates and Steve Case, were setting the standard for customer service in the on-line era. Although I should have been able to figure out the reason for this on my own, the answer did not occur to me until I visited a converted warehouse at Broadway and Houston Street, in the heart of Manhattan's SoHo neighborhood, to investigate a two-year-old company called Bell Technology Corporation.

It was the creation of Marc Bell, who at age twenty-nine had already spent half his life on-line. He had been a preteen hacker, insinuating his way into the Internet when it was still a Pentagon project. In high school in Westchester County he trained small businesses to use PCs, and later, working at Fordham, taught the rudiments of programming to nonspecialist faculty members, earning as much as $200 an hour when he could get his mother to drive him to an engagement. Hackers, it appears, do not grow into slackers, for following grad school at NYU Bell became an extremely successful hardware middleman—a so-called value-added reseller. But as computers became plug-and-play devices and there was less value to add, Bell Technology leaped into a new niche, becoming a small-scale Internet service provider.

New York has many such service providers, each of them ultimately connecting to one of five fiber-optic cables ringing Manhattan. Most providers connect their services to whichever of the five cable operators offers the best rates. But through acts of God or occasional ineptitude, each of these five operators has a failure history. Marc Bell refused to rely on any single one of them, instead linking to no less than three fiber lines while also developing an elaborate monitoring and control system to detour smoothly around any failures. Right off the bat he had an automatic 200 percent improvement in reliability over the typical carrier.

Marc Bell began conducting training classes for Web designers while providing Internet access to their employers. As his trainees jumped between positions in the frenetic world of Web design, many of their new employers turned to Bell for on-line connections. Before long, these same customers were also asking Bell to host their Web pages on his computers. But instead of taking on all comers he refused new clients until he had installed more phone lines and computing capacity than he could ever possibly need—and then some. When I visited him in early 1997, Bell was tearing down walls that he had erected only four months earlier to make room for additional servers. He did this *before* taking on the new business. Unopened boxes of switches, routers, and servers sat everywhere.

"We guarantee our clients will never get a busy signal," he said proudly, walking along rack after rack of servers. "This," he said, pointing, "is *Penthouse* magazine"—well-known (infamously to some) as one of the busiest sites on the Web.

To finance all this, Bell took his company public in an $8 million offering—a crossroads, to be sure. It was short-term earnings pressure from Wall Street, after all, that caused hardware companies to book revenue before they sold product, that pressured software companies to push out products prematurely, that motivated on-line suppliers to sell access they knew they lacked the capacity to serve. Would Bell Technology succumb to the pressures of growth?

A crucial test was soon at hand. Marc Bell had been planning a new venture to install high-speed Internet access in Manhattan office buildings, a plan that caused Wall Street analysts to recommend Bell stock enthusiastically. But after Marc Bell had wired his second Manhattan office building, he realized that using inferior connection technology was the only way to make the plan economical. Just like that, he pulled the plug on the new venture—to hell with Wall Street. "I'm not going to make a bad business decision for the sake of hype," he explained to me. (Wall Street took the decision in stride.)

None of this was wasted on the customers of Bell Technology (which later renamed itself Globik Corp.). At a 1996 trade show called Internet World, Marc Bell met Greg Harper, the technology chief for a planned new venture called MSNBC Desktop Video. Harper was looking for a vendor to host the service without drowning in a torrent of audio, video, and text. There were plenty of companies assuring Harper they could handle the load, but when he visited their places of business he could see they didn't have nearly the capacity to do so. High-tech companies with household names also pitched the business, their seasoned salespeople presenting proposals in snazzy binders. But Harper was bothered that it was salespeople, not systems engineers, making the promises; indeed salespeople are traditionally compensated for products sold, not for products successfully installed.

Then Harper visited Bell's converted warehouse space in SoHo. Almost no one wore a suit. The proposals did not come in snazzy binders. But the place was teeming day and night. Marc Bell himself lived in the neighborhood and wore a beeper and a cell phone on his belt. And unlike the other would-be vendors who had promised the moon, Bell Technology frankly admitted that it couldn't immediately handle the demands of the MSNBC venture. "You'll have to give us thirty days," the engineers said. Harper was so impressed with the combination of candor and commitment that Bell Technology won the prized job. "I can shove pizza under the door and get things done," Harper explained. "I really have the feeling these guys are going to take care of me."

I confess that I had walked into Bell Technology bearing a few of the baby boomer prejudices about Generation X, and my initial impressions failed to dissuade me. Body piercing abounded. A few employees stared at the kind of 3-D video game that provoke nausea in people my age. And although Marc Bell himself was a vision of respectability in his wire-frame glasses and a brown suit, his office, too, bore the trappings of a generation: a collection of "antique" video games, as he called them, vintage 1980–83.

At the risk of unfairly overanalyzing people like Marc Bell and his associates, I suddenly understood why people of his youth seem to perform so impeccably when serving customers. When you grow up in a frantically affluent era, with hand-held remote zappers, five hundred channels, video games, and images that change every 1.6 seconds or so, you're keenly aware of the power of choice. When a TV program becomes boring or a Web site takes too long to load or any product fails to delight, you're outta there and on to the next. It's another variation of reciprocity: The least loyal customers are often the most loyal vendors.

∽

One thing is not new in the new economy: Customers who are burned will find detours around the suppliers who burn them—especially business customers, who, after all, have their own customers to worry about.

Consider first the improbable fact that grease recycling is a golden business. The Dausey family has been at it for four generations. George Dausey, a native New Yorker, watched his grandfather and father broker slaughterhouse by-products—fat, bone, and organs—to the makers of soap and munitions. George, who was sixty when I interviewed him, worked in the industry as an owner and manager most of his life.

As the onslaught of French fries swelled the supply of grease, the surging production of pork and chicken increased the demand for its use as a feed additive. Profits rose in lockstep with the price of grain. By 1996 a grease renderer could expect to pay about $50 for a half-ton container of kitchen grease; with the chunks and water removed, the same load might bring roughly three times as much at the feed plant. It is miserable work, collecting and preparing all that grease, but it paid well because it was economizing in the most direct sense.

It was inevitable that the big money would move into rendering. The billionaire Bass Brothers of Texas acquired a major rendering plant on Maryland's Eastern Shore, which they hired George Dausey to run.

After a few years he was downsized out, but his son Tres, who was working as a bartender in Charleston, South Carolina, was itching to enter the business. So the father and son launched Dausey By-Products on a remote thirty-acre plot surrounded by Carolina bobcats and moved into a home trailer with a dog, a cat, and a fax machine. In the field out back they installed a processing center, where every evening they would unload the day's worth of grease from their green-colored vacuum truck, seven or eight tons in all, pouring the putrid stuff through a filtering screen and raking out the food chunks as they went.

They came quickly face-to-face with the region's Goliath of grease processing, Carolina By-Products. CBP, as it was best known, was a formidable competitor. It had an annual revenue of $100 million and was controlled by such well-heeled Wall Street interests as the U.S. affiliate of Bank of Switzerland and the billionaire Bronfman family of Seagram fame. Ominously for the Dauseys, it was not uncommon in the grease collection business to make "bonus" payments in cash to discourage restaurants from selling their grease to a new collector. But the Dauseys figured they had a fighting chance to win over restaurants anyway because in its years of monopolizing grease collection in the region CBP's service had slipped—and as any restaurateur will admit, a stinking, overflowing container full of old fry grease is no way to beautify the parking lot or keep the health inspectors off your back.

Father and son were soon stunned to see CBP's "bonus" payments soar from hundreds to thousands of dollars each. "They wanted a first-round knockout," George Dausey would recall. A regional barbecue chain called Sticky Fingers, for instance, initially agreed to let the Dauseys instead of CBP pick up its grease—roughly $30 worth a month at each of two locations. Sticky Fingers was a small business, after all, just like Dausey By-Products, and the restaurateurs liked Tres Dausey's hustle. CBP immediately moved to win back the supply by offering Sticky Fingers a $500 "bonus" on top of its regular payments by the pound. Sticky Fingers, to its credit, stuck with the Dauseys. Then CBP upped the offer to a staggering $5,000. At that point, as one of the restaurant owners sheepishly put it, "We caved."

Tres Dausey began keeping a meticulous diary of such defections. A Chinese carry-out, a steak house, some burger joints—all agreed initially to make room for the Dauseys' collection containers only to renege in the face of a pile of cash from CBP. Meanwhile, Tres noticed a mysterious car in his rearview mirror following him on his rounds.

Tres was a hunting pal with a sheriff's detective who traced the car to a CBP employee holed up in a local hotel. When I asked CBP's president, David Evans, to comment on the Dauseys' hair-raising tales he made no effort to deny them. "As far as I'm concerned we're competing on a legitimate basis," he said. "The engine that drives this industry is raw materials. We must protect our raw materials source." His company spied on the Dauseys' operation, he said, just as he presumed they spied on his. (Indeed, the Dauseys were making regular drives past the CBP processing plant, though they conducted their reconnaissance themselves instead of hiring dicks to do it.)

Daunted but undefeated, the Dauseys pressed on. And after a while, they realized that Dausey By-Products was actually hanging on to more customers than it was losing. Restaurateurs appreciated not just the youthful enthusiasm of the tall, blue-eyed, twenty-seven-year-old Tres, who drove the truck from account to account. They also noticed that instead of making pickups at the last minute he showed up well before the containers were in danger of overflowing, allowing an extra margin of error. He was part of their community. And even if the Dauseys weren't paying bonuses, they made the standard payment by the pound more regularly than the restaurateurs were accustomed to. By 1997 the Dauseys had locked in about 150 restaurants. By 1998 they were up to 400.

Ed Dickerson, the owner of a Chik-Fil-A restaurant near Charleston, refused cash three times from CBP. Like many Chik-Fil-A franchisees Dickerson was a deeply religious person. "I don't do business that way," he told the CBP people. When they offered instead to donate $3,000 to his favorite charity, he still told them to go away. He had, after all, committed to the Dauseys. "I'm a man of my word," Dickerson said. It would be different if the Dauseys had reneged on their commitments to him, he said. But they had not. "They've followed through to the fullest extent. They're very, very punctual and they're sensitive to what we're doing." He went on: "These are the kind of relationships we need in the business world."

A business commentator named Napoleon Hill once put it very nicely: "Render more service for that which you are paid and you will soon be paid for more than you render."[21] Which draws us to the bizarre new world of pricing.

CHAPTER

4

What Am I Bid?

Conventional economics falls to pieces in the new economy. You remember Econ 101, the law according to Paul Samuelson's *Economics,* the fattest book any undergraduate ever had to lug? You know, supply and demand curves forming an X, with the intersection representing the perfect "equilibrium price"? Many colleges still teach this stuff with a straight face, even when the most expensive basketball shoe sells out before the mid-price one or when the supply of microchips goes up as the price comes down. Undergraduates also are taught that prices vary with cost, even though anyone in the visitors' gallery at the Chicago Board of Trade can watch a hundred screaming, gesticulating traders fixing the price of the corn harvest without the slightest idea of what the farmer is paying for seed, water, tractors, or fertilizer.

However perfectly it may apply to pig's feet and codpieces, economic dogma has trouble dealing with products built on networks, which account for more and more of the economy these days. The iron law of diminishing returns holds that the value of an item will decrease as its supply increases, yet the second fax machine made the first more valuable, not less, because it gave the first something to fax to, while the third, in turn, made the first two more valuable. In the case of computers, the power of networks has been shown to increase in proportion to the square of the number of terminals hooked together.[1] Similarly, fads and fashions create their own kinds of networks, explaining why something so ridiculous as a Beanie Baby can increase in value as the supplies increase. According to classical economics, there should be no such things as fads or fashions. Most economists still dismiss them as irrational trifles unworthy of analysis—never mind that they play a more vital role than ever in economic activity.[2]

Where scarce commodities display the law of diminishing returns, goods based on knowledge and information display the law of increasing returns. Increasing returns is another way of saying that crowds attract crowds, that success begets success, that he who has, gets. "In a network economy, value is derived from plentitude," writes Kevin Kelly, propounding the "New Rules for the New Economy" in *Wired* magazine. "Power comes from abundance. Copies, even physical copies, are cheap. Therefore, let them proliferate. Instead what is valuable is the scattered relationships—sparked by the copies—that become tangled up in the network itself."[3]

Most amazing (and unsettling, to many), the new economy is decoupling price and value. Today, a product may increase in value, to buyer and seller alike, even as its price drops to zero. For the proof, ask Paul Graziani.

᷇

Graziani was one of the many brilliant engineers whose years of association with the Strategic Defense Initiative would have been a waste except for the great knowledge they took away from it. Clean-cut, trim, blue-eyed, and sandy-haired, Graziani was a young engineer in the space division of General Electric Corporation (a business unit later sold to Lockheed). His specialty was tracking satellites, a vexing task, as you can see by picturing a satellite in orbit. Actually, that's the problem: The movements are too complex to visualize accurately. A satellite may roll, spin, pitch, yaw, rise, sink, and wobble. The solar panels conduct their own motions. Another great challenge is visualizing the signals of the satellite, which cast themselves like invisible spotlights across a necklace of receiving stations ringing earth. Satellites faithfully report their every move to their handlers, but only in raw data. Any calculation—deciding when the sun comes into view for a battery charge, say, or triangulating a ground station and a pair of relay satellites— might depend on dozens of other calculations. Mission planners are famous for picking up their Styrofoam coffee cups and waving them around, sometimes with pencils stuck through the middle. "Okay. Here's the earth . . ."

In his work at GE for a classified customer (he still won't say who), Graziani and his colleagues created a software program that turned all these data into animated, real-time images from any point of view—of the satellite as seen from a ground station or vice versa, of the earth and sky from the satellite's point of view, of the entire system from a fixed point of view in deeper space. The position of the stars, the sun, other satellites, space junk, and even the topology of earth could be included in the picture.

The customer paid $3 million for this product, leaving GE to charge the same princely amount, or any other sum it could extract, from any other customer it could interest in the same piece of software. But the prospects for space-based warfare dimmed drastically in the twilight of the Reagan years. Graziani wanted to cut the price to develop markets in the private sector and among other government applications, but GE was uninterested in trifling with sales too much below the $3 million level. And besides, how big a market existed anyway? There were only a few thousand satellites altogether.

Graziani, however, fervently believed in the commercial prospects for his tool. Like computers, satellites increasingly were becoming hubs through which dozens of far-flung senders and receivers might communicate. From all he could see, every satellite created a large community of owners, managers, analysts, and users. What's more, planning new satellite missions engaged an ever-wider circle of interested parties as telecommunications increasingly overtook the military use of space. It was the reverse of the law of diminishing returns: The more satellites there were, the more valuable each of them became.

So Graziani left GE, taking the rights to the program with him, launching a company called Analytical Graphics Incorporated, and rolling out a commercial version of the product at $9,999—a price cut of 99.6666 percent. The name he gave the product, Satellite Tool Kit, befitted the workaday market he aimed to create for it. As it turned out, GE was far from the only skeptic. Venture capitalists and other financiers, though dazzled by the technology, simply couldn't see the kind of market Graziani foresaw. So on a shoestring budget Graziani and his associates conducted a poor-man's marketing effort, sharing trade-show booths with other distributors and buying ads in obscure trade publications. Little by little the orders came in, totaling $1 million in 1994. Soon there was money to open regional sales offices and to hire programmers to write add-on modules. The company put up a few pages on the World Wide Web, from which it drew a few sales leads a day. Advertising went into the big-selling (and high-priced) *Aviation Week & Space Technology* magazine. It was the "slugfest approach" to selling, as Graziani called it, but it worked. Every time another order came in, a bell rang in the company's offices near a shopping mall in King of Prussia, Pennsylvania.

Even better, Graziani's engineers kept cooking up enhancements to the basic product, each of which became a revenue source in its own right. Before long sales from the add-ons exceeded revenue from the basic Satellite Tool Kit. By 1996 total sales reached $7.4 million a year. There was indeed a market after all for a $3 million software product—assuming it was priced at $9,999.

Still, Graziani remained frustrated. Although sales of add-ons were robust and profitable, they could never grow outside of the market for the company's basic product, the Satellite Tool Kit. And the cost of reaching that market through "slugfest" selling was consuming 51 percent of the company's revenue, cutting deeply into the funds that Graziani wanted to spend developing profitable new add-ons.

Graziani faced another frustration. Analytical Graphics had many stockholders, including Graziani himself, his employees, and the venture capitalists he had finally coaxed into the company. Selling stock to the public was the only way to reap the kind of windfall that everyone's hard work and risk-taking had earned. But nagging doubts about the company's growth prospects persisted outside of the company. Even after selling about 1,500 copies of a $10,000 product and an even greater sum in add-ons, Graziani glumly concluded that Analytical Graphics could probably never convince the skeptics on Wall Street that the untapped market remained huge.

So Paul Graziani considered whether he should cut the price of his basic product again, this time to zero.

His decision was hardly without precedent. Gillette had long given away razors to sell blades. Kodak practically gave away the Instamatic camera in order to sell film—and the film was priced inexpensively so the company could sell more film *processing*. Most conspicuously of all at the time of Graziani's deliberations, Netscape Communications Corporation created a new model of software economics by giving away its basic product—a tool for browsing the World Wide Web—and selling add-ons and upgrades (with mixed success) at a price. A company called Pointcast was giving away a personalized desktop news-gathering service and using the huge subscriber base as a way to sell advertisements. When an outfit called SourceCraft Incorporated posted a free version of some software for program developers on its Web site, it quickly had users in sixty-seven countries, which it then used as prospects for paying transactions. "There'd have been no way we could have sent a direct mail piece to sixty-seven countries," said Ed Chuang, the company's marketing director.[4] Outfits like Netscape, Pointcast, and SourceCraft could accomplish this because there was virtually no marginal cost in producing their products: Once the code had been written, each extra disk cost virtually nothing to produce. By giving away a product in one marketplace, you could make money in another.

But Graziani's idea was far more radical than anything yet attempted with a high-tech product. Not many software or razor companies had turned an established $10,000 revenue producer into a freebie. His board was incredulous at the concept. Satellite Tool Kit represented 23 percent of the company's revenue, a sum that would vanish overnight. The company's existing customers might feel cheated learning that a product for which they had shelled out ten grand was suddenly being given away like free sign-up disks for AOL. Graziani's sales staff all but rebelled. "Tensions are high," Graziani told me at one point. "It's a bold move," he said. "It could easily make or break the whole company."

But one question seemed to overshadow all others: What if someone else beat Analytical Graphics to the punch by rolling out a competing product for free? Thousands of users would undoubtedly give it a try. The competing product would leap from desktop to desktop in the aerospace community like a case of the flu. Graziani could practically hear the echoes: "Hey, man, check out this free software!" Even if the product were slightly inferior, its diffusion across the industry would "lock in" a standard, in the same way that the keyboard had been locked into an inefficient layout ever since the time of the earliest typewriters—the so-called QWERTY standard, named for the sequence of keys that persist in the upper left corner of all keypads.[5] Paul Graziani did not want someone else to become the QWERTY of satellite tracking.

Though incredulous at the idea of giving away an established product, the board of Analytical Graphics trusted Paul Graziani sufficiently to approve his plan.

As the roll-out date approached and I followed the entire drama at a distance, it struck me that Graziani was seeking a new kind of marketing advantage: the advantage of the giver. This is not what you'd call a new idea in human affairs. "One man gives freely yet gains even more," says the Book of Proverbs. "Another withholds unduly, but comes to poverty."[6] But in affairs of commerce, unlike in affairs of heart and the affairs of nations, there is a catch: The payoff comes later, if at all. Creating lock-in with a free software product works only so long as the giver continually improves the product and never charges more than a fair price for it. When a monopolist abuses his position (Microsoft comes to mind) sooner or later (not yet, in Microsoft's case, but inevitably one day) an upstart will come along to topple the industry leader.

On July 21, 1997, Analytical Graphics began distributing tens of thousands of free compact disks in satellite trade magazines, each containing a free copy of the product that had once sold for close to $10,000 and which before that had fetched $3 million. Though stunned by the move, existing customers grasped the logic. "We just can't afford to put it on everybody's desktop for $9,000, but the free release enables anybody to get a copy," explained Roger Ciesinski, satellite mission manager at TRW Incorporated. Analytical Graphics posted the software for free download on its Web site. To stimulate diffusion the company launched a "share the knowledge" campaign, with advertisements offering the chance for $30,000 in free upgrades (plus a leather jacket) to any customer who convinced at least two other people to install free copies.

By June 1998 the company's installed base totaled 13,000—short of the company's expectations, but sharply ahead of where it had begun. More importantly, the company's revenue through add-on sales was soaring, far ahead of expectations. And the size of the installed base was sufficient to set several investment bankers fighting over who would eventually take the company public in an IPO.

∽

I also observed the advantage of the giver at work in an Indiana farm town called Thorntown, population 3,000. Penny Nirider, a whiz with

a spreadsheet, had established herself as Thorntown's installer of
choice when any small business resolved to automate its accounting.
Because she had two small boys, Nirider conducted her work between
9:00 P.M. and 2:00 A.M. Later, when the boys started school, she took a
day job handling accounts payable at a small metal-bending firm,
working in a small cinder-block office attached to the front of a corru-
gated-metal shop. Her electronic spreadsheets made a huge difference
on the bottom line, prompting the owners eventually to make Nirider
a partner.

Metal-bending is a volatile business, so the company decided to di-
versify by purchasing a little plastics shop called Wilmarc. With just five
employees, Wilmarc made composting bins, leaf baggers, and an unusual rounded shovel that scraped away snow without the user's bend-
ing or lifting. They called it the Snow-Ease. Put in charge of the unit,
Nirider discovered that running a small plastics business was nothing
like running a spreadsheet. Wilmarc sold to hardware distributors, an
industry she knew nothing about. There were no uniform sales agreements. Because nobody sets out for the hardware store intent on buying
a leaf bagger, it must be priced to encourage impulse purchasing, and the
margins were terribly small. Nirider also sensed that some hardware
people didn't take her all that seriously because she was female.

One day shortly before Christmas 1995, an elderly woman phoned
Wilmarc headquarters. The caller was desperate to buy a Snow-Ease
but couldn't find one at retail. Would the factory ship her one? Nirider
was uneasy with the request. Wilmarc had never sold directly to a customer, only through distributors. Indeed, each Snow-Ease was packaged in a feeble box designed only for retail display, and Wilmarc
shipped these strictly by the case. For all Nirider knew, distribution
agreements prohibited selling at retail. But the caller was so sweet and
seemed so needful! So a Snow-Ease carton was dispatched to Pittsburgh
for $19.95, or $10 below retail.

Then just after Christmas, the Big Snow of 1995–96 hit the East.
Lynn Cullen, then the host of a popular AM talk show on Pittsburgh's
WTAE, happened to mention on the air that some miscreant had stolen
her snow shovel. The elderly woman phoned in to say she had solved
her own snow headaches by phoning Thorntown, Indiana, for a Snow-
Ease. Unfortunately, word went out on the airwaves that the product
cost only $19.95.

When a Wilmarc employee named Monica Taylor opened up the cinder-block office that morning, the phone was already ringing. It was a Pittsburgher seeking a Snow-Ease. The instant she hung up, another call came in, also from Pittsburgh, then another and another. It was a stunt, she figured; the Pittsburgh Steelers were facing the Indianapolis Colts in the playoffs. But soon it became obvious that some radio personality was raving about the Snow-Ease in Pittsburgh and had given out Wilmarc's phone number, to say nothing of the incorrect price, over the air.

Nirider agonized. Shipping boxes one at a time would be unprofitable and might even violate her distribution agreements. But the Pittsburghers were buried in snow. And whoever was at fault for the price confusion, it certainly wasn't they. "We didn't have a clue what we were doing," Nirider would recall. "But I knew what I would expect as a customer." It was reciprocity in action. So $19.95 it was. Nirider did add a $5 charge for shipping and handling, her best guess at the actual cost, only to find out—after hundreds had been shipped—that UPS was charging her nearly double that per box.

Soon another dilemma was at hand. Never having sold at retail, Wilmarc wasn't a credit-card merchant. But in a snow emergency, how could the company expect people to pay in advance? So Nirider shipped the product with invoices to follow. "It was just common courtesy," she explained. (Barely 1 percent defaulted.)

As the orders rolled in Nirider realized she was having more fun than she had ever enjoyed in business. Partly it was the escalating banter with callers over the approaching Colts-Steelers game. (The Steelers won, forcing Nirider to pay up on a few long-distance bets.) Everybody was so easygoing. Her gender, moreover, didn't matter in these sales. Dealing with the public, she found, "You get to be yourself. You don't have to play any games." Unhappily, of course, the more she sold, the more she lost. With orders unabating after two weeks, she needed an honorable way out. So Wilmarc purchased ads on WTAE notifying people that several days hence, on January 31, 1996, the company would begin charging the established retail price of $29.95.

Yet even at that price the orders flew in, many from Ohio and West Virginia, thanks to radiating word of mouth. By April, Wilmarc had sold 2,100 Snow-Ease shovels directly to consumers across the region, many times the number it sold through the usual distributors. Letters came from people all over thanking the company for responding so quickly and with such a back-saving product. Nirider swelled with pride. "There is nothing I have achieved in my work life that comes close to that," she told me.

Although Wilmarc's established middlemen probably had the right to complain, none did. On the contrary, the company's display of gallantry helped it win favor in the hardware community. "People could see we stood behind our word." Before long Nirider found herself talking to Sears, which asked whether she could make the Snow-Ease with a wider grip and a brighter paint job. Yes, yes. Would she re-name it Snow Pass? Of course. Could her little company go on-line in the Sears electronic purchasing network? Sure! answered the applications whiz.

Late in the summer of 1997 Penny Nirider watched workers loading seven truck trailers with the new-and-improved Snow Pass snow shovel, destined for five hundred Sears stores across the snow belt. From a small shop in rural Indiana came a new national brand, launched on a price that had once been less than profitable, but scrupulously honest.

∽

Pioneering entrepreneurs are not only giving away products, they are also giving away themselves. Certainly this practice, too, has precedents in the old economy, including in my own profession of newspapering. Droves of young reporters have worked for nothing because it was the only way to get a few bylines, which was the only way to get a paying job. In earlier times unpaid "copyboys" ran errands in newsrooms hoping a big story would break when no one else was around to cover it. Today entire firms also work gratis in order to prove themselves worthy of more work. Or, as in the case of a company called Times Direct Marketing, they work for free not only to prove themselves but to test business concepts.

Times Direct was the creation of Chris Peterson, a physics major trapped in the body of an English major. He worked as an advertising writer in New York for several years until one Friday night over drinks in 1987 he and a friend impulsively decided to move to San Francisco. With a '65 Volvo, $4,000 in savings, and a rented cubicle he went into the copywriting business as Times Direct Marketing.

Orders were few, forcing him to spend three years barely afloat on credit cards. Then he heard from a printer friend that Union Bank of California wanted to farm out a new credit-card campaign by mail—

junk mail. As the veteran of much plastic and many credit applications, he suggested using the mailing wrapper to describe the details of the offer instead of the standard practice of teasing the recipient with a cryptic come-on. He won the job and the campaign was a smash. (We have him in no small part to blame for all those envelopes emblazoned "5.9%! No annual fee!") His background in physics made him passably conversant in Silicon Valley, where he next focused his efforts. There he specialized in the tried-and-true use of the "free offer" as a method of generating sales leads for selling to business, usually a guide to some hot topic: *Receive our free 64-page information book if you answer the following five questions* (thereby providing the information we need to qualify you, call you, and close you). Because he was also an experienced writer, Peterson wrote these giveaway booklets himself.

In 1994, while preparing a campaign for the modem maker Global Village, Peterson was writing a giveaway called *The Business Users' Guide to the Internet.* And it hit him: "This is the future of direct marketing!" Within days he had hired a Net-savvy employee (they were few in those long-ago days), installed some networking gear, and leased a ganglion of high-speed lines, all for creating direct-marketing campaigns around the graphical and interactive powers of the Web.

His initial concept was rather simple: using the Web to supplement conventional direct-marketing campaigns. In contrast to a mass mailing, in which the user had to post a reply card, the Web made it possible to deliver the "gift" instantly. The seller, meanwhile, would receive her sales leads just as quickly. And handling costs—postage and phone time—would plunge practically to zero. Peterson imagined building a Web design staff, installing his own servers, and essentially taking over, at a very low cost, some of the work that he traditionally had to turn over to printers, envelope-stuffers, and the U.S. Postal Service.

As humble as this proposal was (and as readily as we take the concept for granted today, only a few years later) no client would go for it, not even the network-product makers of Silicon Valley. No one, it seemed, wanted to test so unproven a medium as the Web for fulfillment in a junk-mail campaign. Junk mail was too sure a bet, with a predictable payback for every dollar spent. "I was frustrated," Peterson later said.

After months of effort, he convinced a single client—NCD, a maker of networking terminals—to let him create a Web page as part of a larger direct-market campaign. But he won over the company solely by waiving his fee for the Web work, accepting a single workstation in return. In the end 20 percent of the mailing respondents used the Web to register their names and download a free booklet. Later, he proposed the same concept in a credit-card campaign at his long-faithful client, Union Bank of California. Once again he did the Web work on his own nickel, but the outcome—again, roughly a 20 percent response rate via the Web—told him he was on to something.

While scoring these small victories, he was dismayed to see a competing paradigm taking hold. This was 1994, and the first banner ads were beginning to appear on the Web—little postage stamps tucked into corners or stripped across the middle of a page. They were annoying to the reader and almost wholly unproductive to the advertiser. Even when they led the reader to a bigger ad they were mostly a waste. Peterson thought touting brands was a job for print and TV. The Web was different! The Web was interactive! The Web was the world's least expensive way to deliver information to the consumer and extract information from her in turn! So he began talking up a different concept. If he could cram the gist of a complicated credit-card offer on the outside of an envelope, he could create Web ads that did the same thing, as in, "Click here for a free CD on Improving Network Performance!"

Yet among clients, the knot of resistance remained tight. When he went to Bay Networks, then a kingpin of the networking world, he offered once again to do most of the work gratis. "Chris realized it was necessary for him to do that to prove his business case," Diane Sheridan, a marketing-program coordinator for Bay, would recall. "It made it easier for us to say yes. It showed commitment on his part and it helped us sell the idea to upper management."

The campaign went ahead, and before long Times Direct had accumulated a pile of respondents for an advertising cost of between $15 and $27 each—less than one-half the cost of each prospect acquired in a parallel postal campaign. Peterson was stunned to beat the conventional method by such a wide margin. He began pitching the idea all over Silicon Valley, presenting the Bay Network case at least a hundred times. People were soon buying in. Even the trend-setting Netscape hired Times Direct to conduct on-line marketing. Before long he had twenty people in his office, with nearly all of his growth due to his Web marketing services—paying services, that is. Working for free was like drilling a wildcat well, and he had hit a gusher.

In some ways the most amazing thing was Peterson's hope, even after giving away his work to prove the concept, that his competitors would make a play for the same business. "We're too small to educate the world," he told me. "I need my competition to get out there with the same message, especially the big guys." Then, he added, once the competition had helped to create the market, "our fleet-footedness, personal service, and focus will always get us work."

᷎

Money was invented as an economizing tool, as a way of uniting buyers and sellers across great distances. But money is not a substitute for a particular set of goods or services. Whether seashells, shekels, or Federal Reserve notes, money is a symbol for all goods. Money is stored matter and energy. Money can be anything. And that has always endowed money with a trace of unexpressed value exceeding that of the specific objects for which it is exchanged.

But ever so gradually, that, too, is changing. The economizing powers of money are slowly being overtaken by the cost of using money. Almost half the cost of long-distance telephone service is consumed by the monitoring, billing, and revenue processing, which is one reason why the telecom companies will inevitably move toward a flat fee for long distance. Money creates other inefficiencies as well. Virtually all the civil litigation in the world's most litigation-prone nation (namely the U.S.) involve questions of money or are ultimately reducible to it. Money forces the parties to a transaction to assign a value even if no objective means exists for doing so. Money causes people to fixate on transactions instead of relationships. And even in an era of negligible inflation, time depletes money of value.

Please don't get me wrong; we're not about to do away with money. What is changing is this: Money is mainly about accounting for individual transactions, and transactions are less important than relationships. Businesses are coming to realize that pushing around a lot of nickels and dimes is less useful than sustaining continuous collaborations.

For instance, the makers of electrical products, as we have seen, are creating real-time links to keep their distributors stocked with only as much product as necessary to meet retail demand. As part of this collaboration, the manufacturers are moving away from minimum orders, volume discounts, and other pricing schemes intended to encourage distributors to overstock their shelves. "If we're going to be partners," asks Tom Kozak of Panduit Corporation, the big electrical products company, "why would I want to sell you more than *you* can sell?"

More firms are also converting work into equity relationships. I know two under-thirty artists, Donald "DJ" Edgerton and Paul Geczik, who operate a prosperous design studio called Draw The Line in Manhattan's SoHo neighborhood. A vendor of theirs, a photo processor, decided to leave New York to launch a new brewery in his native Ireland. He wanted to engage Draw The Line to design labels, logos, and promotional materials, but he could not pay up front. So Edgerton and Geczik threw themselves into the project on a handshake and the promise of a 5 percent interest in the new brewery. Before long they had provided $50,000 worth of free work, by their reckoning. Then, to their increasing dismay, months passed with no word from Dublin. Oh, well, they thought. Win some, lose some. Then, finally, a lawyer called from Switzerland saying he was sending them two plane tickets to Dublin, along with stock certificates for the new Dublin Brewing Company, which had just opened a 17,000-square-foot brewery. Today the brewery supplies distributors in England, Sweden, Finland, and Holland, in addition to Ireland, and is making plans to come to the U.S. Draw The Line, meanwhile, was scheduled to begin receiving dividends in late 1998.

The greatest triumph of relationship over transaction that I've seen occurred in the basement meeting room of the Hyatt Hotel in Bethesda, Maryland. A major contractor called Bovis Construction Corporation, best known for building the 1996 Olympic Village in Atlanta, was putting up a $1 million addition to an office building owned by Kaiser Permanente, the country's biggest private health-care operation. It was a small project in terms of commercial construction, but as any builder will tell you, even a small construction project is a lawsuit waiting to happen.

Two dozen people connected with the project impatiently assembled in the hotel meeting room. The chief architect, Anthony Consoli, conspicuously placed his pocket watch on the table in front of him. When each member of the group was asked to list his expectations for the meeting, a project manager from Kaiser quipped, "My number-one expectation is coffee."

But the contractor's representatives quickly got down to business, dividing the room into three groups—the owner, Kaiser, in one corner;

the contractor, Bovis, in another; and the architect and engineer together in a third. Each group was asked to list its goals for the project. In the strictly commercial terms of this single building, each group had divergent interests: the owner in spending the least money possible, the contractor and architect in getting the owner to spend as much as possible and then fighting over the spoils between them. Yet when the three groups reassembled to read aloud their hopes for the projects, their statements were eerily similar, as if they had been eavesdropping on one another. All three groups said they wanted the project to come in on time and under budget, even though this would benefit mainly the owner and contractor. All three said they wanted to satisfy the people intended to use the building, though this would benefit the owner alone.

And, most tellingly, all three groups said they wanted this project to lead to long-term relationships with the other parties on the job.

Then the real work of the meeting began. In full view of everyone in the room, each delegation negotiated with each of the other two over whatever special accommodations were necessary to fulfill the mission. Kaiser said it expected the Bovis representatives to respond instantly to beeper messages, e-mail, and voice mail—expressing this simply as a requirement to "be there." A lawyer would faint over the legal ambiguity of language like "be there," but the contractor's representatives knew precisely what those words implied, and they all nodded their assent to the demand. The contractor, for its part, said it wanted the owner to make all payments quickly—no surprise, really, except that putting the issue so squarely before the people who would actually write the checks invariably does speed up payment. The architect asked the owner for a fast response when design contingencies arise . . . and so it continued, pair by pair, until several huge sheets of paper were taped to the wall, later to be memorialized in an informal document by which everyone would live for the duration of the project.

From the beginning to the end of the meeting, no one even bothered to mention, much less to review, the draft contracts still under negotiation by the lawyers. In fact there were no lawyers present in the room. In negotiating who would do what, no one said, "That's not part of the deal," or asked, "Who's going to pay for that?" Everyone committed to whatever made the most sense for the interests of the project— knowing that individually and as a group everyone would come out money ahead in the long run.

Among the hundreds of construction projects on which Bovis employed this process in the 1990s, not a single one—not one—resulted in a lawsuit or even the threat of one. On the contrary, this process helped draw Bovis into an ever-thicker and more profitable web of commercial relationships. Indeed, in the case of the Kaiser building, each of the participants was surveyed when construction was complete—owner, builder, architect, engineer—and of a possible perfect score of 100, the project was rated at 101.25 percent. The only deficiency cited during the entire process was ironic and rather irrelevant: The lawyers had failed to finalize the contracts before the building was completed.

CHAPTER
5

From Planning to Playing

Pat Anderson rolled into Dallas in the early 1970s with three daughters in her car, a cigarette in her mouth, and revolution in her heart. Leaving behind a life in Oklahoma and bent on saving the world, she was ready to enroll in graduate studies in clinical psychology. She was a bit of an anachronism at age forty-something, hanging antiwar posters in her home, writing for the local underground press, playing the Animals and other rockers of the era on the stereo at home. She also had a rough and skeptical side, making her known in her new social circle in Dallas for her hatred of insincerity and her brusque rejoinder to "cut the bullshit." What she did more than anything was read—literature, trash, philosophy, humor, a book in one hand and a cigarette in the other, the two calming vices in her life.

Before long she took up with a fellow rabble-rouser named Ken Gjemre. At the peak of the antiwar movement Gjemre had quit a successful career at Zale Corporation, then a retailing giant, out of disgust with the corporate world. (Never mind that Zale sold jewelry, not napalm.) In the era of the Santa Barbara oil spill and the first Earth Day, his cause was the environment.

One day Gjemre told Anderson of his vision for a small business, something at which he might fulfill his personal agenda while also making a living. It was a recycling business, except that instead of recycling trash he would recycle books—a bookstore that sold nothing but used books, not antiquarian books or collector's items but piles and piles of once-read textbooks, travel guides, and dime novels. He needed a few thousand dollars to get started, and was hoping his girlfriend would invest. Would she ever! The idea of "saving trees" while feeding her reading habit was more than Pat Anderson could pass up. Leasing one thousand square feet inside an old Laundromat on Lovers Lane in Dallas, they hung out their first sign: Half Price Books. People arrived with boxes and shopping bags literally overflowing, some tickled with the idea that the books they had enjoyed might bring the same pleasure to someone else, others delighted simply to be rid of the mildewed old things—and everyone grateful for even the few cents on the dollar that Anderson and Gjemre paid.

Their first employee was Pat's youngest daughter, Sharon (known in the family as Boots). At age fourteen Boots assumed the critical task of sorting by genre, which she accomplished quickly by scanning the covers and feeling the weight of the books. A woman running from a house meant Gothic romance; cowboys automatically meant Western; a big, fat volume was usually history. Boots also distributed promotional flyers in the neighborhood, though her mother wouldn't allow her to slip the papers under windshield wipers lest they become litter. There was no book that Half Price wouldn't buy at some price, and if it was too worn or too banal to sell, the owners shipped it to a conventional recycling plant or gave it away.

Within eight months of its founding Half Price Books was moving so much inventory that the old Laundromat was nearly ready to burst. Anderson and Gjemre needed storage at another location, and it occurred to them that they might as well do some selling at that location as well. So in 1973 the second store opened in what had been an old meat locker on McKinney Avenue in Dallas. "She was good at finding cheap property," Boots would recall. Some months later there was a third store, then a fourth.

Then, in 1975, Ken Gjemre's son moved to Austin and was looking for a living. Austin was a book town, a university town—say, why not open a branch there? A year later Boots Anderson, who had given up a college career to work with the company, was likewise ready to strike out on her own, so she opened a new location in the Dallas suburb of

Richardson. Her sister Ellen married a man in San Antonio so a new store went in there as well. Half Price Books was becoming a Texas-wide chain on nothing more than the genius of the concept and the eagerness of its owners to help their children find a living.

Despite paying meager salaries Half Price Books managed to attract just the kind of employee it needed—creative people, graduate students, struggling actors and poets and other such folks who enjoyed being around books. It didn't matter a whit to the owners what the employees looked like or how they dressed, not even through the Perry Ellis era of the '80s. Shoes became mandatory only as a worker's comp requirement. A few employees carried infants in Snuglis. The only rules of the house were a) keep costs low, b) waste nothing, and c) keep the books moving. Each store and each department within each store assumed its own peculiar personality, with hand-lettered signs and homemade display shelves. Sometimes conflict broke out among the eccentric and strong-willed personalities, but Pat Anderson never failed to silence the combatants with her command to "cut the bullshit" and "carry on."

Because experienced employees were so vital, they, like family, became the company's touchstone of strategy, to the extent it had any strategy at all. When a key manager named Ed Sczmanski decided he wanted to live on a beach, Half Price Books decided it was time to roll into the coastal town of Corpus Christi. When a longtime employee named Julian Reipe moved to the state of Washington for personal reasons, Half Price Books staked a claim there as well. Ditto Jack Darsnek, who went home to Madison, Wisconsin, and was soon running the entire Midwest division.

The same down-to-earth emphasis shaped the leadership of the company. Boots came into corporate headquarters as her mother's number two—not on rank order, since Boots was the youngest of three daughters, but simply because her other sisters happened to live out of town at the time. "We did what made sense," Boots later explained.

Pat Anderson delegated almost everything, but she worked overtime keeping a grip on the numbers. Indeed, knowing the numbers freed her from knowing what everyone else was doing. Errors in isolation were no cause for concern, but errors that repeated sooner or later showed up in the numbers. Each day she compiled a tally of store sales, making tiny, immaculate, ledger entries by hand, watching the trends, spotting the anomalies, and informing a store manager or a department head when the numbers signaled an unwelcome change. Using every pencil until there was nothing left but eraser, Anderson kept her arms around her empire with a pencil stub.

Otherwise, Half Price Books bore none of the usual trappings of planning. Every store was different from the next. Each department bore the stamp of its employees. The headquarters was located in a suburban strip mall. "We pretty much made it up as we went along," Boots Anderson would recall. Yet by the mid-1990s Half Price Books had fifty-three stores in eight states and more than $50 million in annual sales, making it the nation's largest used-book dealer by far. Periodically an investment banker would write, offering $10 million or more for the family-controlled business. Pat Anderson, with a raspy chuckle, would merrily feed the letter into a shredder, content to live in her $45,000 house. (Her old boyfriend and original partner in the business, Ken Gjemre, had health problems that forced him to withdraw from the operations; eventually, the company bought back his family's shares.)

At age sixty-seven Pat was still showing up for work every morning, so Boots, by then working in the headquarters operation, naturally grew concerned one day when her mother remained at large at 11:00 A.M. Boots found Pat at home, dead of a heart attack. At the wake, two musicians with day jobs at Half Price sang a country-western tribute.

> If she were here today
> She'd raise her glass and say
> "Cut the bullshit" and "carry on,"
> I wish that I could stay.

Pat Anderson was years ahead of her time. She recognized, to a degree few did at the time, that a business demands a vision of creating benefits that radiate into society; hers was saving a few trees and spreading around a lot of literature. She realized that every business needs an organizing principle but that the simpler the principle the better; hers was providing a source of livelihood and career growth for friends and family. And she realized that day-to-day management required tracking information instead of controlling people. In fact, the more playful people were, the better for the business.

And that's it. That is the entire sum and substance of the "strategic planning" that created the leading firm of its kind anywhere in

America. Anderson's methodology—or rather, her lack of methodology—is more apt today than ever. Obviously, people still plan their days, plan for the seasons, and plan their planning. But these days, there's too much happening in the present to devote so many resources to the future. The spontaneous exploration of the present is a fancy way of saying "play," which is now taking its place alongside planning as a vital element—perhaps the more vital element—of corporate strategy.

∽

"Creativeness," wrote the psychologist Abraham Maslow, the pioneer of motivation theory, "is correlated with the ability to withstand the lack of structure, the lack of future, lack of predictability, of control, the tolerance for ambiguity, for planlessness." In business, Maslow found, creativity required the manager "to forget about the future, to improvise in the present, to give full attention to the present . . . to be able to pour himself totally into the current situation, to be able to listen perfectly and to see perfectly."[1]

Maslow's insights, written in 1962, flew in the face of what nearly every executive held dear (and were accordingly ignored). In those days planning, structure, and the other trappings of control worked (with important limitations, which we shall discuss presently) because all the elements of a system could be controlled. As a discipline in its own right, business planning began in the coal mines of France more than a century ago, when a manager named Henri Fayol began equating men to tons and projecting the outcome five and ten years into the future. This was a major economizing tool: By deconstructing the future, a manager knew how many resources its fulfillment required. Early in the twentieth century, as "scientific management" reduced everyone to a cog, Frederick Taylor hailed planning as the only path to the "one best way."[2] In fact, Taylor's extreme division of labor soon took hold in the very creation of strategy, as planners were segregated into succeedingly smaller operating divisions, first at DuPont, then at General Motors, and later almost everywhere else.

By the 1960s, about when Maslow began to ask the first probing questions, planning had become entrenched in massive flow charts and backbreaking textbooks, creating an entire generation of corporate and government leaders whose influence persisted for thirty years. The principal criterion for stock selection became how closely a company tracked to plan. Career advancement, product development, project management—all likewise occurred according to plan. The economy was controlled through "fine-tuning" from Washington, whether the Keynesian fiscal control of the 1960s and 1970s or the monetarist fussing of the 1980s. Across corporate America "management by objectives" was the order of the day.

Alas, the reliability of planning plunges exponentially with the complexity of the system, and there is no doubt that most systems became a lot more complex in the 1960s. An avalanche of unrest engulfed American society: the civil rights movement, antiwar protests, environmentalism, "women's lib." The Arab oil embargo of 1972–73, forecast by almost no one, proved sufficiently powerful to upset economic applecarts everywhere. A nonlinear enemy in Vietnam dramatized the limits of linear military planning.

"Planning fails everywhere it has been tried," one of the leading figures in the field, Aaron Wildavsky of Berkeley, concluded in a famous 1973 article. Planners began to discover that they had been playing a rigged game: The future of an enterprise could be controlled when it could be predicted, but it could be predicted only to the extent it could be controlled. "Planning is not a solution to any problem," Wildavsky went on. "It is just a way of restating in other language the problems we do not know how to solve."[3]

The vexations of planning—surprise and complexity—become even more severe over greater time horizons, a fact most vividly revealed by the planner's own tool, the computer. In 1963, an MIT professor named Edward Lorenz was making bold new attempts to forecast that most complex of systems, the weather. As described by author James Gleick, Lorenz one day launched a long, highly iterative weather program with a starting value of 0.506. Because he had run this model previously and had a good idea where it was headed, Lorenzo left the room for a cup of coffee while the printer chugged away. But when he returned he found the plots running wildly off the course they had previously taken. The reason was that previous runs used 0.506127 as their starting point. Over the course of so many iterations the tiny difference of 0.000127 compounded to a spectacularly unexpected result. At that moment, by Gleick's account, Lorenz "decided that long-range weather forecasting must be doomed."[4]

Lorenz's findings became codified as the law of "sensitive dependence on initial conditions," or as the frequently cited Butterfly Effect: A butterfly flapping its wings in Rio sets off a chain of events that ends with a tornado in Texas. It also brought to mind the fable that told of how "for the want of a nail the shoe was lost," ultimately causing the loss of a horse, a rider, a battle, and finally a kingdom. In any complex system composed of diverse elements and action, no one can foresee the outcome of feedback acting upon feedback acting upon feedback. Even the most powerful computers using Newtonian calculus cannot predict the effects of gravitation among as few as three objects.

Plans mainly limit human activity. If Pat Anderson had set out to create a $50 million-a-year national bookstore chain, she never would have started out in an old Laundromat—yet by doing so she was able to accumulate the capital necessary for creating a national chain.

It's not that looking into the future is bad, so long as one does not restrict the present according to a future more distant than one can see. Half Price Books spends quite a bit of time putting out more camping books in the early summer, more Christmas books in the fall. Meteorologists, to return to the frustrated Prof. Lorenz, have actually become quite good at planning about four days out—but thereafter weather forecasting remains hopeless, the course of the future too sensitively dependent on the conditions of today. Planning works when it occurs within the range of one's vision or measurements, when one's plan is devised and endlessly revised. "Man proceeds in the fog," the Czech novelist Milan Kundera wrote. "He sees fifty yards ahead of him, he can clearly make out the features of his interlocutor, can take pleasure in the beauty of the trees that line the path, and can even observe what is happening close by and react." Or as the American novelist E. L. Doctorow once noted, life itself was like driving at night: "You can only see as far as your headlights, but you can make the whole trip that way."[5]

Keeping a sharp eye on the road and making constant course corrections is not really planning; it's simply the process of action, feedback, and synthesis. "When planning is placed in the context of continuous adjustment it becomes hard to distinguish from any other process of decision," wrote Wildavsky. He called it "adaptive planning." He conceded, "Others call it muddling through."

Is that the most business can hope for? Merely muddling through? The answer is yes, but that's hardly any cause for dismay. For business muddles well—it best discovers its future—when it uses nature's method, and that method is play. "Life is creative. It explores itself through play, intent on discovering what's possible," write the organizational theorists Margaret Wheatley and Myron Kellner-Rogers. "Life uses messes to get to well-ordered solutions."[6] Accidental improvements survive because they improve fitness; failures are quickly discarded. Kevin Kelly of *Wired* calls it "hacking a living," or trying combinations until you find one that works.[7]

This is especially evident in science and technology. "You can't possibly get a good technology going without an enormous number of failures. It's a universal rule," says Freeman Dyson, who discovered much of modern quantum physics. After all, Dyson says, "it's the numerical accidents that make life possible."[8] The Wright brothers pioneered powered flight not because they were great theorists, but because they threw theory out the door, choosing instead to tinker their way into the air. Likewise in economics. "In its very nature, successful economic development has to be open-ended rather than goal-oriented, and has to make itself up expediently and empirically as it goes along," says Jane Jacobs, an urban-development authority. Growth in economies, she says, no differently than growth in ecosystems, is the result of "improvisational drift."[9] What began as a collection of bicycle-repair shops became the Japanese auto industry through nothing more than an accumulation of experiments.

Control is anathema to exploration, which therefore often flourishes far from the center of an organization—in the outlying divisions, during the graveyard shift, in an overseas operation. This reflects a property of all living systems: Evolution is most rapid on the periphery of a niche. Innovation tends to occur at the fringes of a system because that's where people in the system explore the greatest space of new possibilities. The entrepreneurs who drove the industrial revolution in England were Quakers and other nonconformists who had abandoned London for the fringes of Birmingham and Manchester.[10]

Innovation requires not only freedom but safety—the kind of sanctioned failure that few large organizations have ever been willing to provide. But some are beginning to. Consider, for instance, the transformation of Mercedes-Benz Credit Corporation and the story of a leader name Georg Bauer.

Bauer hailed from the Bavarian region of Germany, a festive oasis in a country (let's face it) somewhat prone to brooding. Bavaria is where the Germans first began brewing beer. The great vineyards and chefs are there. And although all of Germany became more serious following World War II, Bavaria managed to preserve its standing as a place where a kid like Bauer could come of age and have some fun. The son of a brewery official, he loved music and art. But he also breezed through his business studies and his apprenticeships in finance. In the early 1970s, his stellar performance won him a position in the Stuttgart office of the globally expanding Citibank. Practically from day one he had lending approval well into the six figures, authority he would have waited eight or ten years to earn in a German bank.

Bauer drew the notice of Stuttgart's leading corporate citizen, the venerated and conservative Daimler Benz AG, maker of the Mercedes-Benz. Bauer was nervous about joining the hidebound behemoth but was delighted to be sent on the fast track overseas, to financial posts in Italy, France, and, best of all, in Portland, Oregon, where Daimler Benz had just purchased a major truck manufacturer called Freightliner. Bauer's U.S. years were glorious, exposing his family to American culture and himself to the glimmerings of a new post–Industrial Age in management. However oriented around command-and-control principles at the time, American management methods were practically anarchic compared to those that held sway in Germany. Ultimately, in 1992, he wound up president of Mercedes-Benz Credit Corporation, an affiliate headquartered in Norwalk, Connecticut, whose five hundred employees ran a portfolio of $9 billion in vehicle loans.

By all outward appearances nothing needed fixing. The operation had enjoyed years of solid growth, providing financing on something like 60 percent of all the Mercedes-Benz cars sold in North America. Employees could not imagine the new president tampering with such success. Yet Bauer was not only eager to experiment with change, he actually saw the need for it. He was convinced that Daimler Benz and other big automakers would one day cut back on the generous finance subsidies they provided to car buyers. This would thrust Mercedes-Benz Credit onto a level playing field with every bank and credit union in North America. To compete effectively, he would have to cut costs while at the same time improving customer service. This, he reasoned, required tearing the organization apart and reassembling it with low costs and tip-top service as the guiding principles.

But what would the new organization look like? He could not tell.

Employees would have to invent it themselves through trial and error. By keeping what worked and what didn't, a new organization would *emerge*. "Let's let the people in the organization find the weaknesses in the organization," Bauer told the other bosses. "Let's let it grow from the bottom up."

The rules were few but firm. People would attack the service issues in teams because all customer-service problems cut across multiple departments, skills, and specialties. Only through collaboration across functions could these problems be analyzed from start to finish. Another nonnegotiable objective was cutting waste: The headquarters was full of duplication and processes that slowed down service and drove costs higher. These had to be eliminated. Another rule was the eradication of sacred cows: Every job, every procedure was fair game for change.

The next rule was quite a clincher. The rule was *no fear*.

Bauer knew he needed to tap the deepest, even wildest, creativity of everyone in the place. But the employees were accustomed to an organization that had only discouraged risk. Planning was supreme because mistakes—anything to make one "look bad" in the eyes of the bosses—were to be avoided by any means. Only by breaking down these fears, only by encouraging experiment, risk, and sheer play, did Bauer have any hope of attaining the near-impossible. "The future is all about risk-taking," he later explained. "You can't be a faster organization if people aren't taking risks. It's not good enough just to say 'we encourage risk.' The leaders throughout the organization have to support people who take risks and make mistakes. If they don't, you're only halfway there. You have to have a fear-free environment." Bauer was taking a page straight out of Deming's book. "Drive out fear throughout the organization," Deming wrote, "so that everybody may work effectively and more productively for the company."[11]

The no-fear principle also involved a promise from Bauer: Despite his eagerness to cut costs, no one would be laid off no matter how many new efficiencies were introduced. As startling as this promise seems it was actually quite easy to make. For one thing, Bauer wanted the company to grow dramatically, which would create advancement opportunities in new areas. In addition, no one knew better how to find waste than the people creating it. Thus anyone finding a way to eliminate her own job would be rewarded with a new job. Bauer wanted people playing in a safe sandbox.

One team threw itself into writing a mission statement for the new organization, occupying itself in the task for months and ultimately drawing more than two hundred employees into the process. You have seen these mission statements hanging on lobby walls all over corporate America, usually in a wood frame or etched into brass plates. Usually they're full of insipid platitudes that inspire employees to precisely nothing. Mission statements fail because they're written by a small team of flacks or top executives—or worst of all, by consultants with cookie-cutter formulas. A mission statement instead should be thoroughly pondered and long argued over, a document written with such authority that people are willing to whip out a copy whenever they're asked to do something that runs against the grain of the organization. Nobody ever buys into these things unless they have some edge, unless they take a stand—unless they're slightly dangerous. Which this one certainly was.

"We encourage a restless spirit in inquiry," it read. A good word, "restless," rather like the "exploratory curiosity" with which the biologist Sir Alister Hardy once described evolution.[12] "Free-flowing communication is the lifeblood of our organization," the values statement continued—lifeblood, like a living thing—"an information-rich environment where communications flow freely and in all directions." In other words: no management secrets, no confidential numbers, no hidden agendas. This, the document pointedly noted, included the right "to speak frankly without fear of reprisal." It went on: "We must accept and embrace risk-taking at Mercedes-Benz Credit Corporation."

The values statement, in turn, helped guide the teams in figuring out how to alter the day-to-day operations of the place. Ultimately nineteen teams organized themselves around various initiatives. Computers were installed on every desktop (there had been practically none before) and lashed together with e-mail systems and databases so team members could continually volley ideas. The entire office turned into the corporate equivalent of a Montessori classroom, wide open, with walls torn down, cubicle partitions lowered, and conference rooms (ultimately ten in all) encased in glass so everyone could always see who was meeting with whom.

By 1996 the basic outlines of a new organization were in place. Four of the company's eight layers of management were wiped out. (Executive names were also peeled off the close-in parking places.) Every employee became eligible for a leased Mercedes-Benz. New bonus programs compensated people not only for individual performance but for the performance of their teams and the output of the entire company. Boss-to-subordinate performance reviews were expanded to include the views of fellow teammates as well as the members of other teams. A "gain-sharing" program was instituted, in which teams were paid bonuses equal to 10 percent of whatever cost-saving maneuvers they identified. Employees stripped the Connecticut office of its "corporate headquarters" designation and gave it a new name that emphasized collaboration over control: the North American Support Center.

To top it off, a rotating sculpture, a glistening, avant-garde Möbius strip, was hung in the lobby, chosen because the look of it seemed to change continuously.

Indeed the principal outcome of the change process was to assure that the operation never stopped changing, particularly as market conditions shifted. Margaret Brayden, who had spent years as the company's records-retention coordinator, came up with new processes that eliminated her own job. After stepping down to a position called "group leader" of office services, she continued cutting costs, ultimately wiping out her entire department. Her direct reports were all reassigned, while Brayden herself was rewarded with an assignment on a team called "change management."

By 1998 the firm had swelled its assets to $23 billion. Mercedes-Benz Credit was ranked first in the industry for customer satisfaction by J.D. Powers & Associates. Thanks to the constant experimentation of his employees, the organization had diversified into aircraft, boat, and other financing. His employees had created the industry's first real-time financing product, in which a car buyer could apply for financing, receive a credit approval, and drive away with a car in the space of minutes. "That sort of thing is possible only when people stretch," he said, "only when they're willing to step out of their key functions and step into uncertainty."

⟳

If play is so important, of what use is that venerable document known as the "business plan"? Every banker and investor wants to see one, every college course in entrepreneurialism teaches how to write one, and most entrepreneurs are comforted to know they have one sitting in the top drawer. Business plans do have value. They can be fruitful as exercises in imagining the possibilities of a business. They act as a system for capturing and evaluating information. They are models—you might even say toys—for leaders to tinker with and constantly adjust, and sometimes abandon, as you may learn in the story of Dan Harple and his $160 million stock sale.

Harple grew up a teenage rock guitarist, and like any self-respecting garage rocker of the 1970s he was as accomplished with plugs and cables as with picks and capos. His fascination for hooking things together led him to study electrical engineering and psychology, an eminent combination, it would turn out, for the networked 1990s. Ultimately he wound up in Mechanicsburg, Pennsylvania, a small manufacturing town surrounded by dairy farms just east of Amish country, working for an electrical-parts manufacturer called AMP Incorporated.

Harple had a work buddy named Rich Pizzarro, also a guitarist. Pizzarro was a self-taught computer programmer, learning the craft, as so many did, in order to create his own computer games when he was a kid. At AMP he and Harple were involved in networking workstations so that any number of engineers could pass around a single set of electronic drawings. This work inspired Harple and Pizzarro to a vision that went way past their job assignment. What if all those design engineers could watch each other's scribblings at the same time, even while sitting at different desks, on different floors, or even in different buildings? Why stop there? What if they could discuss the drawing by speaking right through the computer network? Even more exciting, what if they could *look at each other* while working on a design? This was work, but it was also play.

The two men quit their jobs in 1992, not out of any disaffection for their employer but because their idea had awakened a deep-seated urge in each of them. Pizzarro's father was a Puerto Rican immigrant who had died young of cancer, expressing regret that he was not leaving behind a business with which to give his son a head start. Harple's in-laws were successful Italian-American entrepreneurs whose example he was eager to follow. In addition, Harple had four children (soon to be five) and nothing quite so concentrates one's ambitions as the thought of putting such a brood through college. Harple also fantasized about creating a legacy to hand over to his children. And both men loved the idea of advancing the connectedness of the workplace. "Computers weren't doing enough to help people," Harple would later comment. "Computers were just slowing people down."

There had been many attempts of varying success to marry voice and video through the years, but each attempt involved the use of ungainly and expensive hardware. Harple and Pizzarro imagined a real-time video network requiring only regular computers and cheap, desktop cameras. Using software alone they would accomplish everything that other teleconferencing systems did with big, expensive hardware. "The solution is in software," they kept saying, leading them to christen their new company InSoft Incorporated.

But not just any kind of software. Their frustrations as network engineers, vainly attempting to connect the hardware and software of many different manufacturers, motivated them to create a product that could integrate with anything. To that end they wrote their code according to the public-domain standard on which the Internet was created. At the time the Internet was still mainly a medium for academics, military, and techies, and Harple and Pizzarro had no intention of creating a product for use over the Internet itself. But using the Internet protocol assured their product a better chance of fitting in with other products—even if that meant making it easier for their customers ultimately to use products from any competitors who happened to follow InSoft into the marketplace. Sacrificing exclusivity, they decided, was better than compromising versatility. Connectedness was more valuable than control.

For months the two men worked in spare bedrooms, Pizzarro in his mother's place, Harple in his house full of preschoolers and preteens. They slept only three or four hours a night. In the summer their workrooms filled with hot air from the exhaust fans of their workstations. But before long they had raised $100,000 from family members. Later they took in another $500,000 from a wider circle of acquaintances. With capital came the trappings of respectability: six hundred square feet of rented space in a building on the edge of a highway cloverleaf near the Pennsylvania Turnpike, plus a board of directors to represent the interests of the outside investors. As they began racking up sales and as word of their success spread, venture capitalists leaped in with a $3 million investment. They began opening sales offices, racking up corporate orders at an average of roughly $20,000 a throw. They lured Russian and Indian engineers to central Pennsylvania to help enhance the product, holding out generous stock options that might prove quite valuable if ever the company succeeded in going public. Before long a Canadian networking company purchased $5 million worth of equity.

To this point all growth had occurred according to plan. Harple, who served as CEO, measured every major decision against a spreadsheet that projected sales, costs, and profits by quarter, a document formulated in conjunction with his directors. He plotted his figures according to the methodology outlined in a best-selling technology book called *Crossing the Chasm,* by Silicon Valley marketing guru Geoffrey Moore. Harple reverentially referred to "the plan" and made no secret of relying heavily on his board of directors for guidance.

But for all the button-down quality of these formal dealings, play was evident everywhere else. Callers waiting on hold had to listen to a recording by the Grateful Dead. Harple hung a poster of rock icon Todd Rundgren in his office. The demo version of the InSoft product was illustrated with a photo of rock guitarist Lenny Kravitz. When the system created a videoconferencing icon for each user, it cried "Smile!" and made the kind of "click" that Pizzarro remembered from the photo booth in a local dime store. Harple's teenage daughter went to work in the company's mailroom.

Nor was InSoft's adherence to plan so compulsive that it turned away from unexpected opportunities. When a sales rep from Sprint walked in one day, he was convinced to recommend InSoft to his own company, leading to a marketing alliance under which some four thousand Sprint salespeople began pitching the InSoft product. When Harple's people heard that the mighty Hewlett-Packard was considering a jump into videoconferencing, they persuaded the giant to adopt InSoft's product instead.

As the corporation's prospects grew, IBM and other suitors came calling. The owners could have sold the company at that moment for something on the order of $50 million, but Harple and Pizzarro would not have it. Although they were eager to one day sell some of their shares to the public, and to give their employees that same option, they had no interest in selling the entire company. InSoft was their identity. They could see a day when every home would have a picture phone and they wanted the InSoft logo affixed to that phone.

Wherein lay the greatest virtue of their business plan: as an expression of their fervent belief in the future of their business as an independent, stand-alone entity. It was like the mission statement that employees created at Mercedes-Benz Credit, or like the growth philosophy of Half Price Books: an articulation of a belief about the future, but not a restriction on the route to reach it. And by 1995 the InSoft dream was becoming a reality. With their staff reaching seventy people, Harple and Pizzarro proudly watched a crane raising giant white and blue letters to the top of the small office building where they worked. It was now the InSoft Building.

But it was just about then that Internet hysteria hit.

Though they had designed their product according to Internet protocols, Harple and Pizzarro had never considered the Internet a medium over which it would be employed. Video demands huge bandwidth (the numbers of "bits," or ones and zeros, that can be stuffed through a wire at once). InSoft video needed the kind of figuratively fat cables that major corporations laced through their ceilings and floors. The Internet by contrast had no more bandwidth than the phone system, which remained largely a network of nineteenth-century copper-wire technology. In the never-ending planning and strategizing intended to keep their dream alive, the principals of InSoft ranked the Internet ninth—dead last—as a potential market for their product. Even as Internet mania swept the software business, InSoft's board, including members of Dan Harple's own family, cautioned against wasting too much time worrying about the Internet. Selling a low-cost, mass-market version to run over the Internet—assuming that were technologically feasible—would cannibalize the corporate sales from which InSoft was recording more than $7 million in annual revenue. "Don't do it," the directors said. "It will kill our direct sales."

But Harple wanted at least to toy with the concept. He quietly convened a two-person skunk works to begin looking at possible new ways of compressing video for the narrow bandwidth of the Internet, and their early work was encouraging. By the fall of 1995 there were fifteen people on the project, by winter nearly the whole company. Meanwhile, the value of anything connected with the Internet was reaching nosebleed heights on Wall Street. InSoft engaged investment bankers to begin plotting the initial public offering that would make Harple, Pizzarro, and their employees potentially wealthy—while still preserving the company's much-prized independence.

One day when the new Internet product was near completion, Harple was conducting a demonstration at Bear, Stearns & Company, a Wall Street investment banking firm that had installed earlier InSoft products on its trading floors. Jeff Marshall, the chief technologist at Bear, Stearns, was eager to get a look at the new InSoft product. "This is unbelievable!" he kept saying. The idea of real-time, face-to-face communication over the Internet—he could scarcely believe it. "This is unbelievable!"

And then came the fateful words: "We've got to get Jim Clark on the phone right now!"

Clark was himself a walking case study in entrepreneurial genius, the creator of Silicon Graphics Corporation and later the business brains behind Netscape Navigation Corporation, whose "browser" software introduced the World Wide Web to millions of desktops worldwide. Clark was diving in the South Seas when the message reached him from Bear, Stearns that a small company in Mechanicsburg, Pennsylvania, had developed a possible picture phone for the Internet. Within hours Clark had climbed into his Falcon 50, charting the improbable course of Fiji to Mechanicsburg with a stop in New York to pick up his tipster at Bear, Stearns.

When Clark arrived Harple and his staff were in the throes of planning not only a public offering but a road show to promote the release of the newly completed Internet product. They were thrilled to have the Silicon Valley legend in their midst, just as he was awestruck by the demonstration of their product. On his way back to the airport in the Harple family van, Clark popped the question. "Would you consider a merger?" he asked.

Harple and everyone else agonized. Selling InSoft would be almost like losing a member of the family. But the world had changed in only a few months. The Internet—and the allied media of intranets, extranets, and the like—seemed at the moment to embody the future of everything. Thanks to his willingness to depart from plan (to the point of going against his board of directors), Harple had assured InSoft a niche in this new world. Yet although there were thousands of small companies developing software products, only a handful of huge ones actually distributed them—including the Microsoft juggernaut, which seemed to destroy everything in its path. InSoft could take a chance by going it alone, but failure meant the loss of a fortune in which all of InSoft's employees were vested. Paradoxically, the safest course, indeed the only safe course, was abandoning the business plan altogether.

A short time later Harple was in a conference room in Sunnyvale, California, accepting a deal for $161 million in Netscape stock on behalf of himself, his employees, and his investors. In the stress of the moment, Harple, then age thirty-six, broke down, weeping. "It's very emotional when you start something and it ends," he explained. "Our little baby grew up faster than we ever thought."

❧

In retrospect, we can see that business, for most of the twentieth century, was not supposed to be personal, much less playful. Business—all work, in fact—didn't count unless you were doing it according to someone else's agenda. As William H. Whyte, Jr., wrote in his haunting 1956 study, *The Organization Man,* "When a young man says that to make a good living these days you must do what somebody else wants you to do, he states it not only as a fact of life that must be accepted, but as an inherently good proposition."[13] *Fortune* magazine published a handbook for managers, also in 1956, asserting that "organization work demands a measure of conformity." How great a measure? For young executives, it said, "a good half of their time is finding the right pattern to conform to."[14]

Even small business was built on rigorously constrained commercial models that submerged individual personality. The rise in the postwar years of franchising in retail and of unionism in skilled trades signaled not an embrace of entrepreneurialism but a flight from it.

But as employers, employees, and entrepreneurs are at last rediscovering, people give their best work when the work conforms to their identities. Identity after all is simply the sum of the features that hold constant (as in "identical") across the scales of one's life—"expression in a self-consistent manner," as *Webster's Third* puts it. Margaret Wheatley and Myron Kellner-Rogers argue that identity is nothing less than a survival tool for every living thing, "the filter that every organism or system uses to make sense of the world," they write. "New information, new relationships, changing environments—all are interpreted through a sense of self."[15] Charlie Parker, the genius of the saxophone, put it this way: "Jazz comes from who you are, where you've been, what you've done. If you don't live it, it won't come out of your horn."[16] Doing what you like and what you're good at turns work to play.

Play can help a business create the future, but can it bring business in through the door? This question leads to the issue of personal style. If Michael Jordan were known strictly for his point scores, he wouldn't be much of an entrepreneur. If he did not electrify his fans and teammates and inspire the best in the kids who follow him—if he were as understated as Hakeem Olajuwon, say—he would still be a great basketball player, of course, but he would never have created an entire industry around himself. Jordan changed the game of basketball not on technical proficiency alone but on the style of his play and the style of his life. This also distinguishes Jordan from the ballplayer Dennis Rodman, who despite his media showmanship lacks all of Jordan's style in play. Show-offs turn heads, but artists win hearts. As Fernando Flores puts it, "Style is not an aspect of things, people, or activity, but rather constitutes them as what they are."[17]

Even in this exhibitionist age many businesspeople remain uncomfortable "outing" their true style. They prefer to craft a cautious image, calibrated in focus groups, brought to life in advertising agencies, and puffed up through PR. They fail to grasp the secular change taking hold throughout the marketplace: that in an era of abundance, when power has shifted from seller to buyer, a come-on is usually a turnoff. Most consumers, from the industrial purchasing agent to the teenage mall rat, can spot insincerity at great distance. "There's a sucker born every minute," said the circus master P. T. Barnum. But today, the real fools are the fakes.

In an era when slickness gets so little mileage, an honest style inspires confidence and trust. It's like the early days of television, when the sincerity of the message was not smothered by production values; commercials inspired more trust because they were live—miscues, stammers, and all. Gateway 2000 ships computers in boxes playfully emblazoned with black-and-white bovine markings because the company makes its home in South Dakota. One of the longest-running and most effective positioning statements in history, "We Try Harder," has survived in dozens of languages because everyone knows that Avis really does have to work harder against number-one Hertz. I often take my car for service to a neighborhood mechanic who displays a stylized Christian cross on his illuminated sign. I go there not out of any particular endorsement of his religious views but because his sign tells me he is honest about his identity, which suggests he may be honest in his dealings with me as well.

The backlash against contrivance is evident in the advertising of Rothman's of Union Square, a Manhattan haberdashery catering to a young crowd. Ken Giddon, who took over the store from the estate of his grandfather, the legendary discounter Harry Rothman, recoiled at the kind of fashion advertising in which Ralph Lauren and other designers declared, "Wear this outfit and you'll get the girl in the picture." Giddon also resolved to lampoon the overbearing boastfulness of many a New York male. So he created a tongue-in-cheek advertising character called the Rothman's Man, someone who "trains personal trainers," who "can make it to the Hamptons in eleven minutes flat," who "has zero percent body fat." The campaign drew in droves of prosperous professional men who hated the oppressiveness of the male fashion scene. "They don't take themselves too seriously here," a customer named Arthur Kennedy told me as he was being fitted for a suit. After all, Kennedy said, "it's just *clothes*." By 1998 Ken Giddon had built Rothman's to more than $6 million in annual sales.

In the new world of marketing, style engages without imposing, teases without taunting. Style is a story—in contrast to an image, which is a snapshot. And on top of everything else, style is fun, and people having fun draw attention, as folks in Minneapolis will tell you about Robert Stephens.

Stephens, like nearly everyone under the age of thirty in this book, is a self-taught coder. The youngest of seven children in a navy family, he received a Commodore computer before he was in the second grade. His father refused to spring for the costly game programs, but he did arrange for the boy to enroll in programming classes at Great Lakes Naval Air Station. He was a mediocre student, but he could program in COBOL, FORTRAN, Pascal, and the language called C. He loved taking apart TVs and VCRs and drawing gory-looking monsters. When he wasn't entranced by a computer screen he was staring at a television screen, absorbed in old cop shows and other syndicated television reruns from the 1960s. He was the only person in the family ever to attend college, but he didn't come close to graduating. He was a classic, Reagan-era suburban geek in a spiky punk hairdo.

He wound up selling mattresses for a distributor in Chicago. Because the company spent eight weeks calculating his commission checks by hand, he took a stack of sales receipts home one day and created a program to figure everyone's commission instantly. The company, every bit as delighted as the salespeople, turned him loose on the delivery logistics system. One day he crashed a meeting where an advertising rep for the *Chicago Tribune* was pitching space in the newspaper's local zone editions. The managers at the mattress company were trying to guess which parts of town their customers were concentrated in. Stephens returned a moment later with a printout he had prepared listing the company's sales by ZIP code. The next day he was an assistant manager.

Before long a friend lured him to Minneapolis, where he supported himself by programming and repairing TVs and VCRs. One day someone in his apartment building brought him two dead computer workstations from a high-tech graduate-research lab at the University of Minnesota. Stephens opened them. One had a burnt fuse, the other a single loose solder. He fixed them both inside of twenty minutes, earning him an overnight reputation as a wizard of computer repair. People called from all over town. "Please fix my computer!" they pleaded. Robert Stephens realized he suddenly had a business on his hands.

He called it the Geek Squad. The name said it all—who he was, and why anyone might want his services, a perfect role because for him it was no role at all. He designed a stylish, oval Geek Squad logo in black and orange. He printed Geek Squad T-shirts, which he distributed in nightclubs because he wanted cool clients. He handed out flyers picturing a geeky Wally Cleaver type holding a glass of milk, an image straight out of a childhood spent in front of syndicated TV. "Geek Squad soothes the painful itching and burning associated with crashing computers," the brochure said. "We'll save your ass." With his income from an installation project for General Mills he bought a 1958 French-made Simca, emblazoned it with the Geek Squad logo, and spent Saturday nights cruising in front of the opera house, drawing stares and exposing his name to the black-tie crowd because he wanted corporate clients as well as cool ones. It all worked.

Despite a widespread mystique to the contrary, fixing personal computers, as Stephens discovered early on, is rarely rocket science. Only a few things usually go wrong. So when Stephens began receiving more calls than he could possibly handle on his own he commoditized the process, reducing it to a few simple procedures, loading diagnostic programs onto a single disk, and rounding up young part-timers at $7 an hour. "The quick oil change," he told me. "That's my model." Stephens's people became part of the corporate identity, outfitted in dark suits, white socks, and pant legs three inches too short; the Blues Brothers, of course! He gave them cards identifying them as "special agents," made himself the "chief inspector," and left behind invoices that said, "Pay up, sucka." He turned a few old ice cream trucks into geekmobiles. With so many metaphors going on at once the Geek Squad was in danger of self-parody. Stephens ultimately simplified things by outfitting his special agents in short-sleeved white shirts, clip-on ties, metal badges, and shiny black shoes from a local cop store. In any case, he explained at one point, "Nobody can make fun of us because we're profitable."

His sense of flair, however, was far more developed than his flair for finance. His books were a shambles. He fell behind with the IRS. He hired a business manager who quit within a year and then engaged an experienced consultant who could see the potential of the business and traded his advice for a 10 percent equity interest. But on the top line, the revenue line, the company just kept on growing. Even IBM, in the throes of a massive contract to convert the agribusiness giant Cargill Incorporated to a global client-server system, brought in the Geek Squad for help in migrating operating systems from old servers to new. "They really enjoy the work they do," the IBM project leader, Mike Hollander, would later explain. "I wouldn't dream about doing one of these big projects without someone from the Geek Squad."

One day someone from the big-box retailer Best Buy saw Stephens's geekmobile, made a few inquiries about the reliability of his service, and then hired him for a cushy assignment: to stand by on the set of a shoot for a laptop commercial, providing any emergency service in case the computer went on the fritz. Collecting a fee of $75 an hour while helping himself to the crew's buffet table, Stephens struck up the acquaintance of some lighting technicians who were gawking over the geekmobile. Sometime later the same lighting crew was working on the film *Clerks,* shot in Minneapolis. A laptop crashed on the set, locking up the film's payroll files. Stephens was called to the scene and quickly effected a rescue, passing out plenty of Geek Squad T-shirts for the cast and crew. The story of the Geek Squad made it back to Hollywood, where the firm was soon on the approved vendor list at 20th Century Fox and Disney. Later Stephens found himself rescuing Emilio Estevez's directing notes on the set of *Mighty Ducks III* in Minneapolis and restoring Daryl Hannah's Internet access while she was in town shooting *Grumpier Old Men.*

As news of his success spread, Stephens was inundated with calls from would-be franchisers. He refused these flirtations, reasoning, with judgment more mature than he outwardly appeared capable of, that the packaging would not work around somebody else's personality. He would grow the business himself, he decided, propelled by good service and the continuing publicity and word of mouth that seemed to ripple in his wake, all without the benefit of press kits and flacks. Indeed, before long he had a weekly computer-repair column in a local paper and a six-figure advance from a major publisher to write a Geek Squad guide to computer maintenance. The local 50,000-watt AM station cast him in a computer-repair call-in show (à la Click and Clack of National Public Radio). One clear day the super-station signal reached all the way to Palo Alto, California, world headquarters of Hewlett-Packard Corporation.

Talk about sensitive dependence on initial conditions.

H-P, it turned out, was launching a contest for small-business owners to win a year's worth of free MIS support, as in management information systems. Was the Geek Squad interested in providing the support? Yes, of course, said Stephens. But without missing a step he urged doing away with the deadening reference to a year of free "MIS support." Instead, he said, "Let's call it 'Geek-for-a-Year Contest!' " And so it was.

᪥

"The creative personality is one that looks on the world as fit for change and on himself as an instrument for change . . . as a divine agent of change," the mathematician Jacob Bronowski said.[18] But there is no rule requiring someone to own a business in order to use it as a platform for self-expression or change. People used to think that corporate strategies had to emanate from a center—from the executive suite or the planning department. America's leading guru of corporate strategy, Henry Mintzberg, has lately debunked the conventional wisdom, arguing that "big strategies can grow from little ideas, and in strange places, not to mention at unexpected times. . . . Almost anyone in the organization can prove to be a strategist."[19]

Notwithstanding Mercedes-Benz Credit and a few other big companies, many, perhaps most, still make things miserable for people who test the boundaries. AT&T is one such company and David Isenberg is such a person.

He grew up in the biology town of Woods Hole, Massachusetts, near Cape Cod, the son of a biophysicist who worked closely with the Nobel laureate Albert Szent-György, discoverer of vitamin C. "If you're going to fish," Szent-György used to tell the young Isenberg in his Hungarian accent, "use a big hook."

Persuaded that people would one day be conversing with machines, Isenberg earned a Ph.D. from Caltech in speech perception. But he flitted from one idea to another, from discipline to discipline—computers, cognition, philosophy, all the while becoming an accomplished harmonica player, a talented photographer, and ultimately an instrument-rated private pilot. He was honored with a postdoctoral appointment from MIT, but after a year's time he showed little promise of making a name for himself in any specialty. "I was always too interested in the big picture," he later explained. The fellowship lapsed, sending him into the real world in search of real work.

It was the early 1980s, and video games were all the rage. Isenberg went to work for Mattel helping to make video games talk in a way that used up the fewest number of digital bits possible, thus freeing up computing capacity for jazzier graphics. He loved the work—it was "history-making" in its own way, in the sense that Fernando Flores describes the work of the entrepreneur—but when Ms. Pac-Man took a dive Isenberg was out on the street. He wound up as part of Exxon's move into office equipment, once again looking for ways to make machines talk, but Exxon's venture quickly proved one of history's most disastrous episodes of corporate diversification, and once again Isenberg was out of work. Offered positions at both Boeing and AT&T in 1985, he chose the latter, reasoning that he was far less likely to endure another layoff at Ma Bell.

David Isenberg felt like he was made for AT&T, which put him to work in the Bell Labs division. Those were the gravy-train days of minimal long-distance competition, and the company allowed, even expected, its scientists to roam widely and freely. Isenberg, it appeared, was finally earning his reward from flitting among all those specialties. Building on his work at Mattel he helped to write complex algorithms so AT&T could stuff more information through the long-distance network. He won a patent for the technology that created AT&T's "True Voice" service (the company's answer to the famous pin-dropping demonstration by Sprint). He acted as the go-between when far-flung engineering departments came together to create Audix, the original voice-mail system.

Neither could Isenberg's timing have been much better. These products were made possible by the substitution of digital technology for mechanical switches, permitting the installation of computers in every nook and cranny of the long-distance network—smart devices that could forward 800 calls, take messages, dial third parties, and conduct a range of services limited only by the imaginations of the marketing people. It was the birth of what became known in the trade as the "intelligent network." For his role in its creation Isenberg was anointed as a "distinguished member of the technical staff."

Bell Labs was always well known (and widely prized) within AT&T as a kind of expeditionary force, monitoring the outside world for clues about the future of technology and assuring that the most important issues came to the attention of the leviathan parent company. Isenberg thrilled to this role, buzzing from cubicle to cubicle and conference to conference, going out of his way to ask pointed questions of management. But however genuinely honored, such activity was governed by unwritten rules. One did not question the economic foundations on which the mighty company was built. One could rock the boat but not question the navigation skills of the bridge. One could experiment but not fool around.

Isenberg began to bump up against the unwritten rules in the early 1990s, when management asked him to prepare a paper examining AT&T's potential business opportunities in a small but growing medium called the Internet. Isenberg's brief investigation revealed that far from being an opportunity for AT&T the Internet was a threat, with its potential to turn the likes of voice mail and other premium phone services into e-mail. But Isenberg's paper never went anywhere, because, as one of the bosses explained, "management is interested in knowing about opportunities, not threats." On a later occasion he co-authored a similar paper which this time went all the way to the top of AT&T, drawing a rare appearance in the Bell Labs offices by the aloof chairman of the board, Robert Allen. Yet when the great leader arrived, Isenberg was not even allowed into the meeting; he was deemed too unpredictable and of insufficient rank to attend. Isenberg was reduced to peeking through the clear edges of the frosted glass in the door of the meeting room, watching the big bosses pondering what he had written, about which he never heard much again.

Though dismayed, Isenberg resolved to help AT&T management see the handwriting on the wall. He wangled an assignment in a small unit with the ungainly name Business Analysis and Scenario Planning Department. One of his first moves was urging the unit to rename itself the "Opportunity Discovery Department," a name in which he took particular delight because of the acronym its initials created. The members of the department became known throughout Bell Labs as the "oddsters." He adorned his office with a huge steel shark hook, his testament to the advice he once received to fish for the biggest catches in the ocean.

He brought in outsiders—musicians, authors, anybody with big ideas about the future—for a series of workshops he called "Not Your Usual Research Seminar." He distributed an irreverent newsletter to hundreds of Bell Labs executives called "No Surpr!ses," calling into question some of AT&T's most dearly held assumptions of the future. He drew cartoons lambasting the cluelessness of top management and signed them Scatt Oddams, a *nom de guerre* based on the name of Dilbert's creator that included the acronyms ATT and ODD. On April Fool's Day in 1996 Isenberg put together a daylong internal conference on a topic as heretical as anything someone could pose within AT&T: "What if minutes were free?" He hosted the entire event wearing a rented fool's costume, complete with a jester's collar, puffy shorts, and tasseled hat, which jingled through the course of the day. Some staffers genuinely began to wonder about the fellow. As the Bible says, "A prophet is not without honor, save in his own country."

At one point Isenberg read an article in the *Wall Street Journal* about a company developing a technology to use the Internet as a telephone system—"Internet telephony"—it was called, by harnessing the power of personal computers at the transmitting and receiving points. Isenberg was blinded with insight. Of course! All that intelligence in the traditional network—intelligence that he had helped to create—would ultimately be worth squat once the *endpoints* were full of intelligence. AT&T was nothing but switches and wires. The switches put together the call and sustained it over the same configuration of wires for the duration of the call—a valuable service all by itself that tied up quite a bit of network capacity over hundreds of millions of calls a day, something for which people gladly forked over a dime-plus per minute. But the Internet—whew! No switches! No intelligence (to speak of, anyway). Just a zillion idiot-savant chips strewn across the computing infrastructure of all America, a self-organizing system like nothing ever built. Every message heaved into the Internet was instantly broken into a multitude of tiny little packets, each announcing its destination to every stupid little chip it encountered, each stupid chip sending the packet on its merry way to the next stupid chip between it and the final destination—until the entire message was reassembled at the end point perfectly intact. Every service offered on the vaunted Intelligent Network of the Bell System—those gold mines of voice mail and call forwarding and 800 service—could be offered over the Internet by any entrepreneur with a few servers and some good code! Sure, it might be a few years before any of them matched the reliability and clarity of the Intelligent Network, but it had the ring of such inevitability that Isenberg could scarcely contain himself. Indeed, the only hope for AT&T and the other Bell companies, he thought, was to seize the moment now and assert their powerful brand presence on the Internet itself, rather than trying to cling to the hoary remnants of a glorious past.

"This is it!" he told everyone who would listen. "This is the really big threat to the network! It has come home to roost and we are hosed!" He felt like the Tom Paine of AT&T, calling attention to the crisis in every way possible, writing a single-page call to arms and ultimately yet another detailed white paper about the threat of the Internet.

Isenberg was still plotting his next move in the spring of 1997 when he logged into a private Web site operated by the Global Business Network. Someone had called Isenberg's attention to a lengthy paper posted there by a former executive of Bell South—a paean to the future of the Intelligent Network and all the whiz-bang products coming down the pike from the established phone companies. It was the Memorial Day weekend and Isenberg's wife happened to be away from home. So in a two-day burst of energy he spewed out a four thousand-word reply. He called it "The Rise of the Stupid Network." It was subtitled, in part, "One Telephone Company's Nerd's Odd Perspective." There was that word again, *odd*.

It was a brilliant piece of work, the culmination of the research and thinking to which AT&T had turned a cold shoulder. "The Internet breaks the telephone company model," he wrote. And the Internet was only the beginning. Fiber-optic capacity would soon become available with the capacity to convey millions of calls simultaneously through a single strand. High-bandwidth satellites by the dozens—shoot, by the *hundreds*—were about to be hurtled into space by the likes of Bill Gates, Craig McCaw, the Boeing Company, and other people with more cash on hand than they could ever dream of spending. Entrepreneurs were already developing amazing ways to send sound and video through wires, spaces, and any other medium.

Though he was offering his "Stupid Network" essay to a private, subscription-only Web site, Isenberg vetted it with the AT&T brass before releasing it; he may have dressed up as a fool, but he wasn't stupid. AT&T blessed the publication of the essay for that limited purpose. But these days most any document that exists in electronic form is a genie in a bottle, desperate to get out and spirit itself into distant corners. "Stupid Network" was soon making the rounds among a small cognoscenti of telecom futurists. A copy landed in the hands of *Internet Telephony* magazine, which immediately published it as "potentially the most controversial paper to come out of the telephone industry, ever." The magazine printed Isenberg's e-mail address with the article. He was inundated with reaction, including from people offering him jobs (as well as a few asking him for jobs). It was becoming apparent that however resistant AT&T might be to the stupid-network concept, there was a world out there ready to hire a consultant with such a specialty.

The coup de grâce occurred after Isenberg was invited to sit on a panel devoted to "the death of telephony" at a major conference at the Rancho Mirage in Palm Springs. The presenters were like a *Who's Who* of high tech—Mark Andreessen of Netscape, Scott McNealy of Sun Microsystems, Eric Schmitt of Novell, venture capitalist extraordinaire John Doer, Internet creator Bob Metcalfe himself—and Dr. David Isenberg! But the idea of AT&T's being represented at such a confab by a technical staffer, even one with "distinguished" in his title, was more than Ma Bell could stand. Was the CEO of AT&T so clueless, people might wonder, that he couldn't speak for the company? So even after the programs had been printed and his airplane ticket purchased, AT&T put the kibosh on Isenberg's appearance. He went to the conference anyway, contenting himself to speak up frequently as a member of the audience.

The fun of being an inventor, an irritant—an entrepreneur—within the vast bureaucracy of AT&T had finally run its course. People who worked in Isenberg's department began fearing that his infamy might cost *them* their jobs, a thought that deeply depressed Isenberg. Others were openly expressing disbelief that Isenberg had not been fired. After twelve years, it was time to quit. The separation was painful; he loved many of the people there, and he was leaving behind much of his best work. But at least the financial sacrifice was tolerable. Within days of quitting, Isenberg set up a consulting business he called "isen.com." Soon he was being featured in the pages of the *Wall Street Journal, Wired,* and *Forbes.* For as far out as he could see he had all the consulting work he could handle, at rates that eclipsed his old salary. David Isenberg would be paid to play, just as he always had. The difference was that he, not AT&T, would reap the rewards of his work.

CHAPTER

6

Nobody's as Smart as Everybody

～

The feeling of the Old West lingers in downtown Dillon, Montana—a few storefronts along the main drag, a set of century-old railroad tracks, a couple of small, seedy casinos catering to the elk hunters and grain traders passing through. The snowcapped Pioneer and Ruby mountain ranges loom on the outskirts of town, where great fields of wheat grow.

It was the wheat that drew Pete and Laura Wakeman to this town of five thousand in the 1970s. They arrived in 1972 after graduating from Cornell University in upstate New York, an education they financed partly by selling fresh-made honey-wheat bread at roadside—not the diluted, stepped-on kind you find in the grocery store these days, but 100% whole wheat, made from flour that the Wakemans themselves ground fresh at a local mill. After moving to Montana they laid out $200 for a bankrupt bakery, in which they developed their own mini-mill for grinding flour on the spot. To promote acceptance of their pure, whole-wheat bread, which was not then common, the Wakemans greeted every customer by holding out a free, steaming slice. Before long people were lined up at opening time, clearing the shelves in a matter of minutes.

The Wakemans did not want to imperil themselves with prosperity.

They pushed back their opening hours when they realized that getting up in the middle of the night did not suit them. They shut down for extended travels. They refused to expand by going into debt because debt meant marching to somebody else's tune. But when someone approached them and asked for a franchise, it seemed like a good way to expand without a whole lot more work. Soon, the success of that franchise prompted still more inquiries and more franchises. As the chain grew the Wakemans remained true to their summer-of-love origins, Pete showing up at the office in a striped tie and a polka-dot shirt, perhaps, with curly bangs dangling in his eyebrows, Laura rarely out of her white apron and baker's hat.

So it was hardly surprising that the Wakemans would quietly make business history as their chain surpassed a half-dozen stores, then a dozen—then finally, by the late 1990s, to more than 100 from coast to coast. They made history because they ran a franchise operation without telling the franchisees how to run their operations.

To be sure, they enforced a one-year break-in period for all new store owners, a kind of apprenticeship in which owners were legally required to use Great Harvest's recipes and baking methods. Newcomers were also required to follow a set of simple marketing rules—no machine slicing, for instance. But after that initiatory year, franchisees became free to modify the formula in any way they saw fit. Indeed, the cover page of the operating agreement that Great Harvest signs after the first year is emblazoned with big, bold letters that state:

Anything

not expressly prohibited by the language of this agreement

Is Allowed.

Now for just a moment think about most every other franchise food operation on the planet. A set of operating guidelines a foot thick. Inspectors from the home office continually cracking down on departures from convention. Thousands of owners and employees so committed to uniformity—to the absence of surprise—that innovation and experimentation are not just unlikely but unlawful. These are what the economist Mark White, who works as a finance professor in Mexico

City, refers to as Roman Law organizations, because, like the Cesarean bureaucracies of old, they prohibit everything they don't expressly permit. "If you prohibit what you don't permit, then innovators must argue their case before they can run an experiment—which would make sense," White notes, "if deduction could tell how experiments will turn out."[1]

At Great Harvest, by contrast, franchisees receive not only a valuable brand name and some proprietary recipes and baking methods, but also a "freedom package," as the company calls it, to otherwise do as they see fit. There are no inspections. There are a few strongly held principles—serve it hot, make it whole wheat—but there are no operating restrictions. White calls these outfits Common Law organizations, because they permit everything they don't expressly prohibit. But a would-be franchisee in search of safety need not apply at Great Harvest; indeed, fewer than one in one hundred applicants is selected. The model franchisees in this organization, as Wakeman once told a convocation of bakers, are "people who love learning for the plain fun of it, who see business as an excuse to play, and love all of life for the sheer thrill of a bumpy ride."

The result is constant innovation—not just new products but new ways of doing business. "Things are certainly deployed here—almost weekly!—but the odds of them finding fertile soil in every bakery are nil," says Wakeman. "The only way the thing really works is if the bakery owners love inventing and installing and de-bugging custom solutions on their own."

In these circumstances, what's the point of a franchise system? Why operate a chain? What economic value is created by connecting so many autonomous bakeries? The answer is in the network itself.

The Great Harvest home office, located in an old J.C. Penney store along South Montana Street, with the prewar fittings and the mahogany woodwork intact, maintains a vibrant electronic-mail network so store owners can remain in constant contact, with each other as well as with headquarters. In addition, the home office pays half the travel cost when any franchise owner (or for that matter any store employee) visits any other store anywhere in the country to pick up some knowledge or spread some around. The travel reimbursement occurs through a reduction on the franchisee's royalty payments. As Pete Wakeman puts it, "The highest-traveling owners will pay the lowest percent royalties and will gain the most from the system for their royalty dollar—which is as it should be, since they are the glue holding the system together."

Ed and Lori Kerpius are such glue. He had been a currency trader in Chicago, she a retailing manager, and like many young career couples who came of age in the go-go 1980s they never saw each other. So they quit Chicago, moved to the Main Line suburbs of Philadelphia where Ed had grown up, and acquired a Great Harvest franchise. Once their yearlong apprenticeship had passed they added cookies to the menu. They launched a coloring contest for kids that ultimately brought in five thousand entries a month—all of them posted on the store walls, a riot of color that prompted kids to beg their parents for repeat visits so they could see their entries on display. (Can you imagine a McDonald's with five thousand Crayola drawings adorning the walls?) In addition to inventing their own ways of business the Kerpiuses shared their successful experiments with other franchisees, and in turn learned from them. In 1997 alone, for instance, they studied counter-service concepts in a visit to the Northfield, Michigan, store; explored new signage ideas while visiting the Great Harvest owners in Chapel Hill; and, with two years' experience running a bakery with a child underfoot, went to Boston to share tips with some new parents there.

Thus Great Harvest is a network more than a brand, a community more than a corporation. Indeed, while offering traditional training in baking and store management, the home office also counsels the stores on the techniques of networking itself. "A strong, distributed system doesn't over-communicate," Pete Wakeman once explained. "It reinvents its wheels ten places at once, then, after a while, looks up from its work and compares wheels." At a conference of franchisees he depicted Great Harvest as an intelligent network in which the best ideas take flight and the worst simply die off. "Celebrate wildly conflicting signals," he urged the franchisees.

> One harmonious hum eventually emerges. Let people scatter off in all directions on a search. As the best answers are found, they gain converts, who teach new converts, and soon a chaotic mess gets aligned in a stampede toward a single point. . . . All of this has a dramatic and dangerous sound. I am positive that, on the contrary, it is the only course of safety, and will make us wildly successful and unstoppable as a group. Hit us with something bad, and we're multi-redundant, quickly self-healing any branch

in the cross-linked net. Throw us a problem and one hundred separate eight-to-twelve member groups work in parallel to solve it with head-spinning speed. Send the whole system in the wrong direction and renegade groups quietly assemble, perfecting and proving themselves, until the system turns.[2]

This explains why a great idea like a new kind of gift-box package or a recipe for cinnamon swirl quickly gains acclamation, while bad ideas like mindless price promotions and closing on Mondays are usually stifled.

We will return to Pete Wakeman and Great Harvest again. For now, the lesson is clear enough: Freed to do their best work and free to test it against others, the people in a group become a single intelligent being, much as billions of neurons become a single brain or millions of intelligent citizens become a single nation. Although the people at the top might discover what's good for an organization, contrary to centuries of received wisdom they will never discover what's best. Because nobody, as the saying goes, is as smart as everybody.

Great Harvest is but one example of knowledge, learning, and self-organization in firms—just one story of how pioneering companies are conducting some of their most amazing work and recording some of their most amazing results.

It's already a cliché to say that business has entered the knowledge era—and nearly a cliché to argue that the greatest knowledge is scattered among the many minds of an organization. Peter Drucker coined the expression "knowledge worker" in the early 1960s.[3] He also points out the delicious irony that Marx's prophecy has come true: Workers at last own the means of production because the means of production is in their heads.[4] As products assumed shorter life spans, producing them became less valuable than inventing them, and inventing them, as we have seen earlier in these pages, requires intense interaction within firms and between them. "Business has become terribly complex," Konosuke Matsushida of Matsushida Industries wrote in 1988. "Therefore, a company must have the constant commitment of the minds of all its employees to survive."[5]

Unfortunately today, a lot of companies are corrupting the idea of "knowledge work" to fit the same command-and-control structures once used on shop floors and in secretarial pools. They squeeze workers into a few hours of training and pass themselves off as "learning organizations." They proclaim their commitment to knowledge-sharing even as they erect new barriers to its fulfillment, such as individual incentive payment plans that reward the hoarding of knowledge. And just as the advent of the electronic network finally beats back old-fashioned hierarchies and controls, the consulting world invents a new specialty, "knowledge management," which has reintroduced hierarchies and controls in a different form. A restaurant employee can't take a special order because the touch-screen of the computerized cash register has no button for it. Massive databases catalogue the "best practices" of the firm, signaling workers that they need look no further for a better way of doing things.

Too many big companies and consulting firms don't understand the most basic, vital fact of knowledge: It cannot be controlled or compiled. "Knowledge management" is another great oxymoron. Although information can be managed—in spreadsheets, books, and databases, for instance—no one can manage knowledge. This is not just a subtlety of semantics. Knowing about knowledge and respecting it will help prevent companies from backsliding into the twenty-first-century equivalent of Taylorism.

In the same way, instructing someone *how* to apply his knowledge in an organization eliminates the special value of his knowledge. Drucker points out that a knowledge worker is useful to an organization only to the extent he knows more than anyone else in the organization about something in particular. Accordingly, Drucker says, "Knowledge workers cannot, in effect, be supervised."[6]

However, knowledge can be shared, and the very act of sharing multiplies it exponentially. A human mind alters its state forty times a second, with each cycle creating additional knowledge. When you expose it to another mind—also brimming with knowledge, also cycling at forty times a second—learning explodes. Each mind changes in accordance with the other mind; they co-evolve. Put three or more together and amazing things really start to happen. "I not only use all the brains that I have," Woodrow Wilson said, "but all that I can borrow."

After twenty years of studying creativity in teams, Fritz Dressler puts it this way: "When connected together and lifted into a team mind, each individual mind becomes the interactive environment for every other mind. . . . The creative magic that is a team mind resides in both the many parallel interactions and the larger actions common to all members." This process very quickly begins to organize itself through sheer iteration and feedback, Dressler says. "Many parallel and independent sub-interactions and sub-sub-interactions result. All of these are channeled into the common effort by repeating rounds of team-wide interaction that follow the familiar pattern of action, feedback, and knowledge synthesis."[7] Or to repeat Pete Wakeman's words, "One harmonious hum eventually emerges."

In this respect, the knowledge of a firm grows through dynamics analogous to those of the brain itself. The billions of neurons in the brain each serves as the hub to hundreds or thousands of connections, known as synapses, each linked to other neurons. Some synapses are long, while others run no farther than next door. In contrast to the mechanical image of neurons firing like relays (or, in a more updated view, like transistor gates), the individual "spikings" of neurons form whorls, which combine into larger whorls, all of which are shaped by other activities elsewhere in the brain. "Feedback trajectories," some call them.[8]

"Who or what within the brain monitors all this activity?" asks biologist Edward O. Wilson. "No one. Nothing. . . . The mind is a self-organizing republic of scenarios that individually germinate, grow, evolve, disappear, and occasionally linger."[9]

So it is for groups of minds. Will they explore a wider, more creative space through social interaction or through outside command? Though the answer should be obvious, consider the case of the heart surgeons from five hospitals in New England who spent 1996 observing each other's practices and talking about their work. The result was a stunning 24 percent decline in mortality rates in bypass surgery, the equivalent of seventy-four saved lives,[10] a result they never could have obtained through the traditional continuing education regimen of listening to lectures, reading articles, or even logging into artificial "knowledge management" systems. Another classic study found that medical interns diagnosed with significantly higher accuracy when working in groups.[11] By all outward appearances science marches forward through rigorous publication standards and peer review, but such due process only validates a faster, messier, and more creative process hidden from public view. "Real science is done through gossip, through phone calls, rather than through scholarly publication," says Bernardo Huberman, an authority on complex problem-solving at Xerox Palo Alto Research Center.[12] As one biologist quips, "I link, therefore I am."[13]

Thus pioneering companies not only put employees in charge of their own knowledge but their own knowledge connections. At Charles Schwab & Company in San Francisco, employees began organizing fifteen-minute team meetings every morning to swap information and insights on the fly—"back routes through computer menus, whom to call within Schwab to get fast information, and improvements in how to do the job without changing it . . . what you really needed to know to get the job done," recalls Malcolm Brooks, a former Schwab official. To any outsider "these lessons would have been highly technical and hard to remember," Brooks says. "But team members understood the context, so explanations were rapid and easy to remember because the information was discovered and explained by a fellow worker."[14]

Another vivid case involves what Ken Baskin, the author of *Corporate DNA,* calls the case of the desk clerk and the housekeeper. Someone in housekeeping management at a Ritz-Carlton hotel was talking to a friend who happened to work on the front desk. The housekeeping manager was sounding off because the department had hit the wall in efficiency gains. Later, the desk clerk began wondering whether the computer system used for tracking guests might be adapted for tracking the makeup status of every room. The result was a new system and a tremendous increase in housekeeping efficiency.[15] No one ever could have "managed" that connection into existence.

Freed of institutional constraints, individuals can make the connections that make the most sense. Consider Northwestern Memorial Hospital in Chicago, which, like all big-city hospitals, is fighting desperately to bring hospital-born infections under control. Under requirements of the Centers for Disease Control, the hospital maintains a formal infection-control committee, designed to include the obvious departments and staffers of certain rank. But when a virulent new strain of the bacterium *enterococcus,* resistant to all antibiotics, began hitting urban hospitals, two infectious disease specialists named Lance Peterson and Gary Noskin began meeting informally every Monday morning to attack the problem. They reviewed patient charts and bacterial DNA taken from infection victims. Some outbreaks were random. But when the doctors identified a cluster of genetically linked cases, they knew to counterattack with the most targeted countermeasures possible.

As the pathogen struck into new hospital wings and departments—hematology, transplant, dialysis, and so on—representatives of those units joined the Monday-morning task force, not out of bureaucratic obligation but medical emergency. Each additional delegate brought in vital, new real-time information about how infection might be spreading. Residents, fellows, and medical technicians also began dropping in on Monday mornings, offering their own on-the-job experience or insights gleaned from other institutions. "For complex, changing problems, you need a lot of diverse input," Peterson explained. By 1998 the rates of hospital-born infection had plunged at Northwestern while soaring nearly everywhere else. Yet as an infection-control nurse named Sandra Reiner explained, "We didn't set out to do anything special. We set out to do our jobs."

Left to their own devices, shop workers are also effective at making knowledge links in and out of the organization. At one time, the New York City Sanitation Department counted fully half its six thousand vehicles as broken down and unusable on any given day. Among those fit to leave the garage, fully one-third went kaput on the road. New management came in and told mechanics they should not just fix trucks but come up with programs to maintain them—a duty previously conferred to engineers in white shirts. Breakdown rates soon plunged, yet that was just the beginning. Mechanics realized they needed to influence the work of the agency's R&D department. Soon they had actually moved into the R&D department and were inventing (and patenting) their own devices to improve reliability—a switch that shut down a vehicle if the oil pressure fell below a critical level, for instance. There was more. The mechanics soon worked their way into procurement, evaluating the equipment the city was planning to buy. Before long they were collaborating with engineers at major manufacturing companies to help them adapt their equipment for the mean streets of New York City. The Allison Transmission Division of GM, for one, changed the design of its electronic transmission controls by acting on the mechanics' ideas. FMC Corporation commended the mechanics for helping it to improve street sweeper design. Explained Roger Liwer, a deputy sanitation commissioner at the time: "The ones who fix the trucks know best how to design them."[16]

Some people think the organization charts of the future won't show where or for whom someone works but the connections created by each employee's ensemble of relationships. "A sign of value to the organization will not be standing at the top of the heap but having the most hyper-linked roles," says David Weinberger, a strategist at Open Text Corporation, a leading developer of intranet systems. "Integrative knowledge will become at least as important as specialized knowledge."[17]

If a corporation is a network of conversations, as the business philosopher Fernando Flores maintains, technology makes it possible for many to speak at once and for one to hear many at once.[18] People at Mercedes-Benz Credit candidly acknowledge they never could have hit on so many new commercial opportunities and business processes without their torrid use of e-mail, even within the same office suite. At DuPont Corporation, a senior internal consultant named Lester L. Shipman once described how communities of practice emerge spontaneously via e-mail networks as people post their most vexing research problems and others gravitate toward a solution. People at DuPont call these "go fish" networks. "It is simple and effective and works well with a minimum of administrative overhead,"[19] Shipman explained. But the key point is that people must hunt for their own connections, because it is in the chase as well as the capture that learning and organization occur.

To act as a force for economizing, knowledge exchange and self-organization require boundaries. Some companies find success using values as boundaries, a fact we will explore later in this and other chapters. But first we must deal with the role of rules—what they prevent, but more importantly, what they permit. Consider, to begin with, a great moment in music history.

On February 10, 1967, a colorful collection of musicians filled Studio One in the Abbey Road recording facility of EMI records. Mick Jagger and Keith Richards of the Rolling Stones were present, wearing the flowing scarves and crushed velvet that trademarked the era. Graham Nash of the Hollies and Mike Nesmith of the Monkees were there. So was the singer Donovan. But these famous rockers were present only as observers of a seminal event. This night belonged to a group of forty-one classical musicians—half a symphony, most of them from London's New Philharmonia Orchestra—outfitted in formal evening attire in a room filled with festive balloons. They had been summoned to record just twenty-four measures of music.

Scratching their heads, shrugging their shoulders, the performers stared at the sheet music before them. Each score began with the lowest note of which a particular instrument was capable. The score ended with the highest note for that instrument. Across the twenty-four bars in between was nothing more than a squiggly line from the bottom of the staff to the top.

The music had been scored by producer George Martin, who stood at the podium in a tuxedo. Next to him stood Paul McCartney of the Beatles, wearing a paisley shirt and a red butcher apron. "You start with the lowest note in the range of your instrument, and eventually go through all the notes of your instrument to the highest note," McCartney explained. "But the speed at which you do it is your own choice." He corrected himself. "You don't have to actually use all your notes."

Soon the playing was under way. McCartney noted bemusedly how various sections handled the ambiguity of the assignment. The strings, accustomed to their unison playing, darted glances at one another and quickly fell into order ("like sheep," McCartney would comment). Meanwhile the brass section, many of whose members were accustomed to jazz, charged off at wildly different paces. The result was a vast, swelling improvisation, a crescendo of sound that was at once organized and disorganized, a single chord that seemed to capture the beauty and horror, the simplicity and complexity, of postmodern life. A short time later McCartney, John Lennon, Ringo Starr, and a Beatles roadie stood at four grand pianos and struck a sustained E chord, which was electronically enhanced to reverberate for nearly a minute.[20]

Thus ended "A Day in the Life," the most critically acclaimed song by history's most influential recording group—and a vivid display of the stunningly purposeful outcome that may result from what some complexity theorists call "a small set of simple rules."[21] The rules established by McCartney and Martin created the potential for an infinite number of possibilities, yet the result was as close to perfection as anyone might dare imagine.

To shift examples, consider the flocking of birds. No one really knows how they do it, of course, but a researcher named Craig Reynolds has simulated perfect flocking behavior on a computer screen by programming his "boids," as he called them, to follow only three simple rules: maintain a certain minimum distance from other boids, match the speed of surrounding boids, and move toward the flock's center of mass. The complex and richly organized behavior of the group emerges from the bottom up, through local rules that somehow seem to fulfill a global purpose. As in the brain, no one is in charge.

The Newtonian world of businesses demanded a large set of complex rules. This was in keeping with the image of the world and the image of business as a great machine. Machines are rules incarnate. The design, purpose, and range of interaction permitted of each part must be spelled out in detail, whether the parts are pistons or people. The new world of business by contrast requires what the Canadian organization theorist Gareth Morgan calls "minimum critical specifications," or, better still, "min specs." "If a system is to have the freedom to self-organize it must possess a certain degree of 'space' or autonomy that allows appropriate innovation to occur," Morgan says. "This seems to be stating the obvious. But the reality is that in many organizations the reverse occurs because management has a tendency to over define and over control instead of focusing on the critical variables."[22] Too many managers, in other words, wield Roman Law. Morgan's idea of "min specs" is the equivalent of Common Law, a small set of simple rules that can provide a wide-open field for baking better bread, creating avant-garde music—or perhaps even building better health care.

An organization called VHA Inc.—the Voluntary Hospitals of America as it was originally known—has embraced the principles of "min specs" and self-organization in an effort to grapple with the wicked problems facing health care. By 1998, several VHA members, all nonprofit and community hospitals, were substituting small sets of simple rules for the kind of Byzantine procedures that bound most hospitals. One group adopted the concept to smooth the merger of several organizations into a regional oncology clinic. Others explored these ideas to create a strong bond between a local hospital and a variety of physician practices. Week upon week, a VHA official named Curt Lindberg pumped out articles describing the latest thinking about the theories of complex adaptive systems. Ultimately several groups of VHA members coalesced into Internet "learning communities" that continually self-organized around new issues. I attended two VHA conferences in the space of a year, and have never seen an organization more unified in the efforts to conquer deep vexations. How ironic, it seemed, that they were doing so by eradicating rules rather than creating new ones.

Fine, you might say. A small set of simple rules can lead to a complex piece of music or even a deep exploration of health-policy issues—but what about pushing a product out the door, day in and day out, in a punishing business environment? For an answer, consider what I found one day in Dayton, Ohio, watching people build bar-code printers.

The company—Monarch Marking Systems, now a unit of Paxar Inc.—had been making price-marking equipment for more than a century, including the hand-held "guns" that spit out price tags. For a time, Monarch did a good job of keeping pace with technology as bar-code machines helped usher in the digital revolution in wholesaling and retailing. But Monarch was a cash cow and its former owners were content to milk it. By the mid-1990s product innovation had slowed to a crawl.

Even worse, the shop floor, with some five hundred workers, had become deeply hidebound at a time when many other plants were vaulting to new levels of efficiency. With employment stuck on a plateau very few new hires came aboard, causing the tenure of the production employee to reach an astonishing sixteen years on average; many had even been with the company twenty-five years. Management had assigned each of these people to a single machine and left them to perform the identical work, year in and year out. Job specialization was extreme, creating 120 different job descriptions, a modern-day version of Taylor's "you are not paid to think" syndrome. It was a small-scale version of the General Motors Lordstown plant.

"A mind is a terrible thing to waste," as they say, not just because society needs minds but because individuals need to use them. Through the years a deep despair took hold in the plant, not over money, since the money was pretty good, but over the mindlessness of the work. Management recognized the problem, but treated it with a Band-Aid instead of a cure—programs like "employee involvement" and "empowerment" that encouraged people to make suggestions that went into a black hole, which in the end only deepened the despair.

In 1995 Monarch Marking came under new ownership by private investors, who installed a turnaround artist named John Paxton as chief executive. Paxton was appalled when touring the plant for the first time—the workers blankly repeating the same motions, machinery bolted in the same location for decades. The manufacturing operation, he recognized, would be a ball and chain on whatever efforts the company launched to reinvigorate the product line and sales effort. "Without the shop floor behind us, we'd have limited success in everything else we did," he explained.

Paxton brought in a hard-charging, gravel-voiced production chief named Jerry Schlaegel, who, in turn, recruited a hyperkinetic quality-assurance engineer he knew named Steve Schneider (who had spent much of his career steeped in the teachings of W. Edwards Deming). Their outward manners might have easily led one to mistake them for classic Industrial Age managers, Schlaegel with his gruffness, Schneider with his zealotry. But after spending several years on high-tech shop floors they had acquired a keen respect for the mind of the worker and for the combined mind of workers—and for the difficulty of unlocking them. Every program to put this knowledge into action seemed to fail miserably, not just at Monarch but just about every plant they knew of.

Schneider and Schlaegel brooded at length over these failures. In time they realized that most companies treated worker-involvement programs as corporate cure-alls, as turnarounds in a pill. Promising the moon, consultants designed these programs so broadly they could accomplish nothing specific. Instead of attacking down-to-earth problems like parts flow or cycle time, these programs invariably wound up in amorphous issues ("worker morale") or trifling ones (more picnic tables for outdoor lunch breaks). Just as vexing, meetings invariably led to more meetings.

Schneider and Schlaegel resolved to involve the shop floor in ways that avoided problems, combining intellectual freedom with the kind of discipline demanded of a commercial enterprise. Although it had not occurred to them in precisely these terms, they needed "a small set of simple rules."

Their first rule was an uncustomary one: Participation in the new exchange of knowledge would be compulsory, not voluntary. That simple rule altered the entire cast of the initiative. This was not a sop to employees, not a feel-good thing, not "empowerment." Indeed it was ridiculous to think that employees needed "power." They already had power! The power was in their heads! Schneider told people that Monarch was paying them to come to work and from that point forward they would be expected to bring along their brains. Every employee in the shop would receive training in problem solving and team communications, and anyone, at one time or another, might be required to sit on a team studying ways to improve the processes of the shop floor.

But how could they ground the process in meaningful business issues, in things that could be changed rather than merely talked about? Schneider and Schlaegel realized that every genuine problem in manufacturing can be measured. All told, Schneider identified 162 measurable variables—"metrics," he called them—involving everything from traditional quality and productivity statistics to such unusual indices as the number of unsolicited letters of commendation received from customers. Teams would form only with the intention of improving one or more specific metrics. There would be no open-ended, pie-in-the-sky committees.

There were just a few more rules. Teams not only had to come up with their own solution to a problem, they had to implement it as well. If other departments had to make changes, it was the team's duty to persuade them to do so. If vendors had to change how they served the factory, the team was charged with making the necessary arrangements. Combining ideas and implementation would motivate people to think hard for the most practical possible solution. "This is your job! This is your life!" Schneider told people. "Change it! Just go make it happen and tell us about it when you're through. In fact, you are required to make the changes and tell us when you're done."

The final rule: No project would last longer than thirty days, from the formation of the team to the implementation of the solution. "It's a project," Schneider told people, "not a process."

Those were the only rules. Anyone could create a team, management or labor. Anything and everything in the plant was fair game for review—so long as it could be measured. A team could come up with any solution at all—so long as it was willing to carry it out on the shop floor. Management forswore any and all veto rights. There were no limits on spending. Schneider and Schlaegel drew a deep breath, gulped, and rolled out the new rules.

An early test came from a group of a dozen workers who built Monarch's hottest product, a hand-held bar-code reader known as the Ultra. Monarch urgently wanted to reduce delivery times while cutting assembly costs. A group of Ultra assemblers was assigned to study whether there was a better way of putting the product together. And as if on cue, every one of them said, in effect, no way. They had no interest in participating. "I thought it was a big joke," recalled Effie Winters, who in her twenty years at the plant had seen one degrading and embarrassing episode of empowerment after another. "I wanted no part of it." Steve Schneider was facing an outright rebellion and went to his boss, Schlaegel, in a panic. So the raspy Schlaegel went before the group and declared in no uncertain terms, "You *will* do this." Recalls assembler Linda Viets: "We figured we would just go through the motions."

But when they found themselves alone with a deadline, the ideas came with startling ease. The dunderheads who used to run the company had installed a clunky, chain-driven assembly line for the assembly of the Ultra. Yet the product weighed two pounds! The workers knew they could easily pass it by hand from one station to the next, eliminating the oversize conveyor that actually limited their assembly speed. Then they realized that by getting rid of the mechanical equipment, they didn't have to sit in a row. They could sit in a large circle, facing one another, talking more easily, and tracking each other's progress. When anyone got ahead, she could help someone else catch up. The team not only changed the manufacturing process but soon realized that the new system exposed inefficiencies they had not seen before. This time, Effie Winters and the other team members launched a new round of investigations at their own initiative, inventing a way of moving parts in and out of the assembly area on rolling carts. In doing so they cut the time spent in switching to a new model from a few hours to a few minutes.

By the time it was all over they had reduced the square footage of the assembly area by 70 percent, freeing up space for new products. They had cut their work-in-progress inventory by $127,000. They had slashed past-due shipments by 90 percent. Best of all, they had doubled their productivity.

By the time of my visit Monarch had seen some one hundred teams form, create change, and disband. One team reduced the factory's ridiculous number of job categories by 75 percent through cross-training. Another figured out how to synchronize the changing of paper rolls in a production line that makes two-ply labels, reducing setup time by 25 percent. Yet another came up with a method for reporting production figures through an on-line system, saving 7,600 staff hours wasted on photocopying and delivering reports by hand. By forming these committees on their own, employees were not only answering questions but coming up with the questions to answer.

On two occasions teams had failed, once because a team leader was promoting a personal agenda, another time because of bad chemistry in the group. On a third occasion, Schneider and Schlaegel became alarmed that a group of engineers had concocted a gold-plated solution to a simple problem. Intent on conquering the problem of missing tools, which caused tremendous downtime, the engineers resolved to create a central tool-keeping area and requested $100,000 in capital funds. Schlaegel was mortified, but signed for the money. "You've got to believe in the process," as Schneider later explained. No sooner had the money been released than the engineers reconsidered their solution and came up with minor modifications of existing procedures that ameliorated the problem. Capital cost: zero. When an inspection team from Arthur Andersen reviewed the entire change system, they were stunned to note that "most improvements are not large, capital-intensive projects. Focus is on doing simple things."

Before long Monarch's operating income hit an all-time high. The company's adroit application of knowledge received many commendations. Schneider and Schlaegel began freely teaching "practical process improvement," as they called it, to Monarch's suppliers and customers. Most interesting of all, a new culture emerged spontaneously within the workforce—a culture that did not permit but that insisted on brain work. Even those who were the most cynical to begin with became eager converts. "We're using our brains instead of sitting here like little robots," Effie Winters put it. "We're not just pieces of equipment anymore."

ᔕ

Monarch helped convince me not only that the answers exist across the fabric of an organization but that the search for answers is itself an organizing influence. The connections that people make in the search for knowledge are most often the connections on which they rely to turn information into action. When people are free to search for answers across the spectrum of an organization they blaze many a false trail, it's true, but the trails over which discoveries occur become well-worn paths. Learning has a similarly physical connection in the brain: A frequently used synapse becomes stronger.

Managers can guide self-organization but can't control it. Control turns self-organization into mere organization, a dynamic process into a static condition. No central authority can sort through the myriad possibilities that the individual members of a system can explore—the process, as Pete Wakeman described it, of inventing ten wheels at once, then looking up and comparing wheels. Self-organizing networks not only acquire information at lower cost, says the conservative scholar Thomas Sowell, they often also apply it more efficiently.[23]

But even when organizations want employees to self-organize, they often find people to be cowed by years of command-and-control management, if not by their parents' tales of corporate oppression. Monarch Marking Systems took the chance of forcing people into self-reliance. Other organizations, such as Georg Bauer's Mercedes-Benz Credit Corporation, moved first to drive fear from the organization. Another manager I know, Jane Biering, accomplished the same thing largely by listening.

When I met her, Biering was the vice president of operations at Staples Direct, the catalogue sales division of Staples Incorporated, the office-supply retailer. Short, blond, age thirty-eight, and clad in white denims, she had grown up with a single mother in a family that considered business school a place where you became a secretary. Though ultimately pedigreed to the extreme (Yale B.A., Harvard M.B.A.), she remarked, "I have a deeply ingrained respect for people without degrees."

Biering worked in an office near Boston adjacent to a sprawling room where hundreds of clerks and dispatchers coordinated the movement of five thousand products, most of them sold for next-day delivery. Near the entrance to that room hung a sign reading, "Let the people who are closest to the work improve the way things work." On the day of my visit Biering was holding a meeting of clerical employees from around the Staples system to swap ideas. She sat on a rolling office chair scooting toward whoever happened to be speaking, acting less as a boss than as a facilitator intent on making good ideas spread through the group. Her skill at listening and her eagerness to act on ideas created a culture in which everyone else was eager to do the same. As a telephone clerk named Elaine Rabbit told me, "There's no nervousness in dealing with Jane."

The episode that drew me to Staples Direct was a story I had heard about the organizing powers of this knowledge exchange. Biering had a group of customer-service managers who fielded problems from customers, usually errant shipments or damaged merchandise. These people worked in the big room near her office. But shipping errors and furniture bang-ups occurred elsewhere in the system, either at one of Staples' massive distribution centers, where orders were picked and packed, or at one of the many regional hubs, where they were loaded into local delivery trucks. This geographical division often pitted one employee against another.

"We've got an angry customer up here!" came the cry from customer service.

"Hey, you have no idea of the headaches I've got down here," came the answer from the loading dock.

Mark Spanek and Mike McDonald frequently found themselves locked in such conflict. Spanek was a customer-service rep whose territory included the region around Boston. McDonald managed a shipping hub in Westwood, south of the city. "Things got heated at times," Spanek would recall. So one day he decided to visit Westwood, a trip that opened his eyes to another world. He could see the pressure-cooker atmosphere of the loading dock, with contract truckers constantly streaming in and out. There was a rhythm to the workday—hard times and easy times, although special situations made every workday slightly different. None of this had been evident from his computer console back at the call center.

Spanek could also see how problems occurred through sheer random acts—a metal desk dented by a forklift, an order for three filing cabinets filled with just two. Wouldn't it be something, he thought, if he could see these problems before they went out the door? That way he could contact the customer in advance to figure out whether to hold back, make a partial shipment, perhaps substitute the goods later—or at least notify the customer sooner that a snag had developed.

A solution immediately became clear. "We had to bring our worlds together," Spanek recalls. Information was driving organization.

He approached Jane Biering for the authority to move himself and his customer-service terminal into the Westwood hub; his request was a mere formality he never would have made had he not known the answer in advance. Spanek and McDonald were soon working at adjacent desks, batting back and forth the status of every problem order. "Mark tracks down the problem on the computer," McDonald told me. "I track the real-time problem of the trucks on the road. We're like two kids building a Soap Box Derby racer."

֍

Phrases like "a small set of simple rules" and "min specs" are redolent of the greatest experiment in learning and self-organization in modern history: the United States. For the entire industrial era the success of the U.S. was available as a large-scale model of organizational success to managers and business owners. Yet most leaders ignored this model, choosing to run organizations more like something closer to Franco's

Spain or Stalin's Russia. Employees were treated like subjects instead of citizens. Learning by the led occured at the sufferance of the leaders. It was not the stifled atmosphere within businesses but the free and wide-ranging collaboration between and among them that has accounted for the stunning prosperity of America.

Among the tycoons of big business, I know of only one who explic-itly pulls the concept of American political freedom inside the four walls of the firm. He is Charles Koch of Koch Industries Incorporated. "Complex human systems, whether societies or organizations, can only function properly by spontaneous order rather than central control," he says.[24] Koch has drawn much attention for a high-stakes money feud with an estranged brother, as well as for his years of bankrolling liber-tarian political causes. Practically unknown is how he applied his phi-losophy of personal liberty in building a $30 billion-a-year empire in energy, agriculture, and financial services bigger than any other pri-vately held corporation outside of United Parcel Service.

One day in the early 1960s, as a newly minted engineering graduate from MIT, Charles Koch found himself in his father's study surrounded by books, shelf after shelf of right-wing literature. The old man, Fred Koch, was an ardent anti-Communist who had built up a prosperous regional oil and gas firm in Wichita, Kansas. Amid the ideological writ-ings Charles pulled down a thoughtful book by the economist Leonard E. Reed dealing with the so-called Austrian school of economics, which describes free economies as systems of spontaneous, unplanned order. He was transfixed with the concept and spent the next two years run-ning from one library to another, studying economics, history, science, and human nature. "The free society is the form of social organization most in harmony with reality and the nature of man," he would say. As one would expect, these notions caused Charles to share much of his father's anti-Communist passion. But the young engineer was troubled to realize that for all its economic freedoms, America was full of minia-ture totalitarian regimes. They were called corporations.

The American economy, he realized, was vibrant and robust because knowledge and decision-making were distributed across its wide expanse. In a corporation, knowledge was no less widely distributed, yet most of it lay fallow. The longer he looked at other businesses, the more stupefying he found them. "A business is a vehicle for integrating knowledge," he would say years later.

So Koch Industries gave employees personal jurisdiction over their own little corners of the company—the freedom to operate the property under their individual control, the right to sell it or improve it, and the opportunity to earn a return on it through incentive-based pay, treating employees, as Koch liked to say, "as if they were entrepreneurs in a free society." He enjoyed telling the story of a refinery employee whose job for years had been to follow regimented procedures, such as "turn the valve when the pressure reaches a certain level." Then the operator was told to use his judgment and experience in controlling the process, within the tolerances of the equipment and the requirements of the adjacent processes ("min specs"). The performance of the refining unit shot up by 20 percent—a quantum leap in a process-driven commodity business in which gains of 1 percent are joyously celebrated. Taking all of the company's refineries into account, freeing individual workers to apply their particular knowledge has added hundreds of millions of dollars in revenue to the company's books *each year.*

"The free market is a discovery process bringing about creative destruction," Koch tells people. Operating the firm as a "discovery" process means building on new knowledge from the marketplace and combining the ideas of employees in the most imaginative ways possible. Thus through the years Koch and his employees have guided the firm into one new business after another—petroleum leading to chemicals leading to pollution-control services; fertilizer leading to grain farming, which leads to cattle raising, and so on. None of these businesses constitutes a "division" in the sense that it is divided from anything else. Everything is integrated. Everyone talks to everyone.

Of course liberty is not licentiousness and entrepreneurialism is not anarchy. Through the years Koch formulated a series of principles, his own set of "simple rules," to foster the integration of knowledge. "Decisions should be made by those with the best knowledge, which will vary with the type of decision," he says. Figuring out how to get the most oil through a pipeline is a task that ought to be conducted by the person with his hand on the valve, but integrating that pipeline with a sales or refining function is work that ought to be performed by someone with broader if shallower knowledge. These responsibilities, which he calls "decision rights," do not depend on rank or job title. Rather they are conferred on a person-by-person basis, expanding as the assets under that person's domain increase in value.

Another of Koch's simple rules is humility, which he preaches constantly. "Humility involves acknowledging our weaknesses—that is, what we don't know—and realizing that we can and must learn," he tells employees. "Humility is essential to social progress since learning begins with the recognition that none of us has all the answers." To this end he enjoys quoting the historian Daniel Boorstin: "The greatest obstacle to discovery is not ignorance, but the illusion of knowledge." The flat earth was one such illusion. A more contemporary example involved the near-universal conviction in the 1970s that oil prices were headed for $100 a barrel, a belief that defied any basis in reality and that Koch Industries resisted, thus escaping the worst of the price crash that followed. Closely allied with humility is tolerance. "Tolerance requires admitting that a radically different perspective may be as valid as ours," he says.

Another rule of the house is complete candor, since information and knowledge are no good if corrupted by politics or wariness. Once a company vice president was meeting with Charles Koch when his assistant interrupted with a phone call. Tell him I'm not in, the man said. Koch was horrified that his executive would tell even a white lie. "I got a lecture like I was an eight-year-old child," the vice president recalled.[25]

Charles Koch called this entire set of principles "market-based management," and though it turned Koch Industries into the second-largest privately held company in the U.S. and attracted some academic interest along the way, it has remained confined pretty much to Koch itself. Other big-business executives, Charles Koch told me, "aren't interested in this stuff." And it's easy to see why. Relying on the knowledge of employees—not just their possessing it, but on their freedom to act on it and organize around it—requires management to give up a huge quantity of control. Koch happily accepts the fact that at any moment his company might change shape or dimension without his prior approval, even though he and his family own most of it. Even if he knows where things stand, he has little idea where they are headed. There are no central budgets. There is no five-year plan; how could there be, when no one knows where oil prices will be in five years or how American food tastes will affect the agricultural markets?

As recently as 1997 Koch was telling his employees he thought the organization had only attained 40 percent of the potential of market-based management, while noting that even that modest progress had enabled the company to grow two hundred-fold over thirty years, "and to be growing and hiring today," he noted pointedly, "while many of our competitors are shrinking and laying people off." In another context he spoke of the properties of emergence (though he did not use the term). "The whole is not simply greater than the sum of the parts; it becomes a different entity. Just as a living thing is a different entity than a collection of molecules, an organization that combines all these elements becomes something different than an ordinary collection of people, activities, and assets."

ᔕ

Whether hippie bakers or button-down CEOs, everyone in business is united by the goal of creating more than he consumes and by the iron law that no one long succeeds without helping others attain success. But the execution of even such simple principles opens plenty of room for tension.

Consider once again Great Harvest, which, despite its élan of togetherness, is built on a big fat paradox that brings Pete and Laura Wakeman frustration as well as reward. It maddens them that some stores install mechanical slicers after their yearlong apprenticeships have expired. (You can't run hot bread through a slicer, so anyone using a slicer is selling bread at room temperature.) The Wakemans also look askance at stores selling cookies and concocting recipes that stray too far from the whole-wheat vision. But while jawboning to remind people of the core values of the company, the Wakemans actively tolerate such departures, because there's no telling when one may produce the next great leap forward against the competition in the increasingly crowded field of handcrafted, hearth-baked breads.

"It helps if you understand that much of the culture of Great Harvest has come out of a dynamic tension between two antagonistic ideals," Pete explains. "On the one hand, we love quality. We are stubbornly opinionated about the best way to run a bakery." But at the same time, "we believe that no person, society, or institution can be great without freedom."

A dynamic tension between two antagonistic ideals. Order versus freedom, consistency versus playfulness—opposite poles between which a creative and robust new reality emerges. Creativity, it seems, is poised on paradox.

This is hardly in keeping with traditional management theory, which seeks to drive ambiguity out of the organization. The standard view has no better spokesman than Al "Chainsaw Al" Dunlap, the downsizer extraordinaire. "Business is very simple, black and white," he says. To anyone who tries to complicate an issue with nuance, he snaps, "Bring me three pages."[26] That was fine when the world was predictable and organizations were controllable. Now they are neither. Today organizations require teamwork and diversity at once, goals that hardly seem in sync. Businesses must lower costs while increasing quality; balance work and family; create local control in global organizations. Economies seek greater affluence without damaging the environment. The list goes on and on.

But a paradox is not the same as a contradiction. Though they seem at odds, both elements of a paradox hold true at a higher level, like hot and cold water taps joined by a faucet that combines them in infinite possibilities.[27] Leonard Bernstein once said, "A work of art does not answer questions. It provokes them, and its essential meaning is in the tensions between the contradictory answers."

Complexity science offers a keen insight into the dynamics of paradox and of the potential significance for business. Using computers to model everything from rodent populations to chemical reactions, scientists have found that dynamic systems seem to poise themselves in a state somewhere between order and disorder, between rigidity and anarchy—a zone they call "the edge of chaos."[28] Certainly it's a descriptive phrase, with a faint ring of excitement, risk, and vaguely directed purpose—like a border town, maybe, or a backstage with two minutes to curtain. Most people intuitively recognize the edge of chaos in daily life, a bustling place somewhere between total control and absolute anarchy. A happy family is a rollicking one. A busy desk is a slightly messy one—but only slightly messy. The edge of chaos is the exquisite point where neither freedom nor control has the upper hand.

The science of this involves the study of communication, of a sort. Whether genes directing the creation of a newborn zygote or ants filling the larder, the ability of the system to self-organize seems to vary directly with the degree of connectedness among its members—the ability of genes to switch one another on or off, the ability of ants to let other ants know what they are doing. If the connections are too dense, the system locks; adaptation cannot occur. If the connections are too few, the system goes random. "The edge of chaos," says the computer scientist Christopher Langton, one of its discoverers, "is where information gets its foot in the door in the physical world."[29]

Pete Wakeman is no complexity scientist, but he has intuitively made the same discovery. The most effective franchisees maintain tight communication with just three to five other stores, plus friendly but irregular dealings with another ten or so. "An overconnected network binds up, becomes brittle, calcified, slow to react," he says, while an underconnected network isolates people and stifles learning.

Of course there are skeptics. "Embracing paradox, 'min specs,' market-based management, or tuning a network to the edge of chaos may succeed in narrow, limited situations," they might reasonably insist, "but is it a way of business?" To be sure, anything smacking of a "system" or a "methodology" may well succeed in its birthplace and die ignominiously everywhere else it is tried. But fostering knowledge, self-organization, and constant change is not a "program." Rather it represents the *removal* of behaviors that inhibit natural systems from taking over. And while not every organization is pregnant with paradox, any organization can benefit by pausing to hold and examine the opposing pressures it faces.

The proof is in the marketplace, as the following story suggests.

ᔄ

For years, the best part of AT&T was the division that sold equipment instead of long-distance service—the part once known as Western Electric, now called Lucent Technologies. AT&T's longtime chairman, Robert Allen, committed some spectacular blunders through the years, but in one true act of genius he cleaved away the AT&T equipment division. As a stand-alone business Lucent became one of the most spectacularly successful major companies of the late 1990s, expertly riding the wave of telecommunication expansion sweeping the globe, thanks in no small part to an experiment in Mount Olive, New Jersey.

In 1994, just before its spin-off from AT&T, the division's leadership was dismayed to learn that some customers considered it slow to change. Just as bad, customers warned that Lucent's equipment was getting too pricey relative to the market. Top management recognized that things had to change. As part of that change, the company decided to set up a few new businesses with no preconceived design, with no AT&T culture, with no baggage from the past. It would simply bring together a few of the best people from all levels of the organization and say, "Create a new business with paramount speed, cost, and quality—any way you choose to do it."

One of the groups, consisting of seven engineers and production workers, built a paradox into itself from day one. The group decided to build a new business on what it called a core set of unswerving principles, which were set forth on a single sheet of paper: "We live," it read, with "speed, innovation, quality; a strong sense of social responsibility; a deep respect for the contribution of each person . . . integrity and candor." It swore to "an obsession with serving our customers." This was intended as a blood oath: Everyone coming to work in the new business would have to sign the document—with some formality, using a special pen. As Steve Sherman, the senior engineer in the group, liked to say, "This applies to everything and everybody."

That document served as the hard half of a paradox—the zone of order, if you will. The other side, the designers thought, would be as loose as anyone from a big company could imagine. They called it their "organically adaptive structure."

Among their other early tasks was picking a product, then designing it, then figuring out how to make it. In virtually every major corporation these functions reside in separate departments, sometimes in separate cities. But by the time the core crew had leased a manufacturing hangar in Mount Olive in the summer of 1994, there was no time for a long, drawn-out design schedule: At that moment, beyond anyone's wildest expectations, the cellular industry was exploding. So the team at Mount Olive resolved to build a new kind of cellular transmitting station operating on digital technology—the large boxes sitting at the base of the huge antennas then beginning to pop up in vacant fields the world over.

Before long some thirty engineers began showing up for work every morning in what was then a cavernous, high-ceilinged plant of a quarter-million square feet. (Several people got around on Rollerblades.) This large group spent the day around a giant table, with whiteboards filling the perimeter of the room. "Circling the wagons," Sherman called it. On the edge of the circle, a group of manufacturing engineers and production workers began figuring out how to manufacture a product that hadn't been fully designed yet. Design and manufacturing are natural adversaries; designers strive for performance while builders strive for efficiency. But with the clock ticking and everyone in the factory committed in writing to "speed," each side had no choice but to take account of the other's point of view. In the intensity of their dealings, the two disciplines were essentially fused.

The result was a new product—nearly one thousand pounds heavy, costing several hundred thousand dollars—that was designed for ease of manufacturing, plus a manufacturing process that was designed for superior product performance. A rank-and-file assembler named John Lezak, recruited from a union job at another Lucent plant, was among the main contributors. "I always felt enclosed by the system, and I saw an opportunity here to see what I could be. I came here and I felt like a manufacturing consultant." Along the way Lynn Mercer, a fast-tracker from a Lucent operation in Columbus, Ohio, came in as plant manager in Mount Olive. Wasn't it difficult for her as the boss, I later asked, to delegate so much authority as many as three levels downward? No, she said, deadpan. "I know how to do my job better than the guys three levels above me."

The first commercial operations took the plant all the way to the edge of chaos. A single large team began bolting and wiring the base stations together in the middle of the plant, surrounded by parts and tools. People assigned themselves and each other. They wandered from machine to machine. But they talked, demonstrated, and switched positions continually. As the first few units transformed from simple shells of metal to fully loaded transmitting stations without ever moving, the workers surrounding them quickly fell into a pattern, like termites building a massive structure. "It was total self-organization," Sherman would recall—the same principle that Rowe Furniture applied to a $499 sofa, except that Lucent was applying it to a highly complex cellular station worth roughly one thousand times as much. Soon, with orders arriving from Indonesia and the United Arab Emirates, production hit about fifteen units a day. The plant was forced to hire more workers, and suddenly the informal system no longer worked. There was simply no way for the assemblers to do their work while training the new recruits, and there was no way for the recruits to find their own way into the system while they were preoccupied with whatever training they got.

It was time for an altogether new system. Fortunately, Sherman had insisted that none of the heavy manufacturing equipment would ever be bolted to the floor.

So the plant switched, just like that, to a traditional assembly line, with a day shift and a night shift. Immediately Sherman was concerned that the plant would become too ordered, so he insisted that as soon as anyone completed his training in a new job he switch into yet a new one. It was the same principle that Dana Corporation's Mark Schmink had applied in building truck chassis for Toyota: Move people around to keep their eyes fresh and their minds on edge. Indeed Sherman moved at every turn to fight the onset of rigidity, to block the plant from moving too far back into the ordered zone. "We needed rules to keep our rules under control," he later explained. "Anything that smacks of rigidity makes me nervous." For instance, everyone agreed that any written shop-work procedure would have to fit on a single page.

These rules against rules—another paradox—became especially important when the plant decided to seek quality certification from the International Standards Organization. This pedigree, known as ISO 9000, requires documenting and standardizing every process in a manufacturing plant as a way of maintaining consistent quality. Though laudable in intent the process can easily turn a facility into a bureaucrat's dream. Despite that, ISO 9000 had become extremely fashionable in Europe, a de facto requirement for any major foreign manufacturer intent on selling into the European Community. Feeling they had no choice but to qualify, Sherman and his team conceived a kind of edge-of-chaos solution. Any process change was "legal" under the ISO regimen so long as it was documented and occurred under an existing process. So Mount Olive wrote a process saying that any worker at any moment could unilaterally alter any process in the plant solely by writing out a note by hand. "Anyone can do a handwritten, self-approved write-around in five minutes," Sherman explained. The plant later installed a huge bank of computer terminals so workers could consult every written process and change it then and there (although the five-minute write-around remained legal as well). Later the plant laid in a supply of laptop computers so production employees could design new processes from home, if they chose, including on company time.

In 1996, the year following the move to the assembly line, Mount Olive's productivity had surged 2,600 percent, with lots of tension—continual tension, in fact—but no failures. Despite that record, Sherman, with Mercer's concurrence, insisted that it was time it change again—the third major structural shift in as many years. "Love our customers, love our values, but don't love our structure, because it's going to change every year," he told people. The distinction between the first and second shifts was blurred; the various clusters of workers were asked to schedule themselves in whatever way made the most sense.

But the net effect of the constant change and ambiguity was that nothing was ever seen as impossible. When a major customer began making inquiries about a possible new product, the developers and builders had put together a prototype before anyone had prepared a budget and before the home office had given its approval. It turned out that the customer's needs changed and Mount Olive never got a dime for its efforts, "but they're buying a lot more of our standard product because of the credibility we've built with them," says Sherman. "We never have to tell a customer that we need approval to do something."

The turbulence, paradoxically, also enhanced product quality while reducing cost. Quality in manufacturing, at bottom, is a communication issue. Errors always occur; the question is how long it takes to recognize them and how much product gets out the door before they've been remedied. The constant reorganizing and self-organizing of the plant had created vast, redundant communication networks—e-mail, TV monitors, break-room conversations, bathroom conversations. When problems come up in the field, design engineers in the plant know about it instantly. "We actually make and evaluate changes before most people would've had a meeting," Sherman would later say. Timely delivery is another quality issue: Employees had created an "urgents board" listing orders that were behind schedule, enabling any employee with a few spare minutes to jump in where most needed— flexibility made possible because so many in the plant knew how to perform so many different jobs.

As for cost, the key was constant experimentation—unsupervised play, as the people of Mercedes-Benz Credit Corporation were also demonstrating at that very moment. In the case of Lucent, the idea was to "drive accountability down to the level of the people actually doing the job," Lynn Mercer explained. She might just as well have been quoting Steve Schneider of Monarch Marking Systems, for in addition to insisting that workers identify the problems that needed correction, Mount Olive was also insisting that they take the necessary action.

Delegation and duty had infused Mount Olive by the time of my visit. "We don't send things through a management loop here," a technician named Tom Guggiari told me. "Here everything happens on a real-time basis." To prove the point, Guggiari dragged me to an associate named Phillip Dailey, who, a few days earlier, had figured out how to eliminate a major bottleneck along the production line with the addition of a single additional worker—and had borrowed a team member from elsewhere in the plant to prove his theory before ever informing anyone in management. A quality inspector named Richard Denning told me he had more say-so in this billion-dollar factory than he had working in his father's small electrical contracting business. "My friends and family don't believe how much people listen to me here," he said. Worker-inspired improvements were happening so constantly that David Therrien, who wrote the original assembly instructions for the product, no longer recognized them two years later. "My instructions were nothing but a starting point," he said.

Regardless of the manufacturing layout of the moment, the design engineers were mixed in with it, combining potted fronds and cubicle partitions with power tools and parts dollies. (Overhead sound baffles made it possible to conduct engineering and office work amidst the squeal of the power tools.) In the plant's fourth year, when Mount Olive began its own limited software development operations, Lynn Mercer took the radical step of throwing a few dozen software and hardware designers into the same room, enabling their designs to co-evolve.

Sherman felt that the richness of these connections made a formal employee-suggestion system unnecessary. Some managers were appalled at the lack of a formal system, but Sherman hated the idea of creating a routine of so vital a function—another splendid paradox. The informality of the system requires people to go to the source of a problem rather than pass it off on some index card, and going to the source of the problem creates more intimate interaction: more learning, more chance of identifying necessary changes, more opportunities to self-organize.

Of course, it also means using judgment and tact—learning not to say, "Hey, your design sucks!" for instance. In fact this entire process presupposes not only some sophisticated judgment but some political savvy on the part of employees, knowing how high a problem or idea should go, for instance, or how to handle a disagreement. "People have to know which levers to pull," Sherman says. He tells them: "We work in a large corporation. There are levels in this organization. There are ways to get support." A lot of people resisted the system and do to this day. Many technicians declared their reluctance to "play political games." They refused to be seen as "sucking up." Managers who once passed out $50 gift certificates in recognition of superior performance instead began requiring team members to make the awards, a practice that aroused much unease among some. Flextime became extremely difficult for teams to manage, not just from the sheer complexity of the scheduling but because of the fairness issues it invariably raised. Management, however, was unyielding, creating an irony so obvious it became a standing joke: "We're going to have flextime, dammit!" Workers were also being asked to make speeches at other Lucent offices and plants and even customer locations. Many expressed discomfort about getting up in front of groups, especially in big auditoriums. "Isn't it enough that I do a good job?" they asked.

The answer was yes—but the job included communication, persuasion, and personal interaction. The left-brain skills get you in the door; the right-brain skills help you earn your security. "We're cascading a lot of freedom to people and they're starting to understand it's a lot of work," Sherman told me not long ago. Although the endowments are not spread equally in society, everyone has a kernel of social skill that can take root in the right environment.

"We have a lot of dynamic tension here," Lynn Mercer told me. She smiled speaking these words, because she knew that for all the tension, her workforce remained astonishingly unified. "After it's all said and done, our success is the result of people working together." When tension boils over—as it does—the tie-breaker is Mount Olive's one-page set of working principles—its inviolate code, its one foot in the ordered regime. When worker confronts manager and vice versa, when managers take on managers and workers take on workers over what's to happen next, "that document is the first thing out of the holster," Sherman says.

In its first several years Mount Olive had never missed a single order deadline, not once. The elapsed time between the conception of each new product version and the first shipments was an astonishing nine months at the time of my visit, with six months soon to come—compared to an industry average of eighteen months. The labor cost of the product averaged 3 percent and was headed lower. Said Mercer, "That makes me competitive with any Third World country." Every worker in the plant knew the name of every customer, the status of every order, and the identity of every competitor. Orders were roaring in—from Puerto Rico, South Korea, Thailand, Canada, and, biggest of all, a $1.8 billion deal from Sprint. In time the organizing principles of Mount Olive began spreading elsewhere in Lucent. "As a corporation we're getting more adaptable and speedy. We helped pioneer that," Sherman told me.

A crowning moment came in 1998. One of Mount Olive's best customers was a consortium of major cell-phone operators called PrimeCo, owned by Bell Atlantic, U S West, and AirTouch. PrimeCo was one of the hottest players in digital cellular, a customer that every equipment supplier fell all over itself to serve. Motorola Corporation, once the leader in cell-phone systems, shared PrimeCo's business with Lucent. But PrimeCo began experiencing network outages—linked to the boxes from Motorola. Over the course of a year the failures, heavily concentrated in the Chicago area, amounted to more than one hundred. So PrimeCo fired Motorola from a $500 million contract and ordered it to remove the offending equipment.

Motorola's business went instead to Lucent.[30]

But with about five hundred people in the plant, the leadership began wondering how much more growth Mount Olive could stand. "I don't think I can be bigger than five hundred people here," Lynn Mercer told me. To some degree the degree of connectedness in any system is a function of the size of the system; the number of internal connections cannot scale as quickly as the number of agents in the system; there are simple laws that regulate how large a system can grow without compromising its dynamics, as studies of ant colonies and other complex systems show. I don't mean to suggest that ants could ever construct a digital cellular base station, but mathematical abstractions hold constant across levels of scale.

There was also a physical limitation to how many Mount Olive employees in any year could conduct a visitor tour of the plant, no trifling matter as far as Mercer and Sherman were concerned. They urgently wanted everyone in the plant to come eye-to-eye with customers and say, "Yes, we can make delivery," or to observe firsthand the enthusiasm that customers expressed when they beheld the purposeful pandemonium of the plant. Sherman also worried that size would lead to rigidity, and that rigidity would compromise the strengths that enabled Lucent to win victories against the likes of Motorola. Above all, he feared that size would ultimately force the standardization of procedure, which could snuff out the very variety of views and actions that gave Mount Olive its strength.

At one point he administered a small test. Speaking before hundreds of plant employees he described at length the paradoxical, alternately loose and tight structure of the plant. He recalled the "scientific management" practices of Frederick Taylor, with its extreme division of labor and no-brain work, contrasting them with the soft-and-fuzzy teamwork investigations that the social scientist Elton Mayo conducted fifty years earlier at Western Electric, the forerunner of Lucent. Knowing that his techie audience had more than its share of Trekkies, he also recounted a *Star Trek* episode in which Captain Kirk was divided into two people—good Kirk and bad Kirk, neither of whom was effective on his own. It was between good and evil that the whole man lay.

Sherman listed all these opposing characteristics on flip charts at opposite sides of the room. Then he asked everyone to get up and stand between the two lists in relation to where he or she believed Mount Olive stood on the scale of loose to tight.

People stood everywhere. They were scattered across the entire room. That was good, Sherman thought. Everyone had a different view. Excellent.

Then he asked everyone to move where they thought the plant *ought* to be. There was some minor shuffling. People moved one step, maybe two. Some stepped left, others right. In the end, the distribution of people was practically identical. Even better, Sherman thought. Nobody had the same opinion about the plant, but everyone thought it was just about where it ought to be.

CHAPTER

7

All Together Now

Hal Croasmun, a business consultant in Austin, Texas, tells the story of his father's becoming the pastor of a church that had voted out its previous two leaders. The Rev. Croasmun made it his practice to invite a different family every Sunday to the parsonage for chips and dip, following the church service. "He spent time just getting to know them," Croasmun recalled. "He'd also ask what they thought others thought about the sermon." Then, each day through the week, the pastor phoned a different member of the congregation to exchange small talk and inquire what they had on their minds—their conflicts, their concerns, their hopes. "Then, on Sunday, his sermons contained all kinds of references to their situations. He addressed their issues and concerns without pointing out anyone specifically, but he was always talking about their lives. And in some way, every sermon became about them."[1]

Then, following the sermon, another round of feedback occurred over another round of chips and dip.

The methods of the Rev. Croasmun say more about leadership than 99 percent of the leadership books ever published. The best leaders today aim their flocks nowhere without some sense of where the flock wishes to be taken. This isn't some cute tautology and isn't meant to be coy. It's also not an original concept. "The leader guides the group and is at the same time himself guided by the group, is always part of the group,"[2] the visionary Mary Parker Follett wrote in 1918. On another occasion she said, "Authority, genuine authority, is the outcome of our common life. It does not come from separating people, from dividing them into two classes: those who command and those who obey. It comes from the intermingling of all, of my work fitting into yours and yours into mine."[3]

It's fair to say that Follett's views have been slow in taking hold. For virtually the entire Industrial Age and beyond, business managers, especially American business managers, took their inspiration from the guts-and-glory school of leadership. This is perfectly understandable. The corporation is the newest major form of social organization, and when it began forming the people in charge had to look somewhere for models. So they looked at the people who led other major institutions, such as armies. Nonmilitary leaders also tended toward the commanding. "Follow me," said Jesus. "I am the way." In later years professional sports provided more than their share of fodder, making football coaches and team captains the toast of the corporate lecture circuit.

These models of leadership have led to such spectacles as "Chainsaw Al" Dunlap posing in war paint, pistols, and bandito belts for a publicity photograph, and Robert Crandall of American Airlines cultivating the nickname "Fang." An acquaintance of mine who worked in a high-ranking position for Frank Lorenzo, former chairman of Eastern and Continental airlines, became so stressed after a long flight with his domineering boss that he stabbed his hand with a pen, drawing a trickle of blood. Harold Geneen, known for building ITT Corporation into one of the first and greatest multinationals, dressed down subordinates so mercilessly they were said to cower in his waiting room. ("Geneen" was pronounced with a soft "G," as in the messianic Jesus, company people said, rather than with a hard "G," as in God.[4]) These leaders gladly persisted in their Attila-like personae in part because we celebrated their doing so. For years *Fortune* annually beatified "America's toughest bosses." Best-selling books and M.B.A. case studies hailed their boldness and decisiveness. Although it's true that different times require different leaders, it's hard to say whether some of these organizations prospered because of their leaders' styles or despite them.

Organizations will always need individual leaders, of course. Legal convention demands it: All corporations must have a president and other titled officers. Efficiency demands it: Few groups can decide as quickly as an individual. And finally, someone must always take a first step, whether in the search for a vision or the execution of a mission. Leading, to take the word literally, means showing the way by going first.[5] Any official position of leadership thus imposes moments of solitary action and reflection, a fact evident in centuries of culture.

What's new is that if organizations are to marshal brains over brawn, if they are to promote collaboration rather than competition, if they are to do everything else required for success and survival in the postmodern age, they must begin to see leadership as a system—of leaders and followers as two elements of a single system, an unbroken cycle in which both parties continually co-evolve as a result of what each learns from the other. Organizations themselves are becoming leaderful, as Mary Parker Follett had once dared to envision. This institutional leadership emerges from the interplay of the few and the many, the top and the bottom, the individually powerful and the collectively powerful. A study of British string quartets found that the least successful were led by domineering first violins or by participatory democracy; the most successful quartet, by contrast, operated between these extremes, with an ambiguous, unresolved tension operating between the first violin and the rest of the group.[6]

Highly complex, adaptive, successful organizations—Sun Microsystems, Lucent Technologies, the Chicago Bulls under Phil Jackson—wouldn't last five minutes under a George S. Patton or a Vince Lombardi (much less a Chainsaw Al). "I've never had control and I never wanted it," says Herb Kelleher, founder and chairman of Southwest Airlines, the most financially successful airline in history. "If you create an environment where people truly participate, you don't need control. They know what needs to be done and they do it."[7] Once I visited Robert Shapiro, under whose tenure Monsanto Corporation grew into arguably the world's leading biotech company. On his credenza Shapiro had stockpiled copies of a single book, which he was distributing as must reading to visiting officers and associates. The book was Kevin Kelly's *Out of Control.*

Even the military itself, which perfected command and control leadership, is backing away from traditional strictures as Newtonian anachronisms. An updated version of the official Marine Corps doctrine—still published under the title *Command and Control*—calls leadership "a process of continuous adaptation."

> Like a living organism, a military organization is never in a state of stable equilibrium but is instead in a continuous state of flux—continually adjusting to its surroundings. . . . Command and control is not so much a matter of one part of the organization "getting control over" another as something that connects all the elements together in a cooperative effort. All parts of the organization contribute action and feedback—"command" and "control"—in overall cooperation. Command and control is thus fundamentally an activity of reciprocal influence—give and take among all parts, from top to bottom and side to side.[8]

If the individual leader is not a commander, then what shall he be? In a world of adaptability rather than rigidity, how shall the leader help instill a sense of purpose? The leader is the standard-bearer of the organization's identity, the spokesman for its vision. Says Warren Bennis, author and well-known former business school dean, "The first basic ingredient of leadership is a guiding vision."[9] One language authority has written that leaders above all must find the words to describe "already shared feelings arising out of shared circumstances."[10] Michael D. McMaster of Great Britain, who as a consultant has helped create a generation of leaders on the oil platforms of the North Sea, puts it this way: "The distinguishing characteristic of leadership— whether it is an individual, a team, or a company—is to see the world in a unique manner and to be able to engage others in the development and pursuit of that view."[11]

A simple enough concept, but more easily described than accomplished. The leader brings the vision to an organization, but the vision is authentic only if it resonates with the values of her followers.

൭

The most deeply shared visions come from a process called dialogue. Most business people think of "dialogue" as another word for "discussion," but they're very different kinds of communication. Discussion is ideas coming together, clashing, hitting, or bouncing off one another, as in per-cussion or con-cussion.[12] Discussion is worthwhile, but dialogue goes much further. "Dialogue" means "flow of meaning," or as the leadership theorist Peter Senge puts it, the "flow of meaning through a group."[13] The flow changes—alters course, increases or decreases in speed and volume—as it passes through each participant. But here is the emergent, seemingly magical part: As the flow changes, so do the participants. They are influenced not just by what they hear but by the awareness that what they say is influencing others. There's no guarantee (and often no intention) of consensus, but there's every likelihood of shared purpose.

When people contribute to the process, in other words, they become part of the process—even though they may start out poles apart, as a few hundred angry fishermen learned one night along the Oregon coast.[14]

At one time the commercial salmon boats headed to sea whenever the captains had a hunch that enough salmon were schooling to make the venture worthwhile. Usually the boats went out around May and quit for the season around September, or whenever the value of the day's catch fell below the sum of the day's expenses. This system worked fine for everyone until two opposing events converged with disastrous results: an explosion of fishing boats and the use of radar dramatically increased the daily catch rate, while the elimination of spawning streams from logging and development reduced the population. A 1980 act of Congress gave states the power to establish and enforce seasons.

When Oregon began the process in 1982, the timing couldn't have been worse. That particular spring, ocean and climate conditions had concentrated the salmon into a dense, narrow band close to shore. Officials knew the boats would never have it so easy. They feared grave long-term damage to the population from a single season's overharvesting. Using unproven methods, the officials shortened the established season from the traditional four or five months to a mere twelve days. Unrest swept the coastal fishing towns. State and federal officials were burned in effigy. With emotions still raging, the Oregon Department of Fish and Wildlife scheduled a public meeting in the coastal town of Newport to ask the fishermen for their input in hopes of improving—and defusing—the process for the following year. State officials expected the worst. Police were arranged in case things became ugly.

But in the midst of all these security arrangements a state biologist named Cliff Hamilton was making arrangements of his own.

Hamilton's regular job involved him in education programs for kids and teachers, which kept him safely distant from the fishing wars. But because he had taken (and taught) a few courses on "meeting facilitation," he was the closest thing the Wildlife Department had to an expert in the handling of angry mobs. Applying the rudiments of dialogue, he thought, couldn't hurt—making everyone feel welcome, putting all participants on the same level. So he asked that the police show up in plainclothes. He said there should be no podiums, raised tables, state uniforms, logos, or flags. Authority symbols work great when the mission is enforcement, but not when it's understanding.

Just as everyone feared, the fishermen, about 250 in all, showed up on the verge of a boil. It was well past dinner hour; many had been drinking and a few were drunk. As Hamilton vainly tried to lay out the agenda a group in the back heckled him with obscenities. One drunk was especially vocal. When a specialist began a presentation on the science of salmon populations the drunk continued yelling. Finally a fisherman sitting near the front turned to the back and bellowed, "Will you shut up!" There was a stunned silence, "one of those incredible points when time freezes and life hangs in the balance," as Hamilton would recall. Then, instead of fists and bottles flying, the entire room erupted into thunderous applause. No one wanted to be in the same class as that drunk. "Shared vision? Yes," Hamilton recalls. "They wanted to demonstrate a vision that commercial fishermen were more than just a bunch of ill-mannered drunks."

Of course, neither Hamilton nor anyone else could have planned such an event. But leadership did play a role in what happened next. Hamilton broke the crowd of 250 into a half-dozen groups, insisting that each discuss how to improve the system. In the small meetings, someone from the agency wrote down every idea, no matter how outlandish, on a big sheet of flip-chart paper. When someone suggested "Kill the director," it, too, went up on the list. But as people realized the big sheets would be taped to the walls of the main auditorium for all to see, the ideas became decidedly more constructive. When people understand that they are contributing to a record—when the talk is serious, not showy—confrontation edges toward collaboration.

Still, as the note-takers continued scribbling, the broad range of serious suggestions revealed something of which most were unaware: The fishermen themselves were divided over how to maximize the catch without killing off the future. "Us versus them" became "us versus us."

The fishermen also realized there was no point in sloganeering or grandstanding; the challenge of putting ideas into words forced them to probe and challenge each other for specifics, as in "What do you mean by that?" or "How specifically would you do that?" Again, the fishermen were doing this work themselves; the state was simply providing the flip charts, the scribes, and an extremely elementary meeting process. "This whole aspect was part of the fishermen beginning to learn how to interact rather than just reacting to what had already been proposed by the agency staff," Hamilton says. The ivory-tower agency staff learned a lot, too, beginning with the fact that fishing was not simply a livelihood but a lifestyle in many coastal communities. Even if the fishermen could earn a fabulous income in a season of only twelve days, many experienced a deep fulfillment from fishing that a few days a year could never begin to satisfy. "It was certainly a new and interesting insight to me," says Hamilton.

When the groups reconvened, they found something interesting under way in the main auditorium. A knot of hard-core dissidents had refused to break into the small groups, remaining in the main auditorium to heckle and jeer the agency's director. But the director was nowhere to be found! Hamilton had suggested he avoid showing up until 10:00 P.M., specifically to deprive the fishermen of a target. So the fishermen who resisted the small groups were reduced to waiting in the auditorium, where the agency's salmon specialist happened to be killing time himself. The fishermen started yakking at him for want of something better to do. "What spontaneously evolved right there, without any planning, was another small discussion group that involved the holdouts expressing themselves in a constructive way," Hamilton recalls. "Pure good fortune of circumstance."

Partly. Hamilton and his colleagues could no more have planned that circumstance than scripted a drunken heckler in the back of the room. What they did do was walk into the meeting with the intention to accomplish nothing except dialogue. And in that they succeeded. There was nothing close to a consensus coming out of the meeting, but consensus is rarely as powerful as common purpose, and the common purpose that emerged was a recognition that the state and the fishermen were on the same side in a highly complex issue of science that required all their brains and best intentions.

When the director walked into the auditorium at the appointed hour, he was shocked to find a quiet and thoughtful crowd awaiting. When the meeting finally broke up, the fishermen gave the people from the state a rousing ovation.

In the months and years that followed that night in Newport, conflicts still arose and fishermen still complained. But the tone of the proceedings had been altered dramatically. Fishermen learned biology and biologists learned fishing, and that put everyone in the same boat, so to speak. Cliff Hamilton moved on to a new line of work, but years later happened to find himself near the hearing room on the day when the season's regulations were being formally promulgated. The same hearing room that had once been annually thronged with angry people was now virtually empty, a few commissioners, clerks, and witnesses formalizing the process in less than an hour. As Hamilton realized, "The processes of involvement, dialogue, discussions, participation in councils and advisory groups, better relationship on the coast, and so on, had had their way. As a result, the final commission enactment now was more of a footnote, a minor closure process."

         ~

Unlike churches and state agencies, businesses can't declare victory through dialogue alone. Businesses have to knock out a product every day. Dialogue is only good insofar as it results in action. But even in the most competitive industries, leaders are finding that they can help align the values of an organization by taking account of the values that are already there. "It's bogus to pretend to be at some top, or in some kind of control," says Pete Wakeman of the Great Harvest Bakery chain. "I'm a player. I love my job. I have a role; I love my role. But I more *respond* than influence. The network of connections teaches me, informs me, hints to me of directions to go, and asks my assistance and commitment to what it already knows it wants, or needs."

Or consider what happened in one little corner of the massive DuPont Corporation in the 1990s, when shared vision helped to commute the death sentence hanging over a factory and the surrounding community, a story that begins with the personal transformation of a leader named Richard Knowles.[15]

Knowles was a research chemist with a Ph.D. from the University of Rochester and had forty DuPont patents to his name, the kind of potent chemicals that people once used without a second thought—animal repellants, flame retardants, pesticides. But for all his laboratory genius Knowles was also a hard-driven achiever who rose through progressively higher positions in the DuPont organization, first as a research supervisor and later through a series of corporate and plant management positions. A football player and a lacrosse player in school, he grew up at a time when John Wayne and Vince Lombardi were the role models for white boys. "My bosses were really big, tough, smart, and very accomplished people, and I wanted to be like them," he recalls today. When he once took a personality test he was categorized as a "driver," and sometimes, he admits, he drove by fear.

Knowles hit a midlife crisis while managing a DuPont plant in Niagara Falls, located just three miles from the infamous hazardous waste dump at Love Canal. In the midst of pondering some major questions about his own life, his marriage of twenty-seven years fell apart. It was a wrenching time. "In a very real sense," he later commented, "I grew up at around age fifty." Knowles handled the delicacy of community relations well, always candidly acknowledging the risks inherent in a chemical plant; the toxic release that killed thousands around a Union Carbide plant in India had left little doubt of that fact. His up-front attitude about such risks endowed credibility to his assurances that the company did everything possible to minimize them.

Eventually he was dispatched to the greatest challenge of his thirty-six-year career: as the manager of a massive old plant in Belle, West Virginia. Among the hundreds of facilities in the global DuPont empires, only one plant handled a greater number of dangerous chemicals than Belle. Though serious releases had never occurred, the plant had a mixed record for worker safety that Knowles was intent on improving. Mounting economic pressures made the mission all the more pressing. The Belle plant was some sixty years old. The patents protecting its products had long since expired. In an intensely competitive global economy some companies were churning out the same products for 50 percent less. Knowles knew that without a miracle the plant's days were numbered. Shutdown orders could arrive at any time—and with them, the termination of 1,300 jobs in a small, single-industry town.

Like many other managers you've already read about in this book, Knowles realized the plant had no hope without the focused intelligence of every member of the plant. But he needed even more than that. He needed energy and commitment. He needed emotional involvement. He needed to put the operations of the plant front and center in the lives of everyone who worked there. But how could he accomplish that? He began by walking the length and breadth of the plant—a mile long, a third of a mile wide, hour after hour, day after day.

A generation earlier, executives had been swept up in a fad known for short as MBWA—"management by walking around." In the era of the imperious CEO, when the *Fortune* 500 ran the world, MBWA was a way to put in face time, to review the troops, bless the flock, or shake a few hands in the manner of generals, popes, and presidents. Some executives of the 1960s took this a step further and actually listened to what people might tell them. One was Edward Carlson, who helped saved a foundering United Airlines in the 1960s by constantly talking to pilots, flight attendants, and mechanics, whipping out an index card whenever anyone posed a question or raised a grievance to which he couldn't immediately respond. Carlson would then pass one of these cards—"Ready Eddies," they were called—to an aide tagging behind. The cards wound up on the desks of the appropriate managers, who were given forty-eight hours to respond directly to the employee.

Dick Knowles was going way past MBWA and way past Ready Eddies. He was interacting in real time, putting his own head together with everyone else's, engaging in dialogue—the "flow of meaning," as you'll recall. In addition to drawing out workers on the day-to-day challenges in running the plant he turned their attention at every chance to the big picture. Who are we as a group? Why do we do this work? Can we do it differently? It was, he recalls, "an endless conversation, a walking dialogue." Knowles spent five hours a day, on average, talking to people who didn't report to him.

Part of his purpose was persuading people of the plant's bleak economics. There was no mincing words. Even in the best case, layoffs were looming. Plant managers have traditionally never talked this way. Fearful of igniting doubts and questions, they kept their anxieties to themselves. Knowles did precisely the opposite. "When somebody's making a product at half the cost that we make it, you sit down and share that information with everybody, not just managers. You say, 'Folks, we've got to do something about this.' " To bolster his case the company began teaching production workers how to read financial statements.

Knowles quickly discovered that "when you ask for help in an authentic way, people give it." Knowles himself was stunned at the outbreaks of purpose and initiative. Workers became involved in adopt-a-customer programs. They helped design the first random, mandatory drug testing anywhere in the DuPont organization (outside of a few places where the EPA mandated them). The workers chose a new supplier of safety shoes and worked out the details of a plan to switch schedules in the maintenance department to four days a week. As he continued walking the plant Knowles could see "webby connections" forming before his eyes. "Spontaneous teams would form when people got so frustrated with the rules and procedures from the old culture they'd just get together and fix it." As the plant won the capital necessary to switch its process controls from old-fashioned pneumatics to high-tech electronics, groups of workers sprang up to conduct the integration. One weekend alone 125 teams came together. "I quit setting goals because I was always setting them too low," Knowles says. A number of mechanics became certified trainers in Stephen Covey's "seven habits of highly effective people," a program that ultimately drew in about one-third of the workforce.

The significance was not so much that people were working in teams or working with their minds but that they had *found new meaning* in their work. Knowles would later reflect:

> What happens when people begin to operate in this kind of environment is that they discover they can make a difference, and they're no longer just a pair of hands. We've tended to treat people in our factories as just a pair of hands. So they do the minimum to get by at work, then go home and do creative things, political things—be mayors, church leaders, scout leaders, all kinds of neat stuff in their communities. That's where they've found meaning. That's where they've put their effort and energy. When they discover that they're making a difference at work, some of that energy flows into the work. . . . The work gets done more effectively. There's a huge amount of buy-in because they're all creating it as we go. And the commitment to make it work is just breathtaking.

Knowles and his assistants began to call this "discretionary energy," a huge repository of intelligence and enthusiasm beyond the minimum required for an employee simply to keep her job. "This discretionary energy is a gift people will give if the conditions are right for them to discover meaning," he told me. "The only loss for me in letting go like this was my ego, since I couldn't claim all the credit."

Belle had become a chemical plant on the edge of chaos. "There was a constant level of turmoil, which is where complex adaptive systems need to be," Knowles later commented. Yet the threat of explosion or toxic release makes a chemical plant a potential tragedy. Was this really the kind of institution that ought to be operating on the edge of chaos? Knowles wrestled with the ethical dilemma. How could he assure that the turnaround from within the plant did not spill into the community with catastrophic consequences?

In fact, the solution was already in evidence. In a refinery accident, as in airplane crashes, oil spills, and reactor leaks, human error almost always plays some role. By motivating operators to devote their most unequivocal attention to the processes for which they were responsible—to become unwaveringly vigilant, to never stop anticipating—Knowles figured he could make the unthinkable far less likely. Commands and controls could never create such commitment. Only deeply held values could. As part of this values-building effort Knowles set out to diminish the distinction between the plant and the community, between "out there" and "in here." The boundary around the plant had to become a "permeable, flexible membrane," as he later put it—firm enough to maintain the vital identity and team spirit of the factory community, but sufficiently porous to allow an exchange of information and values with the outside community. So instead of turning regulatory issues over to lawyers, Knowles gave them to workers. When a chemical release of some kind occurred, the offending worker was expected to face the community in any necessary meetings outside the plant.

In time the standards, principles, and expectations of everyone in the plant seemed to assume an almost physical form, something like the force of gravity, pulling people toward a center while giving them the opportunity to explore the perimeter of the system. At times—usually, in fact—it felt to Knowles as if he and his people were sloshing inside a large basin, which he came to refer to as "the bowl." Being inside the bowl confined everyone to a certain way of business, while giving them the freedom to experiment without seeking permission. "In my experience," as he later explained it, "most questions we ask our bosses are for sanction or permission to do what we already know we need to do. If we have a good sense of the bowl, then the answers to, say, 90 percent of our questions are already there." And when people could act without stopping to ask and waiting for an answer, the entire organization could initiate change, practically at an instant.

Knowles's metaphor of the bowl had more literal significance than even he could see at the time. In their flight from the rigid, linear dynamics of Newtonianism, scientists have developed a rich abstraction called a "strange attractor."[16] When richly plotted through thousands or millions of iterations, the seemingly erratic changes in insect populations, for instance, or the outcome of human game-theory exercises begin to reveal a pattern. The data, in time, course through a cycle that never quite repeats but seems to surround a wandering point. Mathematicians call the point the "attractor" since it seems to attract the data toward it, even if the point seems to migrate (hence, "strange"). Researchers call the field around the attractor a "basin of attraction," because it's in that space that the data invariably fall. It is a deep, possibly universal law of complexity: An attractor is an organizing force whose power resides not in controlling the behavior of a system, but in shaping its tendencies.

Strange attractors suggest that in any system, a great number of cycling actions can show organized, purposeful behavior even though the actions vary on every cycle. And there's no reason why the constant iterations of a factory process, or any other organized human process, should not betray the same characteristics. If so, then what precisely *is* the attractor in an organization? What is the force or influence that creates variation within unity? Says business theorist William Frederick, "The corporation's strange attractor—the component that permits change within constrained limits—is it values system."[17]

In the case of the Belle plant, the basin of attraction—Dick Knowles's "bowl"—was a culture, a system, "a network of knowledge and knowing," as he later described it, "our vision and mission and principles and standards and expectations." Over the course of hundreds of thousands of conversations the entire organization began to feel the bowl holding its efforts together, providing focus, direction, and boundary to otherwise open-ended and largely uncoordinated initiatives. "I would encourage folks to do what they thought was the right thing within these constraints and I would support their experiments," he later explained. "I found that this was a powerful way to free up the organization to move into action. When they knew the bowl, they didn't have to wait for me to sanction what they already knew how to do. They just did it. . . . I trusted the process and lived in the ambiguity. I didn't know what would happen next, but as long as it was in the bowl we were okay."

One morning Knowles received a pleasantly startling lesson in how the bowl had freed employees to act on their own. One of his plant operators was listening to a country music station while driving to work at 6:00 A.M. The disk jockeys were ragging on the plant for its supposedly noxious emissions the previous evening, when clear skies and a bright moon illuminated the plant's billowing plumes. The operator, who served on the plant's environmental committee, knew that the emissions were pure water vapor. She was outraged that the radio station could permit such a fundamental and unfair error. So she called the station and invited the DJs to the plant the following Monday. She did this without checking with anyone. In fact she bothered to notify Knowles only because she hoped he would spend an hour meeting with the DJs to speak for the entire plant. The plant's "external affairs" coordinator nearly fell over when he learned of the operator's actions but Knowles refused to get in the way. The visit inspired the DJs to spend weeks telling listeners about the plant's safety commitment.

Dick Knowles left Belle after six years for a headquarters job in Wilmington. By then injury rates had plunged 95 percent. Emissions had fallen 87 percent. Productivity had increased 45 percent. And earnings had tripled. In the course of his tenure layoffs eliminated four hundred of the plant's 1,300 jobs. But almost no one left without something as good to go to. Knowles arranged for DuPont to underwrite a two-year associate's degree for everyone laid off. Many went to DuPont plants elsewhere. Those losing jobs received as much as eighteen months' notice. In 1996, when Knowles finally retired from DuPont after thirty-six years, he bored deeply into the study of complexity, including the concept of attractors, which made him understand why the Belle plant had been so successful. He developed a theory of corporate sustainability that involved fluidity of structure, strength of identity, degrees of diversity and connectivity, and the depth of human reflection, and applied his thinking as a consultant to groups in the U.S. and Australia.

"I've seen this happen over and over again in organizations where everyone has access to all the information," he once commented, "where relationships are open and trust is building, and where everyone has a strong sense of their identity and the intentionality of the organization. The organization can and does become leaderful."

∽

A lot of people in business think that a homogenous work group is a tighter work group. This view is easy to understand. People learn about togetherness in classrooms and sports teams, where everyone happens to be the same age, often the same gender, and, until recently, usually the same color. Business, however, isn't school or sports. The workplace is infinitely more complex. As we've previously explored, a diverse economy, like a diverse ecosystem, makes far more efficient use of resources. And although diversity sometimes introduces the potential for conflict, it can just as easily provide the kind of ruggedness and flexibility that makes conflict easier to absorb. On balance diversity—and I don't mean just race—fosters unity in the workplace, as Joyce and Vic Williams of Atlanta will surely tell you.

Vic was a young architect who was early to grasp the potential of computing in his profession. After several years of working for other people he and Joyce opened a company in 1985 called Architectural Support Services Inc., or ASSI, which performed computer-aided drawing and printing services that many established architectural firms were eager to farm out. Joyce, who had worked for contractors as a bookkeeper, had a talent for keeping track of lots of little pieces. She organized the turbulent flow of electronic versions and the jumble of floppy disks that Vic's work generated.

Before long they landed a big contract helping an up-and-coming local retailer named Home Depot churn out construction diagrams for its new stores. Joyce and Vic were eager to provide quintessential service; they did not want to cut a single corner. So in gearing up for the expansion they adopted a rigorous recruiting profile, hiring strictly hotshot new graduates from the best schools. Though it wasn't their intent, they wound up creating a look-alike staff of a dozen people between twenty-one and twenty-three years old, most from well-to-do backgrounds, all but one of them white.

Joyce, meanwhile, moved to create a culture of teamwork, autonomy, and self-organization. Employees were invited to form their own project teams. They helped train one another. They created their own job titles. For a while this worked: The client list swelled to thirty and annual billings to more than $1 million. In 1994, ASSI's workplace-of-the-future policies landed the entire team on the cover of *Fortune,* a dozen sparkling, fresh-faced employees smiling broadly over a headline hailing theirs as "a company where the employees take charge of their futures."

It was just about then that Vic and Joyce sensed a deep tension brewing. Employees were expected to schedule themselves, but they seemed to resent when Vic pointed out they were behind. They were supposed to deal directly with the firm's customers, but they bristled when customers made major demands. When every employee began clamoring for a seat next to a window, the owners leased an extra large workspace so everyone could be accommodated. Yet once their wish had been granted, employees complained about the glare on their monitors. "We couldn't do anything right," Joyce would recall. Intending to create a sense of fulfillment in the work, Joyce and Vic had unwittingly created a sense of entitlement.

ASSI might have recovered except for one thing: the monolithic characteristics of the employees. With their similar backgrounds and attitudes they fed into one another's resentments. There were no older role models to follow, no alternate points of view to discuss. The only people who were different from the workers were the owners, intensifying the us-versus-them tensions. When Vic took people out to lunch to discuss their grievances privately, they presumed he was seeking to divide them. "It was like a spontaneous unionization drive," Joyce recalls. In the space of two months, ten employees, virtually the entire lot, walked out. The owners were devastated.

One Friday after an intense week of trying to save the business, Joyce was waiting for a carryout pizza. Behind the counter she noticed a sign. "When all else fails," it said, "lower your standards." She didn't take the message literally; she was too much the perfectionist for that. But it did seem to hint at an answer. By hiring a single kind of employee—the best kind, so far as the owners knew at the time—they had practically assured the company's decimation. Perhaps by hiring to a different standard, by considering personality over pedigree, ASSI could build a new and stronger staff.

So they began looking for qualified designers who showed a capacity for getting along, regardless of where their degrees came from or how recently they had graduated. Though not consciously seeking diversity, that was the inevitable result. In came a Korean-American, an Indian-American, an architect from Vietnam. By not hiring from the top northern design schools ASSI wound up with more locals, creating a better mix of Yankees and Rebels. The age range reached to about forty years old instead of twenty-three. There were married people in the new group and parents, too. All this meant that when problems erupted—business problems, personality problems, or both together—the diversity of views tended to dampen rather than magnify them. In addition, the greater number of sensibilities created a greater number of potential solutions to any problem. Business and morale quickly recovered.

In time ASSI adopted an additional element of diversity, using free-lancers, part-timers, temporaries, contractors, and even employees it shared with other companies. The purpose of these additional arrangements was adapting on a daily basis to the level and profitability of the work, the variety of employment arrangements enhancing the stability of the entire group. "In a self-organizing system there must be room for some elements to come and go and for that to be okay," as Joyce put it. "It seems that freelance, temporary, and part-time people are more used to self-organization than the traditional employee." Some employees want such arrangements, others don't. ASSI can accommodate them all, and leave itself stronger as a result.

෨

In any living thing, good traits persist through the generations while bad ones ultimately shrink away. This doesn't mean that time creates perfection, only that everything alive today embodies the best of what preceded it. Maybe that's why we honor our forebears. We put their photos on the piano or construct elaborate genealogies not just to remember them but to remind us who *we* are. This is no less true of organizations. When organizations preserve and honor their past, they remind present generations of the good work and best values of earlier generations.

History, in short, is another unifying force in the workplace, an organizing principle that can inspire emotional commitment in a way that command and control methods never could. In addition, a look backward facilitates a vision of the future. There's nothing new about companies honoring their histories (notwithstanding Henry Ford's assertion that "history is more or less bunk"). What's new is the discovery by some companies that the past can serve as an antidote to the poisonous effects of a fixation on short-term results—that "remembering what we're all about" or "remembering where we came from" helps shift the focus of the organization to the long-term. That in any case was another important lesson I learned in visiting Avedis Zildjian

Company, which I introduced in an earlier chapter as the oldest business operating in America.

Throughout its existence—providing cymbals for Middle Eastern
armies, for the speakeasy drummers who invented jazz, for Ringo Starr
and the Boston Symphony and thousands of marching bands in
America—the company guarded its seventeenth-century alloying technology as if it were the Hope diamond. Even today, when the moment
arrives to pour another supply of the copper and tin material, only a direct descendant of the original Avedis is permitted in the smelting room.
From the outside it's impossible to say how much of a trade secret the
company really is protecting. Regardless, the mystique surrounding the
product sustains the company's exotic history, not just among the drummers who make it their business to know their suppliers but among the
employees who make the product in the first place.

In the late 1970s, for the first time in the company's history, there
was no Zildjian son ready to receive the business. Into the void stepped
Craigie Zildjian, the first woman ever admitted to the secret smelting
room (and the first permitted to own stock in the company). Craigie
had never been quite so steeped in the company's culture as the male
heirs who preceded her. "Girls didn't study drums," she says today.
"Girls took piano lessons."

So for several years Craigie Zildjian entrusted management of the
company to "professional" outsiders, who, as such managers are wont,
immediately moved to attack costs and concentrate on quarter-by-
quarter results. But this caused the company's fabled product-
development efforts to languish for lack of an immediate payback. The
company's tight relations with the drummer community began to
weaken. Dark years followed in which the company seemed to lose its
soul. Although the back shop continued to employ a great number of
amateur and semi-professional drummers working as lathe operators,
quality inspectors, and design engineers, the front office lost nearly all
connection with the essence of the product.

Awakening to this horror, Craigie, in the mid-1990s, presided over a
housecleaning and hired a search firm to seek a new CEO with an
important qualification: Any candidate had to "care about music."
Into the position stepped a longtime bass guitarist named David Bryan,
who had been a senior executive at Sara Lee Corporation. While moving into the position Bryan also began taking drum lessons. Quickly,
the artist relations department was beefed up (most were also drummers themselves) and a new R&D team was launched.

Once again the music was integral to the business. The company coaxed its most famous customer, Ringo, into visiting the plant. A studio in which visiting drummers could test new products was outfitted in the middle of the company's headquarters building, where any employee walking past could see (and hear) a reminder of what the business was all about. In the hallway sat the quaintly simple drum kit of Buddy Rich, who from his deathbed asked the Zildjian family to take care of it after he was gone. The walls were lined with photographs of famous drummers, Zildjian devotees one and all.

The company also launched a program to encourage front-office and other employees to learn to play the drums themselves during lunch breaks. "We cherish this business," Craigie Zildjian explained. "We hope people will feel a part of what we make"—as worthy a definition of shared purpose as you'll find anywhere in the literature of leadership.

CHAPTER

8

Money and Motivation

In the spring of 1997 outfielder Al Martin of the Pittsburgh Pirates made professional sports history: He left money on the table.

Not chicken scratch, either. Though already handsomely paid at about $2 million a year, his contract was up for renewal and he was free to talk to another team. He could easily have locked in additional millions elsewhere. Everyone in the league was positive he could double his salary. Yet with hardly a thought he signed a new contract committing him to the Pirates until the year 2000, with a modest salary increase. Sports agents cringed. The players' union was aghast. It seemed almost un-American. It was definitely un-baseball. What kind of elite athlete walks away from money?

Martin grew up in a working-class neighborhood near Los Angeles surrounded by great athletes. He watched an uncle build a long and rewarding career as a defensive back with the Oakland Raiders of football. Then he watched a brother wind up with much less after jumping among the Raiders, Pittsburgh Steelers, and Buffalo Bills of football. So when Al Martin left USC for professional baseball he resolved to start and end his career in a single city, wherever he happened to reach the major leagues first. After seven years and 963 games in the minors, that turned out to be Pittsburgh. He was a .300 hitter with a reliable glove in left field, and his salary climbed steadily.

Pittsburgh happens to be where I live these days. And although I have never been much of a baseball fan, you can't live here without recognizing that Pittsburgh has very demanding and moody fans. This was especially so after the 1994 players' strike. Diamond-studded ballplayers go over poorly in a lunch-pail town like Pittsburgh. So despite a solid playoff record and the presence of many league-leading players, the Pirates were losing favor with their fans. Attendance at the Sovietesque Three Rivers Stadium, never a sellout to begin with, plunged further.

Then, in 1996, some new nickel-biting owners came in, offering to release every high-priced player from his contract in order to rebuild the team with cheap recruits. Freed to sign richer deals elsewhere, every big-name player immediately bolted, except Al Martin.

A short time later Martin showed up at 1997 spring training to find himself surrounded by a bunch of minor-leaguers, many from as far down as single-A. It was like something out of *The Bad News Bears*. They were barely shaving! Many earned the major-league minimum of $150,000 a year. The entire Pirate roster, in fact, made barely $10 million a year, less than the Chicago White Sox paid a single player, Albert Belle. By baseball standards the Pirates were so working class they clipped grocery coupons and treated their clubhouse supper as a feast. "On most teams guys will take a few bites and go home or go out to eat," Martin said. "On this ball club we have guys loading up two and three plates and then wrapping some up for leftovers. I'm not kidding. You see guys carrying food out of here."[1]

The competition laughed, the fans rolled their eyes, and the pundits roundly predicted a hundred losses for the season. There wasn't a soul who followed baseball predicting the Pirates would wind up anywhere but dead last in their division. Even the new owners, stifling their delight at fielding the cheapest team in baseball, could promise no more than a "rebuilding" year.

Looking around him at camp, Martin realized that if leadership were to come from anywhere it would be from him. At barely thirty years old he was the granddaddy of this team, and the only one, it would appear, with the chance of a league-leading performance. So he built a culture of hard work. "This," he told people, "is how we will do business." When everybody else was still eating Egg McMuffins, Martin was already in the batting cage. He was the first to break a sweat, the first to leap to his feet, the first to greet a player returning to the dugout after a big play. "He leads by example," the first baseman Kevin Young told me later in the Pirates clubhouse. "It's something the younger players feed off of."

The youth and low pay of his teammates strengthened his leadership. "If you bring in veterans from other places, they bring in their own baggage," he explained on one occasion. "With young guys, it's kind of like putty. You can mold them and build something that's mainstream throughout the organization. 'This is how we go about our business. This is the way we play. If you don't agree with it, you're not going to be here.' You can't do that with a bunch of veterans that make a lot of money."[2]

In an ingenious (if unwitting) display of systems thinking, the Pirates' marketing people picked up on the team's work ethic and realized how smoothly it would harmonize with the ethos of the hometown crowd. They created a new logo for the team: a lunch pail. They rolled out a new marketing slogan: "Let's go to work." And they filmed brazenly cheap-looking TV spots that featured various ballplayers moonlighting in unlikely jobs: one as a lifeguard, another as a crossing guard. Al Martin was shown in uniform turning a wrench under the hood of a car, an air wrench wheezing in the background. "Come see the team that works as hard as you do," the announcer said.

The season opened, and to the astonishment of everyone, the Pirates were winning ballgames, barely more than half, to be sure, but, in a weak division, enough to propel them to the top. They made as many spectacular plays as they did spectacular mistakes because every player was at full throttle on practically every play. It seemed they either lost big or won narrowly. No single player dominated; on the contrary, their individual statistics were rather mediocre—except in the categories that reflected sheer hustle and sacrifice: triples, steals, and even in getting hit by pitches.

Remember the cycle of action, feedback, and synthesis? Sports is full of it. A dedicated player inspires dedication in others, bringing back the fans, which inspires the players even further, which brings in more fans. Attendance climbed 15 percent despite the worst spring weather in years, including snow in the bleachers. One Saturday the Pirates sold out Three Rivers for the first time in twenty years (not counting opening days). Bursting with pride, Martin hauled the entire team one unseasonably blustery evening down to the gates, where the fans were arriving under umbrellas and stocking caps. Martin told each player to introduce himself to the arriving fans and shake every hand he could. The event was totally spontaneous; the players were as stunned and as thrilled as the fans. Through the determined play of their rookies and the leadership of their veteran, the Pirates were mending their ties with their hometown.

It was in the midst of this Cinderella year that Martin's contract came up for renewal. The Pirates offered to extend him for roughly $3 million a year, a figure he could have easily doubled elsewhere. But why? "I'm comfortable enough," he told people. "What am I going to do? Buy a million-dollar car?" Making a couple million dollars is awful nice—no fooling anyone about that. But there isn't much a family man could do with a second million that he couldn't accomplish with the first—except run up his point total on the scoreboard of bragging rights. Al Martin preferred keeping score on the field. Indeed, as he watched his son's sheer delight in playing Little League, Martin began to see images of himself in the midst of the improbable '97 season. "For the first time in my life as a professional," he later told me, "I realized I'm having as much fun as he is."

In fact, Martin feared that making too much money might penalize his team play. At such elite levels of performance, athletes can easily calibrate between maximum individual achievement and maximum team achievement, and Martin knew that the pressure of additional millions would put any human on the defensive. The owners of baseball, still afflicted with linear mind-sets, figured that any increase in salary could only make for better play, when in fact after a certain point it might well have the reverse effect. At the very least, Martin feared that such high stakes would cause him to feel the chill of self-awareness in the batter's box. "I'd rather be a bargain than overpaid any day," he said.

It was days after Martin re-upped with the Pirates that disaster struck. In the space of a week, injuries felled the team's top run producer, its best defensive player, its clutch reliever—and the top hitter, Al Martin, sidelined with a hand injury. In came more bottom-scale minor-leaguers. Yet the team roared on, the culture of hustle surviving those who had created it. The amazing thing about leadership is how it persists in the absence of the leaders themselves.

Martin made it back into play after a few weeks. The Pirates had fallen a few games out of first place and spent the rest of the season mightily struggling to regain the lead. It came down to the last few days of September. It was close, but not meant to be. But the narrow second-place finish took nothing away from the astonishment over what a bunch of kids and Al Martin had accomplished. One small exercise in arithmetic by the Associated Press, conducted in the middle of the season, said it all: On average, the Cincinnati Reds paid their roster $1.78 million per victory. The Yankees paid $1.64 million. The Florida Marlins paid $1.25 million. The Pirates paid $284,000.[3] There isn't a compensation model in the world that can account for numbers like that, except perhaps the model that says all compensation models are worthless.

Things went a bit differently in the 1998 season. Facing eye surgery, Al Martin slipped into a hitting slump. The team owners began dropping hints of a trade, despite Martin's history of loyalty to the franchise. But the memory persisted of that magical season in which the team had defied all the odds—a season in which money mattered not a whit.

~

I won't pretend that the Al Martin story signals an end to salary inflation, least of all in the corporate world. Al "Chainsaw" Dunlap pulled down $100 million in his final year as chairman of Scott Paper, a fact that delighted him less for the riches it created than for the bragging rights it bestowed. "I'm a superstar in my field," he explained, "much like Michael Jordan in basketball and Bruce Springsteen in rock 'n' roll."[4] At nearly every other level of work life, compensation remains structured as if it were the only source of motivation. Psychologists call this the Law of Effect—"do this and you get that"—an axiom lifted straight from Newtonian cause-and-effect logic. Behavioral scientists legitimized the pay-for-performance mind-set by using rewards to make lab mammals do just about anything of which a mammal was capable (causing the historian Arthur Koestler to accuse psychologists of replacing the anthropomorphic view of the rat with the "rattomorphic view of man"[5]).

There's no point in denying that money is supremely motivating to people who have little or none of it. An extra penny per seam will cause faster sewing when it means the difference between one cabbage and two. But for the preponderance of people for whom the extra penny does not spell such a difference, the "rattomorphic" view falls apart. The reason is that each additional dollar in anyone's possession is less valuable than the one that preceded it. James Baldwin once quipped that money was exactly like sex: "You thought of nothing else if you didn't have it and thought of other things if you did."[6]

Willie Sutton was famous for saying he robbed banks because "that's where the money is." Yet in his autobiography he told a slightly different story. "I was more alive when I was inside a bank robbing it than at any other time in my life," he wrote.[7] If money is not the whole story, then what's the rest of it? Consider to begin with the concept that made the late Abraham Maslow one of the most important thinkers of the modern age.

To a little-known degree, Maslow helped spark the revolution in work and economy that this book is about. A professor at Brooklyn College (later Brandeis) who once scored the second-highest IQ ever tested, he resisted both of the psychological schools that held sway in the prewar years: the darkness of Freudianism and the bleakness of behaviorism. Instead of studying sick minds, Maslow thought it might be interesting to study healthy ones for a change—the whole person within the whole society. In keeping with the retreat from Newtonianism then accelerating in the physical sciences, Maslow began to grasp the relativity of the human condition: the notion that what someone aspired to depended on what he already had. It was a radical approach to human motivation.

"It is quite true," he wrote in the early 1940s, "that man lives by bread alone—where there is no bread. But what happens to man's desires when there is plenty of bread?" The answer was that "higher needs emerge. . . . And when these in turn are satisfied, again new (and still 'higher') needs emerge, and so on." People, in other words, are motivated by the needs they haven't satisfied. The first $1 million meant a lot to Al Martin, but no additional millions could inspire him more than his love of the Pirates organization. By the 1950s Maslow had popularized his famous "hierarchy of needs," a stairstep of aspirations pursued in succession by humans. First they fulfill physiological needs, for food and water, then physical security, such as shelter. With these needs met, humans seek love, through affection and belonging, followed by esteem, through social approval. Having accomplished all this, man finally yearns for what Maslow called "self actualization," or self-fulfillment, of which he said, "What a man can be, he must be."[8]

Maslow attained celebrity for his work. It helped to launch a broad interest in the study of "peak experiences" in sports and the arts. It deeply influenced early feminist writers, establishing much of the intellectual foundation for what became the "women's liberation" movement. And to return to the subject of money and motivation, Maslow's hierarchy convinced a small group of managers that after a certain point, money alone ceased to motivate their workers. Once they had provided for their lower-rung needs, people in the workplace needed to belong. They needed to be loved. And in the best cases, they needed jobs to help them become everything of which they were capable. As Maslow wrote, "The only happy people I know are the ones who are working well at something they consider important."[9]

Though scarcely known for management theory, Maslow also spent a sabbatical at a company near San Diego called (appropriately enough) Non-Linear Systems, which made voltmeters for the aerospace industry in an old blimp hangar. The owner of the business, Andy Kay, had immersed himself in Maslow's writings in the late 1950s—ideas that helped him understand the mystery of why workers at the end of the assembly line were invariably the most productive. It was there, Kay finally realized, that people could feel the fulfillment that comes from completing the job, conducting the last few tasks standing between a long chain of work and the customer's use of a valued product. Andy Kay took this realization and broke his workforce into small groups, each responsible for an entire product, a clear precursor to the kind of self-directed teams that Charlene Pedrolie would one day introduce at Rowe Furniture.

A representative from *Reader's Digest* visited the plant in 1963 and published an incredulous report: "When Non-Linear discarded its assembly line it kept all its people—some with only a grammar school education—but divided them into small teams of fewer than a dozen people. Each team runs its own little business. Each has its own rooms, for which it decides the décor. . . . There are no time clocks. . . . Anyone can get coffee whenever he feels like it."[10] Notably, workers signed their names on the equipment they built and fielded queries from the individual customers who used their machines, extending the employees' feeling of belonging into the heart of the marketplace itself. This was radical stuff for a time when the American Management Association published a popular guidebook called *Tough-Minded Management*.

At Kay's invitation and expense, Maslow spent the summer of 1962 roaming the corridors of Non-Linear Systems, marveling at what he saw and dictating his impressions into an early model hand-held tape recorder. Each day Kay's secretary typed Maslow's comments, which he later compiled into a mimeographed volume he called *Summer Notes*. It was an extraordinary piece of work. In it Maslow coined the phrase "enlightened management." He took an obscure term from anthropology, "synergy," and applied it for perhaps the first time to business to describe how cooperation creates wealth. "The more influence and power you give to someone else in the team situation," he noted, "the more you have yourself." He discussed "continual improvement" as an operating concept before anyone in the West had heard of the Japanese *kaizen*.

But Maslow's main interest was fulfillment as a source of motivation on the shop floor. "Highly evolved individuals," he said in his notes, "assimilate their work into the identity, into the self. Work actually becomes part of the self, part of the worker's definition of himself. . . . You participate in the glory, the pleasure, and the pride of the place." In part, this attitude reflected the growing affluence of society, which, even in 1962, was causing workers to rank the quality of their work ahead of the quantity of the financial reward. "Money," Maslow insisted, "is no longer a very important motivation."[11]

Alas, the Non-Linear story had an unhappy ending for all concerned. The company slipped into a steep tailspin in the aerospace downturn of the early 1970s, and although Kay's innovative practices helped to slow the decline, critics used the company's failure as proof that the newfangled management methods were all wet. *Business Week* published an account under the headline, "Where Being Nice to Workers Didn't Work."[12] Maslow's *Summer Notes*, meanwhile, was published commercially under the ghastly title of *Eupsychian Management*, based on Maslow's coinage ("eupsychia") for the ideal society. Instead of becoming the management equivalent of *The Jungle* or *Silent Spring*—a book that by itself might have ignited a revolution in its field, holding a light against the dark vision of *The Organization Man*—Maslow's book instead slipped into obscurity.

Maslow's summer at Non-Linear Systems did have important secondary effects, however. His notes deeply influenced such eminent management and leadership gurus as Peter Drucker, Warren Bennis, Douglas McGregor, and Peter Senge. I wrote a column on the book that rekindled publisher interest in it, and a new volume was scheduled for publication. By then, of course, Maslow's observations could only reinforce changes that were already well under way.

In my view Maslow's most brilliant insight was that people try to give their best when they can see the widest known effects of their actions. They want to reach to the greatest distance possible. Self-actualized people listen for the "echoes" of their work, he said. "It's like the holistic way of thinking, not so much in chains of causes and effects, but rather in terms of concentric circles or rings of waves spreading out from the center."[13] How do people attain that wider fulfillment? To some degree it gets back to their tools.

శ

Tools, as I've previously discussed, are the technology of economizing, but they are also, as Marshall McLuhan said, "extensions of man." Whether a trowel, a telephone, or a week of training, tools magnify the user. As the British chemist and science philosopher Michael Polanyi wrote in 1957, a carpenter extends his senses to the head of his hammer every bit as much as a blind person to the tip of his cane; Polanyi could just as well have written the same of Al Martin's bat or the webbing of his glove. "We pour ourselves into them and assimilate them as part of our own existence," Polanyi wrote of tools. "We accept them existentially by dwelling in them."[14]

This was certainly the case in pre-industrial times, when excellence in the use of a tool demanded experience, judgment, or "feel." A farmer did not control his plow animal but governed it. A sailor "worked with" the wind.[15] Outside of slavery (which through most of history was an affair of state, not of commerce), no one even considered controlling the execution of another person's work. In art and artisanship alike, apprenticeship arose from the reality that skillfulness in the use of tools involved such ambiguities that instruction alone was insufficient.

The Industrial Age turned tools from extensions of man into extensions of management, deadening the potential of the person holding them. At the Lordstown auto plant, torque wrenches and paint guns fulfilled the will of the planners rather than the judgment of the workers. These tools diminished people and consequently demotivated them, precisely as Maslow would have predicted. Then the changes began. As Dana Corporation discovered at its auto-chassis plant in Stockton, human judgment and feel in welding actually improved the quality and lowered the cost of the job—so long as the tools fit the needs of the worker rather than the requirements of the task. As Charlene Pedrolie found at Rowe Furniture, the most motivating tool in a self-organizing shop was information.

And as I learned from an entrepreneur named Bill Armstrong, the quality of the tools can shape the quality of a culture.

A tall man with a gruff voice, he was seventy years old and slightly stooped with age when I met him at the bustling headquarters of Armstrong Ambulance Company, located in the Boston suburb of Arlington. After returning from the army in 1946 Armstrong's father, a building contractor, discouraged him from going into business for himself. But Armstrong's mother, a farm girl who had become a nurse, cashed in a life insurance policy in order to lend him the down payment on a gleaming new $5,500 Cadillac ambulance. She also became his only employee, joining him on his runs to make sure that the journey to the hospital (or, just as likely, to the nursing home) was comfortable for the patient.

Armstrong wired the family home with alarm bells. "The place sounded like a fire station," he would recall. He also operated the most up-to-date and fully outfitted vehicle, regardless of the cost, even to the point of denying himself personal medical insurance and his own children a few basic necessities. "We had an ambulance in the driveway but no Band-Aids in the medicine cabinet," says his daughter Gail. For thirty years Armstrong made his living on a single vehicle, using his daughters as his dispatchers.

Then, in the late 1970s, the private ambulance business exploded. The reason was a sudden advance in technology and training, making lifesaving acts by paramedics, once miraculous, much more commonplace. Armstrong Ambulance continued its tradition of buying the latest and the best, often in excess of what cash-strapped local fire departments could provide. This made Armstrong Ambulance the workplace of choice for the cream of the paramedic crop, since paramedics measure their pride and professionalism by the extent of their technology and their training to use it. They are flattered when equipped with the best tools and offended when issued anything less. Most deeply resent the intrusion of cost-benefit considerations into questions of patient care.

All of this set off a wonderful feedback cycle for Armstrong Ambulance. Drawn by Bill Armstrong's superior tools and technical training, local municipal firefighters began moonlighting for him. These moonlighting firefighters, in turn, helped Armstrong win emergency-service contracts from one Boston suburb to the next, providing the company with revenue to buy even newer and better equipment, which drew in more experienced paramedics, and so on. The cycle accelerated as the advent of 911 technology in the mid-1980s inspired more municipalities to offer the most high-tech emergency services possible.

By 1997 Armstrong had seventy ambulances and three hundred employees serving some 350 patients a day. If an ambulance was offered with a choice of sixteen or twenty strobe lights, he insisted on twenty; there was no telling when that one infinitesimal degree of added warning might glint into the eye of a motorist unaware. All this cost money, of course—but it made money, too, because Armstrong Ambulance continued to enjoy the most experienced and loyal paramedic workforce in the region.

"We lack for nothing," a paramedic named Michael Forget told me as I watched him unpack the rear of a $100,000 ambulance, looking as if he were setting up a location shot for *ER*. Forget spent seventeen years working for another New England ambulance company that was bought up by a cost-cutting national chain; by the time I visited, he was commuting two hours each way for the chance to work for Bill Armstrong. "A large company has to satisfy shareholders," Forget explained. "But Mr. Armstrong sees his name on the side of the vehicle and he wants the best no matter what."

"The name on the side of each and every vehicle is a pledge to patient care," paramedic Derick Aumann added. "The one word that describes the difference between working for this company and any other is 'pride.' " Though he didn't use the Maslowian jargon, Aumann described the rewards of working at Armstrong as belonging, self-esteem, and self-actualization all in one. "When we're walking into an emergency room and a nurse sees you're from Armstrong," he said, "she knows the kind of experience you've got."

⌇

It's not just tools, of course, but the purpose to which they are put that creates a motivated workplace. As Maslow observed in his *Summer*

Notes, "To do some idiotic job very well is certainly *not* real achievement."[16] Fortunately, idiotic jobs are on the decline as a proportion of all jobs. Organizations are eliminating work that adds no value just as surely as the economy is eliminating organizations that add no value (and all for the same reasons). But some idiotic jobs persist. In these cases, wages are all that matter. And when wages alone matter, motivation becomes a serious problem.

Telemarketing boiler rooms—or "service bureaus," as they prefer to be called—are the air-conditioned sweatshop of the '90s. I visited the flagship operation of one well-established firm, Ron Weber & Associates, at the invitation of the company itself. The company said it wanted to show off its pristine working conditions and its success in recruiting and motivating its workforce. Weber considered itself the Tiffany of call centers, working for the leading long-distance companies and credit-card operations and receiving many of the industry's top awards for quality and integrity. "It's not just a job," founder Ron Weber told me. "It's a career, and there's a career path within it."

The firm insisted on my visiting even after I warned of harboring a personal bias against its line of business. Telemarketing is the lowest form of selling, like junk mail arriving with bells ringing and voices commanding immediate buy or sell decisions. This method of marketing persists only because there are many hapless souls willing to work for wages low enough to make the service profitable. Like many other such companies, Weber & Associates concentrated its operations in the farm belt, where a devastating depression beginning in the early 1980s created a desperate need for work, particularly among women seeking to provide a second household income. I happened to visit Weber's center in Waterloo, Iowa, where the struggles of Rath Packing and Deere & Company had thrown many into unemployment. At the time of my visit Weber started people at $5.75 an hour. Top pay was $8 an hour. The bonus in a good week was $30.

My tour began in the high-tech nerve center where technicians were loading giant reels of nine-track tape, each with thousands of names and phone numbers. A bank of computers dialed numbers and waited for answers, hanging up when a machine took the call. After detecting a human voice, the computers trolled for a salesperson with an open line. Only then, with the would-be customer dangling on the other end of the line, did the call go out to a large room known as the "production floor," where, according to computer manager Jim Strong, "they're constantly being flooded with calls."

On the day of my visit everyone on the production floor was pitching long-distance services to small businesses. (I agreed in advance not to disclose the identity of the client.) The production floor was a large room with rows of operators sitting a few feet apart, separated by gray partitions. There were three narrow windows along one wall—practically no natural light. A low rumble of voices filled the air, each reading from a script, the murmur punctuated by supervisors walking the aisles admonishing the clerks to "convert" the calls into sales.

"C'mon, you guys! We need a sale this hour!"

"Four more! Four more!"

"C'mon, Rosie! One more!"

This is not what Maslow meant by motivation.

In the program under way on this day, the goal was two sales—per day. That's two victories in an average of 160 attempts and 158 rejections, ranging from "No thanks" to "Get lost" and much, much worse.

If you think it's bad receiving these calls, just imagine what it's like placing them. "We do a lot of hand-holding," said Celina Peerman, Weber's personnel chief. "They have to learn rejection isn't personal. There's a lot of stress in the repetition; they're getting phone call after phone call after phone call of rejection." Supervisors watched for outbreaks of the blues, not just to rescue individual employees from burnout but to block despair from becoming epidemic. "If someone's having a bad day, it spreads from one person to the next person to the next person," said Ellen Humphrey, the head trainer.

Some clerks were doing a magnificent job of projecting a little cheer through their boom microphones; others spoke monotonously at best. Some slouched. Some doodled. A few stole precious seconds between calls to gossip over the dividers. (As the industrial psychologist Frederick Herzberg once noted, "Idleness, indifference, and irresponsibility are healthy responses to absurd work."[17]) "After lunch it goes faster," a clerk named Danette Hager told me. "The day is half over." A few rows away, another clerk complained that her headset was broken and no one could seem to find a replacement. Nearby, clerks fretted over an absent employee rumored to have a blood clot in her leg.

By all appearances the front-line supervisors were doing their best to sustain the mood, if only through a routine of token gestures—the occasional pie in the face of a supervisor, a free car wash for good performance, the installation of a few picnic tables for nice-weather lunch breaks, the addition of a second microwave. (It's amazing how popcorn helps people through the day.) "It's so important," said Humphrey, "to make deposits in their emotional banks."

Yet many of the morale boosters only called attention to the drudgery of the work—a dismissal fifteen minutes early after a big day, say, or the right to relax in jeans or sweats the days after a good performance. (A strict dress code was necessary, explained operations chief John Harrington, because "we don't want clients thinking it's some kind of boiler room.") Although the company used such rewards as motivation tools, in reality they only recognized the truth that when the work arouses the loathing of the wider world, the main motivation is reaching the end of the day.

Maybe, one wonders, the work might pass more easily if the pay were better. The answer to that question suggested itself at a different call center, near Boston.

ᴄᴐ

It was the catalogue-sales operation of Staples, the big office-supply retailer, where, as you may recall, the operations manager Jane Biering had created a culture of self-organization. The tools in the Staples call center (a lot of telephone lines and computers) were identical to those I saw in Iowa, and the pay was nearly identical as well (a bit less, in fact, if you accounted for the cost-of-living difference between suburban Boston and northern Iowa). But otherwise the contrast was instantly striking in the look and feel of the place. Partly this was due to the presence of natural sunlight and vastly brighter furnishings, but the major difference was the effervescence and energy level of the people inside. Instead of desperately hoping to snag a few seconds away from the phone, for instance, the salespeople at Staples groaned when the computers temporarily went down.

What mainly accounted for these opposite appearances was simply the direction in which the phones were pointed. The Staples clerks were fielding *incoming* phone calls—contacts from people who actually *wanted* to talk to a salesperson. Everyone in the room was motivated by knowing she was coming to the aid of the person on the other end of the phone—solving problems, providing tools, making someone's work life a little easier. Employees could sense the difference they made to the outside world. A clerk named Nutana Kulakofski had a can of Folger's coffee on her desk because Staples was running a promotion on the product. "It's tactile; it inspires me. If I can see it and feel it, I can sell it," she told me. "I'm one of the best phone jocks at Staples."

This work was also motivating because it used more of the mind. Instead of reciting the same spiel hours or days on end, the Staples clerks sold from a catalogue containing tens of thousands of products. Every item ordered by a customer presented an opportunity to sell something additional—*Need some toner to go with that fax paper?* Grouped in clusters instead of long rows, clerks continually exchanged selling tips and war stories. "I love the philosophy of this company," a clerk named Richard Cohen told me. "I like the way they handle customers and I love the fact that everyone works together." Another, Bill Paul, had managed a Radio Shack store for fifteen years, was laid off, and started working the phones at Staples until something better came along; he never left.

Jane Biering recognized that people don't work for money alone. (As William James commented a century ago, "The deepest hunger in humans is the desire to be appreciated.") So a few years ago Biering asked a committee of call-center clerks to design the best recognition program they could think of. The outcome was a scheme for rewarding people who accumulated written commendations not just from customers and managers but from their fellow clerks. As a result, peers went out of their way to look for good work by peers, causing good practices to propagate while fostering the sense of belongingness (one step along the Maslow hierarchy). Instead of being patronized with an employee-of-the-month parking place, winning employees were honored at a solemn ceremony, with everyone from the call center gathered into a big room. The prize itself, as chosen by the employees themselves, wasn't a night on the town or a pair of Red Sox tickets, but enrollment in a management-development class, time off to pick up new computer skills, or an all-expenses-paid visit to study a Staples operation elsewhere. One popular destination: lovely Chambersburg, Pennsylvania, where Staples operated a major warehouse.

As a call-center employee named Karen Rabbit explained, "It's a chance to really buff up your résumé."

∽

Money, as I've argued earlier, is stored matter and energy. But it also has value as information—as feedback, or as an attention-getting signal for what works and what doesn't, as I learned spending a few days at a Hollywood outfit called Metropolitan Talent.

The owner of the agency was a story in his own right. He grew up in Queens, New York, as Christopher Klaff, the grandson of a prominent industrialist who had commercialized life rafts, high-pressure boilers, and other assemblages of fabricated steel. Chris was a child when he first visited the shipyard his father owned, a business that everyone in the family fully expected Chris one day to run. But he was shocked walking through the cavernous steel-fabricating shops to see cascading sparks and grimy workers in black welding masks. When the workers approached to offer their hands to the young scion, he was frightened by their grotesquely callused hands. "I made up my mind on the spot I wasn't going to make my living there," he told me. Ultimately his father was injured in an accident on the job and sold the business to Bethlehem Steel—then watched the fortune waste away to nothing because of his punitive medical bills.

Chris himself wound up as far from the shipyards as possible in every way, enrolling in the High School of Music and Art, becoming an actor, and assuming the stage name Chris Barrett. Baby-faced, with a dimpled smile, he was successful acting in commercials and in secondary roles on secondary TV shows—the *Bob Crane Show,* for instance, and a drama called *Harry O.* But he could see himself never getting past second-banana roles, and as a whirlwind of energy who could sleep only five hours a night, he urgently needed more stimulation in his life. So in 1981, at the age of thirty-two, he turned to the business side of show business, joining an established firm as a junior talent agent.

As a newcomer he had to tread carefully. Agents typically draw an annual salary plus a year-end bonus—often a windfall many times their base salary. This means that everyone wants the credit for every piece of business she brings in. Turf is sacrosanct. So to avoid raising alarm Barrett confined himself to helping small-time actors find work in second-tier studios. These deals, though not particularly remunerative for the agency, came quickly. Barrett began representing talent still on its way up or already past its prime. Soon he and some partners got together to create their own firm, which they called Metropolitan Talent Agency.

In time Barrett grew troubled. He felt that the individual agents in the firm were the real sources of wealth and that more of it should be shared with them through bonuses. Yet he also hated the year-end ritual of a closed-door meeting at which the owners made all kinds of subjective judgments about individual performance. For such a vital matter from the employee's point of view, the division of the pie seemed imprecise at best. Discouragement over the unfairness of the distribution outweighed excitement over the payment. Bonuses, it appeared to Barrett, were actually demotivating! It was, as he later put it, "a system that beat the creative spirit out of people."

Eager to attempt a radical experiment, he left his partners and bargained to take the Metro Talent name with him. "My partners were not interested in trying this stuff," he said. He leased a magnificent turn-of-the-century mansion full of warrens, cubbyholes, open meeting areas, and outdoor courtyards. And because his was a tiny operation next to the likes of a William Morris Agency, he resolved to turn each of his agents into an ally, rather than an adversary, of the other, guiding them with compensation.

His new system scored every dollar of commission revenue that came into the agency according to any combination of three activities. Thirty percent of the income on each deal was attributed to the agent who originally signed the client, no matter how long ago. The next 30 percent was scored to whoever happened to represent that talent at the time (sometimes the same as the signing agent, often not). The final 40 percent was attributed to whoever landed the deal in question (again, often an altogether different person).

Then, at bonus time, Barrett took a substantial portion of the agency's revenue—roughly one-quarter—and divided it among the agents in the proportions by which it had been attributed to each. There were ten agents in the company at the time of my visit (the agency has since surged in growth). The system assured that every agent was motivated to seek deals for every client on the book, not just for those she had brought into the firm or those she happened to be managing at that moment. The entire firm represented the entire roster of clients. Every agent, moreover, had veto power over the addition to any new client to the firm, assuring that everyone worked unreservedly on behalf of the entire book.

He didn't stop with the compensation structure. An incurable gadgeteer, he hard-wired the old mansion with high-powered Unix workstations and Ethernet cable and installed a state-of-the-art database system that shared every bit of information that every agent entered: what roles the talent was seeking, what movies were casting, which kind of directors each kind of producer was looking for, and so on, a gi- ant brain of the firm reflecting the latest information from every brain connected to it. "Everyone is responsible for data," Barrett explained. "This company is so interlaced that every transaction has value to everyone."

The marquee names of the time—Demi Moore, say, or Jim Carrey— might not have required such guerilla effort. But for every headliner, Hollywood has thousands of actors that require a touch of selling. Around the time of my visit one such actor was Rachael Leigh Cook, a would-be teen star. She was recruited to Metro Talent by an agent named Karen Forman, who assumed the day-to-day responsibility for her dealings. Later, a different agent, Jeff Okin, scored her a role in the Columbia production of *The Babysitters Club*. Yet another agent, Adam Levine, signed her to the Becky Thatcher role in Disney's *Tom and Huck*. Ms. Forman, for her part, landed the girl in *Carpool,* oppo- site Tom Arnold.

It's difficult to describe how radically this system departed from the conventions of Hollywood. Prior to joining Metro Talent, agent Deborah Miller spent fifteen years at the massive William Morris Agency. "I would get information and hold it," she told me. "Information was gold. Here, we all work, literally, for every single client," thereby creating more income for the entire group than they could ever make working at cross-purposes. Another agent, Andy Howard, had spent years at both William Morris and the Hollywood powerhouse of ICM. "I used to go to work with a knot in my stomach every Monday morning," he said. "I used to gag on my toothbrush. This is an adversarial business—and at the big agencies that starts inside the agency."

As Howard spoke, the breeze swayed the white curtains in his office windows facing Wilshire Boulevard. Sunlight bathed his office. People continually traipsed through on their way to their own offices.

"Here," he said, "the whole notion is not 'me' and 'mine.' Part of it is because everybody gets a piece. Everybody here has a stake."

At Home in the Economy

In the shadow of the Great Sphinx at Giza, an anthropologist named Mark Lehner has spent years excavating what appeared to be an ancient bakery. But on closer inspection, the massive operation was a collection of households, each devoted to making bread on a small scale. "Rather than having a large Wonder Bread factory, they did things with a kind of single-loaf method, replicating it many, many times," Lehner, of the University of Chicago, explained. "I am becoming more and more convinced that ancient Egyptian society was a series of households within households, in an embedded pattern. . . . A complex, large-scale society evolved out of the simple household structure."[1] Indeed, "pharaoh" meant "the greatest household." The very word "economics" comes from the Greek *oikonomos,* which meant the management of the household.

Business is older than religion, art, politics, government, and law, but it's not as old as the family. In fact, business was born in the family, through the division of labor among men, women, and children.[2] For virtually all of history, most work was conducted on farms, and most farms were operated by families. In urban life, from ancient Egypt to nineteenth-century New York, most businesses were likewise based in the household.

But in the antiseptic ethos of the industrial era, stigma surrounded family business, as if the involvement of family was somehow unbusinesslike. Family businesses were often thought of as quirky, eccentric, full of childhood neuroses, sibling rivalry, spoiled heirs, and mom-and-pop management—as indeed they often are. Family business was often dismissed as entry-level work for immigrants. In later times, professional people with home-based businesses were quietly discussed as people who couldn't make it in the corporate world.

The disdain for family business reflected a corporate disdain for the family itself. Home life was an unwelcome "distraction"; how could it be anything else when duties at home always threatened to interfere with the mechanics of work? Twenty-five years ago when I was writing about my hometown General Motors operations, a company official blamed menstrual cramps for the shockingly high rates of absenteeism at a wiring operation staffed mainly by women; it had not yet occurred to managers that women phoned in sick because it was the only way anyone could remain at home with a sick kid.

The rift is now healing. Entrepreneurs and employers are rediscovering the natural connection between work and family. More parents work at home, using technology either to extend their reach as entrepreneurs or to economize on time, gasoline, and frustration as corporate employees. In office buildings, warehouses, and factories—some of them, anyway—kids come to the office for lunch, whether the office is in a spare bedroom or a downtown office building. The reunion of family and work life signals a return to what business used to be—in urban retailing at the end of the nineteenth century, village metalworking in the eighteenth century, and family farms throughout history: young children begging for attention, parents pleading "don't touch that," the beginning of informal apprenticeship, instruction by example in the pressures, joys, and morality of business. Anthropologists have long known that work has a completely different meaning—that it is less stressful and preoccupying, more fun—when conducted in homesteads instead of large organizations.[3]

"Our business is all mixed up with our family life," a publisher named Mary Ellen Hammond told me. She and her husband Jim Parham run a company called Milestone Press from the mountains of Almond, North Carolina, publishing three adventure sports guides a year as three-year-old Sidney runs around. Dad handles the business all morning, then hands off to Mom. Whoever's minding Sidney conducts whatever business errands must be run. Sometimes the arrangements are maddening and confining, and overnight travel can be a problem. But the business is solidly in the black. It financed the construction of a home, including a specially designed office. "Above all," Hammond says, "we feel great about the parenting job we're able to do." One can only imagine the kind of work ethic their son will grow up with.

Indeed, the reunion of work and home is only a symptom of a much larger condition: the natural affinity of business and family. The record is convincing. Family businesses innovate at a great rate because they tend to be smaller and less hidebound than bigger companies. They are managed with a legacy in mind, meaning that they do a better job of balancing the interests of the next generation against the outcome of the next quarterly report. They build value much faster than publicly held corporations because they reinvest profits rather than burning them up in dividends and taxes. Family firms also provide greater opportunities for women, though these have been slow in coming.

"Just as families are the building blocks of a stable society, so are family businesses important in building a stable economy," one definitive 1995 study argues.[4] People often cite the high failure rates of family businesses, but these statistics are meaningless: So many family businesses fail simply because so many businesses fail—and because at least 90 percent of all businesses in America are family-controlled.[5] Most of the businesses described in this book are family businesses, not out of any bias in the choosing but because that's what most businesses are. I have only anecdotal evidence to go on, but I suspect that family firms live longer on average than nonfamily partnerships and corporations. The family firm, as *The Economist* has written, is "society's most successful and enduring institution."[6]

What's important to understand is that the family business has become a model for *all* business. The reason is that business, today more than at any time in a century or longer, is built on relationships— the very stuff of which families, too, are made.

Consider, to begin with, the Askew family, whose business, U.S. Aluminate, I briefly introduced in an earlier chapter for its extraordinarily tight, value-creating relationships with vendors and suppliers alike. Why would a family-owned company display such skill at integrating itself into the supply chain of commodity chemicals?

The answer begins with Larry Askew, who graduated from high school and went to work as a pattern maker in Detroit, building wooden gears and other model parts for the machine tools used to make cars. When he and his wife, Sue, began building a family they yearned to live in a top school district, which a craftsman's wages did not permit. So Askew went to work selling commodity chemicals to the plants along the southern shores of the Great Lakes, driving from factory to factory in his car.

On weekends back home in Detroit he and Sue relaxed on a small sailboat on the Detroit River. As their three sons came into the world each was introduced to the water from the moment of birth: David, Tim, and Peter, each born two years apart in the early 1960s. The family began racing as a team, and each son ultimately became expert in a different sailing skill. On a small boat, though, everyone must always be ready to switch into a different job. "We grew up as interchangeable parts," Tim explained. "Sailing is a system where you have to rely on each other." Added David: "No one can be afraid to do someone else's job." Because the Askews weren't rich, the boys could advance to bigger boats and more challenging races only by crewing for other people. "When you crew, you do everything for the owner," Tim said. "We got to see the world as competitive sailors because we were willing to do the scut work other people weren't."

In the early 1980s, meanwhile, with his brood enrolling in college, Larry's sales career took an entrepreneurial turn. Raising $500,000 from a dentist and a raw materials supplier, he set up a small chemical plant in Ashtabula, Ohio, to produce a single chemical for a single customer, years before anyone used the word "outsourcing." During the summers his oldest son, Dave, an engineering student at the University of Michigan, worked to computerize as much of the process as possible. When Dave graduated he joined his father full-time, dashing into the plant to repair a broken motor, whipping on a welding mask, upgrading the local-area network, or doing whatever far-flung tasks the business required, just as if he were crewing a boat.

Tim, also a Michigan graduate, had gone on to earn an M.B.A. at Boston University and to work as a consultant with Peat Marwick. But eventually his older brother, Dave, recruited him to the business as well to help develop new accounts. Tim, in turn, recruited Peter, an anthropology major at Michigan, to join the company and complete the arduous task of writing up every process and procedure conducted in the manufacturing operation. If the founder, Larry, had filled those positions by recruiting from the outside, he never would have selected such an odd mix of backgrounds and skills.

Each of the sons seemed to possess a different piece of his father's head, but each also switched off roles as necessary, just as all of them had in a lifetime of sailing. Dave began designing new plants as well as working as a plant operator himself. Tim took on responsibility for finance as well as sales. Peter became a plant manager as well as the corporate regulatory affairs coordinator. It was unnecessary to isolate their routines in order to stockpile successes or isolate failure, because each came to work every day knowing the boss would automatically give him the benefit of the doubt. As Dave explained, "We just do whatever makes sense." Or as the patriarch said, "We can make any decision in a five-minute phone call."

As the sons dealt with one another, so they managed the company's workforce, which totaled thirty people in four plants by the time of my visit in 1998. Every production worker performed multiple jobs: The truck drivers acted as plant mechanics, the process operators drove trucks, everyone ran forklifts. Such integrated assignments gave workers the opportunity to spot new efficiencies, and because the owners' sons were working alongside the production workers, these ideas were acted on instantly. By watching their father at work, the sons also acquired his sense for integrating closely with customers and suppliers, which explains why, as I discussed in the earlier chapter, the Askews have succeeded in dissolving so many boundaries between themselves and the suppliers and customers. As Tim explained, "We're always trying to make the umbilical cord wider and shorter."

꿍

Family businesses often begin life selling to friends and other family members, customers who look you in the eye as you cross paths in the community or sit down across the Thanksgiving dinner table. This endows family businesses with even more powerful cultures of customer service, further strengthening their value as a model in today's service-oriented commercial landscape.

That was certainly the case in a little Augusta, Georgia, storefront called Aiken Tire Company. The owner, a junior-high dropout named Geddings Osbon, had reared six children by selling and repairing tires.

His son Julian joined him in the business from the age of nine and worked alongside his father almost daily except for his four years at college. "Family, church, business—that was my life growing up," Julian recalls.

One day the father, then fifty-nine, turned to the son and said, "I have this device that helps men deal with impotence." Impotent himself, Geddings, an inveterate tinkerer, had turned his professional knowledge on his own condition, reversing the piston on a tire pump and connecting it to some hardware store piping. By pumping the air from the tube he could create a partial vacuum in his penis, drawing in all the blood necessary for a fully functional erection, which he sustained by rolling a ring from the tube to the base of his penis. With practice and design improvement the device became foolproof. "He had a good feel for vacuums and pressures," Julian would proudly recall.

Some years later the combination of oil price shocks, long-lasting radial tires, and the national tire-service chains caused Aiken Tire to plunge in a way that customer service alone could never prevent. The Osbons needed a new living, and Geddings turned to his "youth equivalent device," as he quaintly called it. Working with his wife and their son Julian, Geddings Osbon began mailing brochures to retirement communities in Florida; because of an anatomically correct line drawing, Geddings was charged by postal inspectors for mailing indecent materials. (He won on appeal.) Even worse, the FDA shut him down for holding out the product as a medical device. But eventually the family won FDA approval, as well as endorsements from Medicare and the Veterans Administration.

As a medical device the product could be sold only by prescription, and building acceptance for such a sensitive product involved battles in which the support of family was essential. When Julian appeared at a convention of urologists one physician snapped, "You belong in a sex show!" For years every publication the family approached to buy advertising—*Reader's Digest,* the *Wall Street Journal,* and others—said no. *Modern Maturity* finally deigned to run an ad so camouflaged with romance it was barely possible to identify what was being advertised. "You're still in love after all these years . . . ," the ad said, with photos of a happy couple advancing through life.

There was a bit of technique in using the device, and with every shipment the company included a twenty-four-hour toll-free line for some coaching. Mother, father, and son all fielded the calls, and Julian carried a beeper because sex—and a call from a desperate customer—might happen at any hour. The three of them were already comfortable providing explicit instructions by phone; Geddings himself was patient number one, after all. But they also learned to tread delicately around the sensitivities of the patients. They were fascinated, for instance, to notice that many customers appeared more comfortable discussing the intricacies of the product with Mrs. Osbon than with either her husband or son. So as Osbon Medical grew, it began hiring additional customer-service call-center staffers, many of them women. The arresting candor and lack of embarrassment among the members of the family quickly made other employees feel comfortable as well in talking to mostly older men about the most intimate aspects of their bodies. "Mr. H—, you can stop pumping once you see your penis rise off the floor of the cylinder . . ."

Geddings Osbon died in 1986. Under Julian's tutelage the company continued pouring everything into the future, as befits a family business with no public investors to satisfy. Osbon Medical paid unusually high salaries and put profits into what Julian called his "growth budget," financing development of a state-of-the-art sales tool the company called its "zone planner," in which field representatives reported on the status of their visits to doctors' offices and received pointers on where to focus their sales efforts. The company also poured funds into the most high-tech customer-service technology available. The Osbon device sold for $395, but as Julian often said, "We give away the device; it's service we're selling."

People in Augusta, a most conservative town better known for green jackets and golf, had once looked askance at the Osbons. But by the time of my visit in 1995 the company was as establishment as the Masters tournament. It had just won the White House small-business exporter-of-the-year award. It had more than two hundred employees, including sixty sales technicians around the country. Julian had become quite the man about town, striding across the street from the former Aiken Tire building to the city's ritziest lunch club wearing a gold lapel pin in the shape of the Osbon tension ring.

Just how important to Osbon's success was its family ownership? Consider what occurred when the family finally sold.

In late 1995 Julian was approached by a company called Urohealth Systems Incorporated, a creature of Wall Street if ever there was one. Urohealth was using its stock to purchase medical device companies all over, ultimately a dozen in all, many dealing with incontinence and gynecological problems. Though Julian owned the majority of the company, his siblings were shareholders and some of them were becoming eager to cash out. Nobody followed developments in the treatment of impotency more closely than Julian, who knew that an impotence remedy called Viagra was in human trials. So he sold the company for roughly $47 million worth of Urohealth stock while remaining at Osbon Medical under contract to the new owners.

It was not a good match.

"A corporate person looks at a business in black-and-white terms," he later explained. "They thought we were selling medical devices. But we were selling services. And that makes human resources so critical." Jobs were eliminated in the interest of cutting costs. Manufacturing was transferred from the Augusta headquarters to California. A particularly harsh setback came when the parent company smashed together the health care plans of several subsidiaries, reducing them to the lowest common denominator—and in the process cutting the level of benefits that Osbon employees had long enjoyed. "They began doing away with things that didn't contribute directly to the bottom line," Julian said. "We had a unique and fragile business. It's sad what they did to the company." (Urohealth told me it respected Julian's views but that it had to manage the business with broader interests in mind.)

Paradoxically, the hysteria over the impotence drug Viagra should have actually been a boon to the business, since Viagra, while inspiring millions of men to seek help for impotence, could not be prescribed to huge numbers of them. Instead, Osbon Medical swooned. But by then Julian had safely cashed out the stock he'd received, using the proceeds to help fund a biotech start-up in cancer research, a hospital services company, a community bank, and the preservation of the oldest continuously operating black church in the South.

‿

A magazine called *Home Office Computing* once interviewed children about sharing their home with a business. To a kid they all expressed gratitude that they didn't roll in from school to an empty house and that mom (or in a few cases, dad) was available when the chips were down. These are right and wonderful reasons for merging work and family life, and the most common reasons why parents choose to work at home.[7]

But they are not the only good reasons. When an employee telecommutes or an entrepreneur turns a home into a headquarters, every day of the year is "take your daughter to work day" (and sons, too, of course). Children who see their parents work not only learn about boundaries but learn about business itself. They see all the frustrations and joys up close and personal. They learn about commitment and service. They see the work ethic in action. It's too soon to know whether the surge of home businesses fostered by technology will inspire more children to follow in their parents' footsteps, but if history is any guide, that's inevitable. Parents were the first mentors, children the first apprentices. The corporate designation "& Sons" is undoubtedly as old as the corporation itself.

And when the family is a healthy one—as many admittedly are not—the passing of the generations signals the perpetuation of a dynasty, as the Koss family reveals.

In 1953 a television repairman in Milwaukee named John Koss took $200 in wedding gifts, drove to Chicago, and bought a pile of second-hand televisions. He returned them to Milwaukee, mounted them on rolling carts, and offered them for rental to hospital patients. With his shop in the family garage, his business and home life were inseparable. The earliest memories of his firstborn, Michael, involved marveling over TV tubes and crawling over TV carts.

Michael also vaguely recalls his father one day coming into a supply of three-inch television speakers for which he had no use. Rather than throw them away the old man attached them to a set of chamois ear pads he had pulled out of an old flight helmet. He mounted the padded speakers on either end of an outstretched length of hanger wire, pulled them over his head, and plugged them into a stereo "hi-fi." They were the world's first stereo headphones, and Koss Corporation, still a world leader in the product, was born.

Even in grade school, Michael Koss dreamed of a career with his father. He scratched out the name on his father's business card and wrote in his own. In sixth grade he acted as photographer at the company's annual meeting. The jazz keyboard virtuoso Oscar Petersen dined at the Koss home, and Michael had the chance to sit in on endorsement meetings with Sammy Davis, Jr., and the rock group Blood, Sweat and Tears (which horrified the elder Koss as the first musical act ever to request his payment for their endorsement). Frank Sinatra, Jr., joined the company's board of directors. On his way to school each morning Michael listened to his father dictating business memos into a recorder.

If Koss Corporation had remained a cottage business instead of growing into a public company with an international product, nepotism never would have been an issue. But Michael's mother said if he had any hope of being taken seriously he would always have to work twice as hard and spend twice as long moving up. So he began his career at the company behind a broom. As a teen he spent summers inhaling solder smoke on the assembly line.

Life was a bit different for the second Koss son, John Jr.—Johnny—who was three years Michael's junior. Johnny had no idea the family name was becoming a global brand until his second-grade teacher introduced herself as a company shareholder. Yet Johnny felt very much a part of his father's life, working, from boyhood, as the founder's regular Saturday-morning caddie. In time Johnny learned not only the sport of golf but the art of selling, since it was on the golf course that the old man did some of his best dealmaking.

Although he was making no conscious effort to do so, the father was sharing part of himself with each son. "We always competed at different things," Johnny would later explain. "I could be good at sports. . . . Michael was more introverted, always up in his room, reading." The two sons intended to study business in college but their father discouraged them. Instead, he urged, "study people." So Michael majored in anthropology, absorbed in the science of how the brain processes art (an interest undoubtedly nurtured by a lifetime under the headphones). Johnny took up English. And when they both finally landed at the company full-time in the late 1970s, the brothers received much encouragement but no entitlement. Michael took a marketing job in London, Johnny a sales territory on the West Coast.

Oddly, misfortune hastened their ascent. In 1979, with the company in a downturn, the founder relented to the conventional wisdom holding that entrepreneurs could not handle growth, turning the top leadership positions over to "professional management." Unfortunately, the purported professionals brought aboard heavy debt loads, which John Koss, like most family business owners, had always eschewed. They built up a vast bureaucratic empire, something else that fast-and-loose entrepreneurs usually succeed in resisting. The hired hands added new product lines in which the company had no experience and for which no one else in the company had much passion. Stereo distributors were dismayed that a company named Koss was no longer headed by someone named Koss. Soon, the company was stumbling badly.

John Koss returned to the helm for the tragic duty of putting his company into bankruptcy proceedings. The resulting housecleaning was so severe that Michael and Johnny Koss were quickly swept into the headquarters operation; there was no one else left to help their father lead the company.

Michael bore deeply into the company's cost structure—this was the family's fortune, after all, as well as the shareholders'. He also moved to reverse a slide in quality—that was his name emblazoned on the side of every headphone. (He accomplished both objectives by tearing apart the assembly line and creating cellular work teams, long before doing so had become fashionable.) During the reorganization Michael felt firsthand the sting of the bankers when the family asked them to settle for less. "Do you know what this will do to your mother?" one banker asked him. "This will kill your mother." Johnny, meanwhile, threw himself into battling against Sony, which had overtaken Koss as the market leader.

Reaching his early sixties, John Koss was once again ready to turn over control. As family members, Michael and Johnny didn't qualify as "professional managers," but nobody had spent more time in the business and nobody had demonstrated so much commitment to its future. Michael became the president and chief executive officer, a tall, rather imperious figure in a bow tie and suspenders. Johnny became the vice president of sales, far more casual, festooning his office with golfing awards. "I sell the stuff and Michael figures out how to make money on it," Johnny says. "I don't have this ego thing. Was it unfair? There's a certain level of responsibility he's good at and certain gut-wrenching things I'm not good at."

In a business driven by brand names, nepotism sells. "That's our name on the door," Johnny says. "We play on that. Growing up, we had the knowledge and the philosophy of the business built into us. We don't have to argue about business philosophy. That's the way we are, and we got that from Dad." Notably Koss was feted in the *Wall Street Journal*'s popular "Work and Family" column when the company's vice president of finance, Sujata Sachdeva, relocated to Houston after her husband changed jobs. Michael Koss took the then-radical step of keeping her in the position from a remote locale, where she stayed in touch with teleconferencing equipment. Michael was besieged with disbelief. "You did *what?*" people asked. Yet the experiment worked so well that when his chief designer had to move out of state, Koss repeated the arrangement.

I learned a lot in my time at Koss. One obvious lesson is that owners and their families lead with a passion that "professional managers" can rarely muster over someone else's creation. I also learned a truism now regaining acceptance after being long-forgotten: that healthy families make healthy businesses.

∽

Today, women create more new businesses than men.[8] They still face obstacles that men do not share, particularly the larger responsibility for children, owing both to biological inevitability and to lingering cultural reflexes. They also face less access to capital, though this difference is diminishing drastically (while capital itself becomes a smaller factor in business). And although in a politically correct era few are willing to say so, women, as a group, manage businesses differently than men. The exceptions are rampant, of course, but women tend to acknowledge the family needs of their employees more than men, whose jobs have traditionally required them to keep the problems of home at greater distance. Culture more often reserves relationship-managing duties to women, skills with greater business value today.

For better and worse, women business owners also tend to maintain businesses at a smaller size than men to a degree for which their unequal access to capital can't entirely explain. Partly this reflects the choice of many women to work at home, a limitation on the size of a business. Partly it reflects the preference that many female entrepreneurs exhibit for nonmanufacturing businesses, where the economies of scale are less apt to apply. Women may also favor small business because they have not experienced the cultural conditioning in which many men equate size—the size of a business, that is—to achievement.

Consider, for one, Leni Joyce, who grew up with textiles in her blood. At the dawn of the twentieth century her father, Nathan Cohen, left Lithuania for the immigrant enclave of Lowell, Massachusetts, where he established a company called Suffolk Knitting. Nat, as everyone knew him, was a pioneer in the use of pile fabrics to make linings, fake fur, and stuffed animals. By the time his daughter Leni went to work at Suffolk Knitting, the mill had grown to a million square feet inside a series of red brick buildings. She loved everything about the place.

Leni Joyce (her married name) still clearly recalls the city fathers of Dixie trying to entice her father into moving the factory south, promising him cheap nonunion labor, tremendous tax breaks, and even a free mansion in which his family could live. But Nat's wife, a strong-willed Polish immigrant, would not consider moving, and Nat, for his part, could barely contemplate the thought of turning his immigrant laborers into the street. He remained stubbornly in Massachusetts, his costs climbing, his competitors closing in. By the early 1970s Suffolk Knitting had failed.

Though Leni Joyce had moved into interior design, it was far from her first calling. She would visit the shuttered brick mill, swearing she could still smell the wet wool and hear the Irish and Russian voices echoing from the inside. "I would stand there and cry," she later said. She kept alive her love of the business in the only way she could think of: by enrolling in weaving classes at Boston College, sitting at looms alongside students less than half her age.

It was the early 1970s, and the psychedelic era had not yet run its course. Joyce marveled at the heavy textures and bright colors of the fabrics her classmates created. Soon she was making outlandish material of her own, dyeing her own mohair on the top of her stove, hanging the wet yarn, burning her hands, and ruining her kitchen. Before long she had installed a hand loom in her basement, a big, old contraption like something out of pre-Luddite England or Colonial America, weaving ever-more-unlikely combinations: mohair with chenille, for instance, or wool with suede. It was pure pleasure—but was it a business? "Make it beautiful," her father told her from his deathbed in 1979, "and there will always be a market."

In fact, when Joyce showed her fabrics on Seventh Avenue they caused a minor sensation, winning her orders from a couple of the haute couture houses. Her success inspired her to buy some massive old power looms of the kind her father once owned. Bigger production runs meant lower costs per yard, after all. But it was an economically futile step. No one had made a living running power looms in the Northeast for at least a generation's time. A bigger operation only meant bigger losses. In addition, Joyce had hired a production foreman to run the power operation and he died unexpectedly. She abandoned the machines after a brief run. "You reach a juncture where you have to go forward or back," she recalled. "I went back."

About that time, she was doing some interior design work at an architectural firm when one of the partners mentioned that he needed new upholstery on the seats of his private jet. (Airplane seats, even on private planes, endure unusually heavy wear.) She showed the client some of the heavier fabrics she had produced on her hand loom. He loved them, and soon she had an order in hand. Before long she was striking off samples containing a dozen different thread weights—a variety of tensions that a mechanical loom could never handle—and slinging them in a bag over her shoulder to business-aircraft trade shows. A few more orders came in, and a new business called Leni's Incorporated was born.

Skeptics, as you would imagine, abounded. "You can't do hand labor in America!" her friends cried. To field a stable workforce in the mid-1980s she would have to pay yearly salaries in the $25,000 range, plus benefits. She would have to purchase yarns in the smallest and least economical lots. She would have to pay through the nose for worker's compensation insurance, as Massachusetts, absurdly, put her hand looms in the same category as power looms. "You'll never make it," people said. But it turned out that in airplanes costing a few million dollars, customers didn't worry too much about paying $250 a yard for seating upholstery when it was the most durable material that could be made, particularly when a small shop such as Leni's Incorporated could customize an order of any size. Business rolled in. Joyce moved the business into an old printing plant in Watertown, along the Mass Pike just outside Boston—a miniature version of the red brick building that her father's business had once occupied.

Like her father, Joyce hired highly motivated immigrant workers, only this time it was a new generation from Cambodia and Vietnam. Most of her hires were women, and many had babies while working at Leni's Incorporated. ("Weaving is a lot of exercise," Joyce told me at one point. "They looked wonderful during their pregnancies.") As the babies came Joyce disassembled her massive hand looms and had them reassembled in the basements or family rooms of her employees' homes, where they could weave with a child at their feet. Ultimately four of her nine weavers were working full-time at home. This arrangement cost Joyce practically nothing but motivated her workers and above all kept them from leaving. Another employee, Kerry Hopkins, also once wove for the company at home. Now that her child is older Hopkins works as the mill foreman, leaving whenever necessary for soccer matches and the like. "Leni was doing this long before it was trendy," Hopkins says. "Having a woman employer makes a difference. She's a mother. She understands."

Joyce is not afraid to be herself regardless of whether doing so plays into people's stereotypes. She brings coffee cakes to work. Some of her customers told me that she regularly sends them boxes of homemade chocolate-chip cookies, a personal touch of which no marketing consultant would even begin to conceive. "I'm older; I have almost a mother image," she told me. "There is a warmth in this business."

A critical moment arrived in the early 1990s. The same recession that was causing corporate America to jettison managers was also causing it to abandon private aircraft. Joyce urgently wanted to keep together her crew of a dozen weavers to await the boom she knew would return, but the capital of the company was quickly depleting. Joyce turned to her son, Mark Albion, explaining that her only way of surviving was raiding the small estate she had hoped one day to pass on. "Mark," she said, "I am gambling your inheritance." Albion, a Harvard Business School professor who would become a force in a group called Business for Social Responsibility, recognized that his mother's identity was vastly more important than any inheritance. "Go for it, Mom," he replied.

And when the economy recovered and the business-aircraft market soared anew, Leni's Incorporated was intact and ready to reap its reward. By 1997 Joyce was up to eighteen employees. On the day I visited the shop, it was turning out a garish purple fabric laced with gold Lurex, created precisely to the specifications of a Saudi prince who was spiffing up his 757. "She weaves at home. She weaves at the shop," marveled Karen Cooper, an interior design specialist at Gulfstream Aerospace, which makes many of the world's costliest executive jets. "It's all-encompassing with her. I think she's a genius."

If so, Joyce says, it is because weaving is her tie to family. "My commitment to the business is tremendous because it is the only thing left from my family," she says. "It's me. It's part of my heritage. I do this because it's what's in my blood." Funny, isn't it? she asks. "I had to fight to win what was there for me all along."

❧

The rise of women in business has had another important effect: It has validated spouses as business partners. This trend, too, signals a return to a natural way of doing business. For almost the entirety of economic history, spouses worked together—their business, of course, was farming. Today, as business and family life reconverge, many couples begin businesses together without a second's thought of how unusual this practice was even half a generation ago.

Is it risky for a marriage to stray into business? Is it risky for a business to involve a marriage? Yes to both, of course—but the risk of disagreement is present in any business relationship. Most corporate business breakups I've seen involved no spouses (or for that matter relations of any kind). Neither does divorce often involve a business. Special problems can erupt when business and family merge (more of which presently) but there is no reason why they must. And the potential benefits greatly outweigh the potential risks. Spouses bring the kind of trust and commitment into a collaboration that other partners might take years to develop.

That much was clear when I went to Sikorski Memorial Airport in Bridgeport, Connecticut, to investigate the story of an air-charter operation called Flight Services Group. The founder was Dave Hurley, an uncommonly handsome man of fifty-six when I met him—a former champion wrestler who had taken college classes at age thirteen. Once, in 1972, while working as an aircraft sales executive, he was delivering a small jet to a customer when the engines flamed out due to a mechanical failure. Hurley glided over Corning, New York, until he found a place to land, narrowly clearing some utility wires and putting down in a two thousand-foot-long field behind a Holiday Inn.

Flying a plane does not involve a small set of simple rules; it involves a large set of fairly complex rules. After starting his own charter business Hurley's passion for rules was such that he hired a licensed lawyer as his chief pilot and put every pilot he hired through many times the required training. He also conducted much of the flying himself, an astonishing two thousand hours a year, more than any other pilot on his system, impressing his corporate and entertainment customers with his snap-to attentiveness and his explicit adherence to procedure. Among his most committed clients was the pop singer Carly Simon, a white-knuckle flyer who refused to travel with anyone else. "He's one of the most attractive people I've ever met in every way," she once explained. "He's completely comfortable with himself, which makes you feel he's completely comfortable with the equipment." In addition, rich investors and big companies entrusted him to maintain and rent out their Learjets, Cessnas, and others—planes worth $3 million to $7 million each, renting for roughly $1,000 to $2,000 an hour.

But Hurley's adherence to the rules of flying was so complete that he was incapable of establishing rules for the business side of the operation. This failure was masked by the booming business Flight Services experienced ferrying investment bankers from Wall Street in the takeover heydays of the 1980s. Instead of establishing "min specs" as a boundary for his managers, Hurley was content with no specs.

Then the recession of the early 1990s hit, and the bottom fell out of Flight Services' business—which is what brought his wife, Johanna Hurley, into the business.

She was every bit his equal in terms of energy and appearance, and like Dave she was driven with entrepreneurial spirit. But while rearing three kids she never dreamed of going into business, contenting herself with painting, organizing community events, even co-authoring a book of humor (called *Cooking for Nitwits*). She and Dave did discuss his business regularly, and periodically he would invite her to apply her organizing or artistic talents to one business project or another, but she declined every entreaty, caught up in the widely held view that business and marriage don't mix. She prized the egalitarian qualities of their marriage: He cooked, she paid the bills, neither dominated. Joining Flight Services meant she would be working *for* her husband, an idea she simply couldn't imagine.

But as Flight Services went into a deep and serious stall in the recession, Johanna saw the effects up close and personal. The livelihood of her family, the happiness of her husband, and the future of many other families were at stake. Each night Dave dragged himself home deeply depressed, bearing a new tale of woe. The low point came when the company was evicted from its office suite for nonpayment of rent, forcing the administrative operations to crowd into the corner of the company's airplane hangar. Layoffs and cutbacks abounded. And Johanna recognized it was time for her to help, if only temporarily.

She showed up to pack boxes, move files, and pitch in where needed. Her unpaid presence signaled that the rescue of Flight Services was not just a commitment of Dave Hurley but of the Hurley family. She also hoped her presence might help to sustain her husband's mood and, when he was off flying, to help buck up the morale of everyone else. Because the company was desperate for revenue she also thought she might look for ways to marshal her skills to the company's benefit— starting a newsletter for corporate clients, for instance, or attempting a direct-mail campaign.

But not everyone appreciated her presence, least of all the chief financial officer, Hugh Regan. The last thing he thought the boss needed was the distraction of a wife or the introduction of some new marketing program. His wariness worsened when Johanna confronted him with pointed financial questions. Was it true the company was losing $70,000 a month? What did that mean for the business? What was the solution? Hugh Regan found her questions impertinent; Johanna Hurley found his resistance arrogant. On one occasion the two simply glared at one another. But Johanna kept asking questions and requesting documents. And before long Regan realized that she not only stood her ground but cared deeply about the business as a business—more deeply, in fact, than any employee could. Perhaps, Regan thought, she might become his ally in an important mission.

In his role as finance chief Regan had been campaigning for months to install a system of financial reporting to make individual managers more accountable for the performance of the assets under their control. But Dave Hurley couldn't be bothered with the idea. As much as he valued the rules of flying, he resisted the creation of rules on the business side. So Regan began to think that if the owner couldn't be persuaded to take this step, perhaps the owner's wife could. If Hurley wouldn't listen to him, maybe he'd listen to her.

Johanna could immediately see the finance man's point. The company indeed needed better financial reporting, a few "min specs." So she began asking her husband probing questions. Was he following the money closely enough? How could he be sure that revenues were covering costs? Was he safeguarding the future of his employees? With her persuasion Dave finally assented to the installation of the new accounting system. Without dampening the free-spirited culture of the business, the new system immediately began providing the feedback necessary to identify winning moves from losers. Before long, Flight Services Group had soon pulled out of its stall. By 1997 it was extremely profitable and pulling in $20 million in annual revenue.

"Dave went through a metamorphosis," Hugh Regan told me. "He began thinking strategically." Or as Dave Hurley himself put it, "Hugh and Johanna forced me to become a CEO."

Johanna remained with the company as the recovery continued, launching precisely the kind of marketing campaigns she had been thinking about. She continued feeling conspicuous as the owner's wife and for a time even resisted answering calls from the outside for fear she would have to give her name. Flying and maintaining aircraft was far too sophisticated a business, she thought, to permit even a taste of mom-and-pop flavor. But in time her wariness diminished. She could see that her marketing efforts were accelerating revenue growth. Like her husband, she brought a level of personal commitment to the business that few outsiders could ever give. So she resolved to stay, so long as she abided by, well, her own small set of simple rules.

First, she would never act wifely at work. Doing so would have a corrosive effect on her relations with other employees. "I have a position here," she says. "I have a role, and it's not wife." Second, she says, "For my own dignity and pride, if I can't add value on a day-to-day basis, I'm out of here." To that end she seeks a performance review from Hugh Regan, the finance man who was once her adversary, every six months. And most important, she resolved that if work issues ever interfered with her home life, she would quit immediately. "I put twenty-five years of marriage first," she says.

In her case, however, there seemed little risk of this. People do behave differently at work and at home, of course, but rarely do they become fundamentally different people. Getting along in one venue is a pretty good signal that people can get along in another. And as in the case of Koss Corporation, healthy family relationships usually lead to healthy business relationships.

Usually, that is, but not always.

⁖

There's no escaping the fact that a family business is a system consisting of two systems, and these systems are vastly different even though the people occupying them are not. Though both involve trust and teamwork, families thrive on emotion and businesses on rationality. To the extent that business tends toward the collegial, families tend toward the totalitarian.

Academic studies and a wealth of anecdotal evidence suggest some of the most inevitable clashes: in-laws against each other, cousins versus cousins, fathers versus children, siblings versus siblings. "A family is a family, a business is a business, and the unfinished business of the family can too easily muck up the company," says Ira Bruck, who runs the Family Business Center at the University of Massachusetts. Often, adds Richard Narva, who once worked in his father's shoe company and who now helps family business owners cope with conflict, family businesses can become, for good and ill alike, "stages on which the dramas of families are enacted," as Narva himself discovered in working with a client called Heat-Fab Incorporated.

If I make any valid arguments about the constructive nature of business in this book, Lloyd Green embodies the best of them. He never got past high school, but he became skilled at operating the lathe in his father's machine shop. Later Lloyd and his wife Millie brought up five kids, then took in several foster kids. Through the years the two of them built their small manufacturing company, Heat-Fab, in their hometown of Greenfield, Massachusetts.

Heat-Fab made metal chimney liners and stovepipes on fabricating equipment of Lloyd's invention. Millie divided her time between the shop and the office. "You're never alone in a business of this type," Lloyd explained when I visited in early 1997. "You got your relations to your suppliers, your distributors. It's extremely important to do what you say." At the same time, he said, "Being an employer is an important part of what we've always wanted to be. I feel good that there's some forty people working here who support families."

Their oldest son, Harold, who was thirty-nine at the time of my visit, had worked with his parents for years, forming a front-office bond so tight they barely had to speak. "We did it all—made it, packed it, shipped it," Lloyd recalled. In the 1980s the business grew to about $3 million a year and held there steadily. Lloyd eventually threw himself into developing a new design for a water heater flue, a product he hoped would one day launch a new growth phase for the company.

Then, in 1992, the three of them—Lloyd, Millie, and son Harold—became five. Another of the Green children, Holly Long, and her husband, Ron Long, were both downsized out of solid careers with Digital Equipment in Atlanta and came to Greenfield to work in the Heat-Fab office while seeking permanent work elsewhere. But after leaving a major corporation with such a bitter taste in their mouths, they loved working in a small business. And with Lloyd's major new product line in the works, Heat-Fab was on the verge of requiring additional management anyway. So they stayed on.

It was a cheerful, garrulous family in which grandkids were revered and occasions were shared—but in the office tensions soon became evident. Harold, the firstborn, was suddenly sharing authority with a sister and brother-in-law who had been absent for many of the struggles in building the business. The past intruded: The sassy teenager that Harold remembered was suddenly contacting his customers. Holly for her part was hurt that the supportive big brother of her youth could be so critical. "Suddenly I'm back in little sister and daughter mode instead of being an experienced business person with a brain," Holly would recall. Ownership issues heightened the tensions: Holly had been assured a piece of the business, but her parents, preoccupied with new-product development and other distractions, had not gotten around to formalizing their plans. "We weren't part of the business other than being employees," the son-in-law Ron would recall.

These anxieties—plain to all, but never fully discussed—elevated minor disagreements into proxies for major fights. "Who lost that invoice?" began to sound like "I can't trust you, can I?" The parties paired off behind closed doors—Ron and Holly in her private office, Harold and his mother in the accounting section out front. Lloyd Green did his best to smooth things over and act as go-between. "What communication there was would go through him," Holly said.

Then, in 1995, the peacemaker was blindsided by cancer.

He was diagnosed with multiple myeloma—"no known cure," the medical literature says unequivocally—and entered an experimental treatment program at Baystate Medical Center in Springfield, Massachusetts. The illness intensified the business conflict, not only because of the founder's absence but because of everyone else's grief. "Emotions were just amazingly through the roof," Ron Long says. Soon, mother and daughter came to sword's point over an insinuation that Holly had purposely fouled up some paperwork. Holly stormed out, vowing that she and Ron were gone for good. It was a loss for which no one was eager. The new products were approaching completion and going through the arduous review process at Underwriters Laboratories. "It would have been a bad thing for them to leave, unquestionably," Harold recognized.

Ravaged by illness and treatment alike, Lloyd Green called in help from the aforementioned Richard Narva, a lawyer who works with a psychotherapist in his family-business consulting practice, known as Genus Resources. Narva and his partner began driving to Greenfield from the Boston area to meet with the parties. Holly and Ron agreed to stick around to see what counseling accomplished.

From the start Narva made one thing clear: that he considered the business itself to be his client. This helped open a small patch of common ground. But it also began to send a message that a business is a real, concrete thing whose success and failure can be guided and measured. Unlike a family, a business is not an ethereal collection of emotions. "The business is neutral," Narva's therapist partner, Tom Davidow, would explain. "It just exists." Heat-Fab was not the same as the Green family, regardless of who had which responsibilities and who held the share certificates. Heat-Fab was forty employees, each with his own family. It was customers all over America, who depended on its products. It was the accumulated genius of its founder, reflected in a host of homegrown manufacturing machines and in a new breakthrough product to which he had given the last three years of his life.

So with the patriarch gravely ill, the family members moved to resolve their individual frustrations according to what was best for Heat-Fab. They came to realize that a business—any business, family-managed or otherwise—sometimes requires snap judgments that might sting in another setting; thus Holly learned that she should not take her brother's criticisms so personally. They came to realize ownership was not just a business issue but a matter of personal finance, so Lloyd and Millie formally brought Holly and her husband into the ownership arrangement. All such grievances were aired, though not all were immediately resolved.

Indeed, there were still some issues on the table when Lloyd Green underwent a harrowing, debilitating, long-shot bone marrow transplant in March 1996. The following morning, Harold met with a potential customer for the newly completed venting system Lloyd had created. The customer was willing to commit to $2 million in orders a year—if Heat-Fab was sure it could deliver. The future was at stake, not only the family's but the company's. "We had to know that day whether we could work together," Harold recalls. For the sake of the business and all it represented, they agreed to gear up for the huge order. A second shift was quickly added. Harold secured a critical alloy supply and the necessary letters of credit. The work pace pushed lingering differences into the background. A big step forward came when the counselors convinced everyone to tear down the physical walls between them, turning the front office into an open bullpen in which everyone could see and hear everyone else working like mad, erasing any doubts about anyone else's commitment or competence. Heat-Fab's 1996 sales nearly doubled to $6 million. "It's unbelievable how far we've come," Holly told me.

The greater miracle was Lloyd Green's survival. The transplant was a success. After a few grave weeks he was soon feeling stronger, his hair and nails growing back, assuring him a place in the medical literature as a survivor of the incurable. On the day of my visit everyone was all atwitter: Holly was in labor with her first child. And everyone was working together. "I don't know what made it happen any more than I know how the chemotherapy and transplant worked," a beaming Lloyd told me. "All I know is I'm sitting here today with my sales up and my family happy."

CHAPTER
10

"All My Sons"

〰

In 1947, America was still celebrating its victory in World War II when a young Arthur Miller opened his play *All My Sons* on Broadway. It told the story of Joe Keller, who had built a prosperous aerospace company by cutting corners on wartime production, delivering engine cylinder heads he knew to be cracked. Keller's greed caused the failure of a number of planes, and the death of their pilots.

In the climactic scene, Joe Keller learns that his son Larry, himself a pilot, had volunteered for a suicide mission after learning of his father's criminality. Overwhelmed with contrition, Joe Keller informs his wife he will turn himself in to the police. She begs him not to go. "Larry was your son, too," she implores him. "You know he'd never tell you to do this."

"Sure, he was my son," Keller answers. "But I think to him, they were all my sons. And I guess they were, I guess they were." With that Joe Keller puts a bullet through his head.

Of all the boundaries that concern economic life, none is blurrier than the separation of business and social interest. For many years, business drew this line brightly. Executives equated what was ethical with what was legal. Corporate conscience was equal to corporate compliance. Displays of social concern were segregated as acts of special consideration—conducting a United Way drive in the corporate cafeteria, say, or bankrolling a pet project of the chairman's wife. These acts, though often generously spirited, were carefully controlled so as not to rob the one, true beneficiary of the business, the shareholder. Some business people persist in thinking that even a trace amount of such giving is pure theft. My favorite foil, "Chainsaw Al" Dunlap, claims that corporate leaders steal from their shareholders even when serving on philanthropic boards. "Corporations become woefully inadequate when CEOs think they are great social messiahs," he says. (Just for grins, I checked out the four executives that Dunlap publicly identified as his models of perfection: the late Robert Goizueta of Coca-Cola, Michael Eisner of Disney, Bill Gates of Microsoft, and Jack Welch of GE. It turned out that Eisner served on seven philanthropic boards and Goizueta six. Gates sat on one. Welch, it's true, served on none.)

The "either-or" era is now coming to an end, signaling a return to business at its most natural, least artificial state. Like competition and cooperation, like diversity and unity, like freedom and control, business and society are two parts of a single system: Like Abbott and Costello, Microsoft and Intel, or Lennon and McCartney, neither would be much without the other. "Business does not stand apart but is an integral piece of the total community ecosystem," says William Frederick of Pitt, who founded the study of business and society many years ago. "Their fates are as intertwined as the doubled helical strands of DNA."[1] Nearly fifty years ago Maslow put it this way: "Good managers and good enterprises and good products and good communities and good states are all conditions of one another."[2]

I'm not suggesting that selfish human nature has changed in the space of half a generation (although scientists now recognize that it can and does change quite rapidly). But some important elements of economic culture have changed. The pressures of global competition and the accompanying waves of "creative destruction," as the economist Joseph Schumpeter called them, force business to operate on merit and objectivity rather than ego and hubris. Meanwhile, breathtaking advances in productivity have moved all of Western society a full step higher on Maslow's hierarchy of needs (and perhaps a half step higher in Asia and Latin America; we can only hope the same for Africa soon). By having more of our immediate, lower-level needs more readily satisfied, we, as entrepreneurs, executives, and employees, can begin to concern ourselves with our longer-term place in a larger society.

Another important change involves the scope of our awareness as businesspeople. We have discovered just how much everything in business, like everything in nature, is driven by the creative cycle of action, feedback, and synthesis. As new technologies widen our field of vision, we absorb more feedback and behave differently as a result. The printed word created the community of interests by which nations were made. Real-time reportage made possible by the telegraph created the "immediacy of participation in the existence of others," as McLuhan wrote, inspiring the crusades of Florence Nightingale, Charles Dickens, and Harriet Beecher Stowe.[3] By the time people were inured to the effects of wire-service dispatches, along came televised sights and sounds from Selma and Saigon, rallying the American public behind the civil rights movement and the antiwar effort. The first distant photograph of earth, taken from Apollo VIII, is widely credited with helping to galvanize the environmental movement.

Today our new tools include the computer, through which we can, for instance, identify patterns in global climate change once hidden from view. Our instruments measure the presence of toxins in parts per trillion rather than mere parts per billion. The ubiquity of the media lens, though often distorting social problems to the point of grotesquerie, exposes everyone to the pressures of inner-city life, the horrors of dysfunctional family life, and other stubborn nemeses. As we learn of new problems we invent new answers, if usually a step behind. DNA synthesizers hold out the promise of reducing cancer; fuel-cell technology may drastically reduce use of fossil fuels.

I have also argued that demographic forces account for new business values, such as the rise of women (many of them mothers) to positions of economic influence. The values of Generation X also have a profound influence. Vanessa Kirsch, formerly an assistant to pollster Peter Hart, was shocked when a purportedly scientific survey by the firm suggested an image of Gen-Xers as self-centered slackers. Kirsch left the firm and set out in pursuit of the truth. First she traveled the U.S. and was astonished at the displays of empathy and citizenship everywhere she turned (particularly in places like Silicon Valley, where young people, it must be noted, can afford to be empathetic). Then she and her husband, a Harvard-trained lawyer named Alan Khazei, conducted a yearlong tour of the world in which they interviewed four hundred leaders of all kinds in twenty countries. Big government, they found almost everywhere, was being supplanted by "big citizenship." Kirsch now runs a venture capital firm in Boston called New Profit Incorporated, which invests capital from wealthy, mostly young, technology entrepreneurs in "socially conscious" businesses.

What's significant is not whether businesspeople are giving more—though the anecdotal evidence is impressive, as witnessed by Ted Turner's $1 billion gift to the United Nations and other boxcar-size donations from the new millionaires of Silicon Valley. Today the quality of giving is also different—in a way that reflects a closer union between business and society. Pioneering businesses provide not only jobs but meaning, fulfillment, and self-esteem to employees. These businesses don't simply train but educate, taking over at the inadequate point at which the public schools leave off. They use technology to cut costs not just so investors will earn higher profits but so consumers will enjoy higher living standards. To these leaders, business is not merely a living. It is even more than an expression of identity. Through nothing more complicated than an honest attempt to economize and create value, business, they realize, is a way of making a better world for themselves and for their businesses. Ted Turner's billion-dollar benevolence, though grand, will do less on behalf of world freedom and economic progress than the news broadcasts that his CNN beams to the Third World by satellite.

Business, after all, has become the dominant institution on earth. As recently as the 1970s most anyone would have attributed this position to government, but business has overtaken the role in no small part through default. In addition to its shrinking in sheer economic proportions (not in all countries, but most), government has been discredited as a source of innovation and moral leadership. Politicians command a smaller following than talk-show hosts, statesmen hold less sway than sports figures. "If this century proves one thing," says Peter Drucker, a trenchant observer of all society, "it is the futility of politics."[4] Even civic duty, once a bedrock value of both parties, has been corroded by partisanship. When the Democratic White House conducted a summit on volunteerism in 1997, the conservative talk-show host Rush Limbaugh growled that "citizen service is a repudiation of the principles upon which our country was based. . . . We are all here for ourselves."[5] Surely he could benefit from a copy of Patrick Henry's call to arms.

Into this leadership void steps business. Business now accounts for virtually every breakthrough in technology, including medicine.

Business is responsible for most of the innovation in leadership and process design. Business alone is leading the revolution in customer service. Cynics may attribute any newfound public spiritedness in business as a response to economic pressures of the era; idealists may think that business is inherently benign, and that by shedding its Newtonian values business is again showing its true colors. I submit that both views are correct. Business is simply realigning itself with the timeless values, incentives, needs, and rewards of humankind.

Business is part of society. Society is part of business. They co-evolve, in the sense that each changes the other—more often for the better these days than before, as I hope my final few stories suggest.

✑

Growing up in Cleveland, Eric Johnson wasn't much of a student, but he knew how to make money. He had barely reached high school when he launched his first business: breeding Siamese fighting fish for tropical fish dealers. He opened a professional photo studio. He went to Morehouse College in Atlanta, but dropped out in his senior year to become a filmmaker. He worked in a film lab in Los Angeles but with no connections and no union card he spent seven years failing to break into cinematography. Returning to Cleveland, he ran a remodeling business and moonlighted as a barber to make ends meet. For a time he worked as a special-education classroom assistant in the Cleveland public schools, where his mother, Gwen, spent twenty-five years as a business teacher and guidance counselor.

In the early 1990s Gwen's mother (Eric's grandmother) could no longer bathe or care for herself in other ways. Medicare provided coverage for home health care services, but the Johnsons were maddened and frustrated by poor service. Being undressed and bathed by a stranger brings out the vulnerability in anyone, and the constant turnover of personnel meant the old woman could never forge a comfortable, trusting relationship. In time the Johnsons, who were black, could see that they faced an additional problem: Many of the best agencies and nurses viewed the inner city as unclean and unsafe—a not altogether untrue image—and they resisted going into minority-populated neighborhoods. Other African-American families faced an additional burden: the presence of drug and alcohol problems in their households, often involving the patient. The toughest cases in home health care existed in the inner city.

This struck Eric as a screaming business opportunity. His mother, by then retired from the school system, readily joined him. They combined their first names, Gwendolyn and Eric, to call the company Geric Home Health Care Incorporated.

While Gwen completed the ghastly paperwork required by Medicare and other authorities, Eric hired a few nurses and began selling to hospitals, nursing homes, mental health agencies, and others who arranged at-home medical services for people. With no track record in an industry full of sleaze and charlatans, the only way he could get a foot in the door was with an arresting pitch: "Give us the cases nobody else will take." They got them: quadriplegics, MS patients, people on ventilators, cases where alcohol and drugs mixed with paralysis or terminal illness; referrals in rodent- or lice-infested homes; neighborhoods with police tape in evidence. But the company quickly fell victim to its early success. As more contracts came in Geric couldn't begin to recruit the licensed practical nurses, certified nursing assistants, and registered nurses it needed to serve the demand. Qualified caregivers were in short supply everywhere, but Geric faced the additional and all-too-familiar hurdle of resistance to working in the inner city. Suburban nurses of all colors said no thanks.

As they pondered their dilemma Gwen and Eric came to the somewhat startling discovery that the answer was in their midst, in the very neighborhoods they had so much difficulty serving. The answer was creating a workforce within the inner city, putting "neighbors to work helping neighbors," as Gwen explained. Or as Eric would put it, "We hire from the 'hood to serve the 'hood."

This was a masterstroke. Here, it turned out, was a pool of potential employees sharing Geric's vision without even knowing of the company's existence. The city, after all, was full of experienced caregivers. They were mothers. Though young, many in their teens, they had learned overnight the meaning of one human's complete dependence on another. In addition many already had informal experience in elder care; inner-city Cleveland, like many urban areas, had seen a generation of African-Americans decimated by drugs and crime. Straddling this lost generation, young women cared for infirm grandparents as well as their own children. And while many of these mothers were getting by on welfare, the crescendo of talk about welfare reform in the mid-1990s was motivating more of them every day to seek out education and work.

Geric's highest ranking and best-educated nurse, Sharon Gillum, had been a teen mom herself. Gillum understood only too well the monumental transportation and scheduling hassles that kept welfare mothers tied down. So in putting together a curriculum to create the new workforce, Gillum crammed the statutory classroom time into three weeks of nine-hour days. "If they can get themselves together for a month, they will have a job," she told me. Not only that, but a job well suited to a single mother. Geric analyzed the distribution of its cases over a grid map of the city bus schedule, matching workers with clients who lived along the most convenient bus lines.

There's no point in sugarcoating things: Geric was recruiting vulnerable people in at-risk neighborhoods and putting them to work in a highly regulated industry. There was little room for slipups. Gwen, Eric, and their staff began probing every school applicant for what they called a "heart of caring." If someone could not convince them he or she deeply shared the company's values, they passed over the applicant, no matter how urgent their need for new recruits. As employment swelled Eric hired two ordained ministers to high-ranking positions. And the company took the dicey step of insisting that all new hires exhibit a "spiritual" dimension—not a commitment to any particular church, as Eric was quick to point out, but the humility to admit the existence of a higher power. "I don't care who you pray to," he said, "as long as you think there's something bigger than you." (Indeed, the office is highly diverse, full of whites as well as blacks, Jews and Muslims as well as Christians.)

As employees bought into Geric's vision, Geric bought into their lives. Eric began providing personal development and motivational courses for the trainees. The dearth of banks in the city was forcing employees to pay high fees at check-cashing services, so he arranged free checking for his employees at a community-minded local bank. Because urban life provides an exceedingly low margin of error, Geric also began advancing wages when someone landed in a bind over utilities and rent. "Not one time have I ever been burned on an advance," Eric says.

Consider what Geric had accomplished: By immersing itself in the community, it offered better service than consumers were accustomed to, created jobs that otherwise would not have been available, and provided income for the owners of the business. Before long the company was applying the same business model in the hardcore inner cities of

Detroit and Gary, Indiana, receiving federal training funds for each student completing its course. At the time of my visit there were six hundred employees in three states doing $12 million a year in business. The company had just passed a Medicare inspection with a 100 percent record. I spent some time in a classroom of eighteen recruits, each in her company-provided lab coat, every one of them female, every one of them a mother, nearly all single, and nearly all on welfare, but not for long. "Right now I'm crawling, but when I get my degree as a pediatrician I'll be walking," said Angela Bailey, mother of four. Another student named Anita Hill became interested in medicine caring for a child with sickle-cell anemia, one of her three children. "I'm in here beating welfare reform before it beats me," she said.

The atmosphere throughout the company's headquarters was as uplifting as the classroom. "The most exciting part is the entrepreneurial spirit," said Alisa Smedley, who once cared for her grandfather and who went on to head Geric's administrative operations. "We're like Tom Sawyer, lying in the grass, dreaming what we can do next."

Since at least the late 1960s, and perhaps since the publication of Rachel Carson's *Silent Spring* in 1962, the greatest tension between business and society has involved the environment. Since that time business has mostly viewed any duty to the environment as penalty or tax—a zero-sum game in which business is punished through higher costs (and consumers through higher prices) for the sake of vague, perhaps doubtful environmental benefits. But some businesspeople—not just the Ben & Jerry's crowd, but even mainstream leaders—are beginning to see that business is part of the society around it, indeed part of the natural world itself, making the environment not an object of exploitation but a medium through which business improves *its own lot* and that of others. This harmonized approach doesn't work everywhere, and there will be some industries that long resist it. But the number of adherents is longer than one might guess.

I know no better way of illustrating that than with the Ray Anderson story.

He grew up in small-town Georgia, studied industrial engineering at Georgia Tech, and landed where many young engineers did in the Deep South of the 1950s: in a carpet mill. He rose steadily through a variety of manufacturing and marketing posts with major companies until it dawned on him at age thirty-three that Alexander the Great had conquered the world by his age and that Jesus Christ had saved it. Discontented, Anderson struck out on his own.

About then he took a trip to Europe, where a breakthrough was sweeping the world of floor covering: carpet tiles. Anderson immediately recognized them as the answer to a major American design challenge. It was the early 1970s, and developers were erecting downtown and suburban office buildings at a breakneck rate. The buildings would stand for generations, but the warren of structures inside them, driven largely by computing technology and changing workplace habits, would continually change. So Anderson founded a company in Atlanta called Interface Incorporated to manufacture and sell the carpet tiles, almost single-handedly ushering in a distinct (and not entirely acclaimed) period look in office design. "We sold flexibility," he would later say. "We sold dealing with an unforeseeable future." His foresight made Interface the largest maker of commercial carpeting in the world, with twenty-six factories on four continents, sales in 120 countries, annual revenues of $1 billion, and shares traded on the New York Stock Exchange. Through the following two decades the company conducted no less than forty acquisitions.

But hard times eventually hit. Interface found itself overtaxed by takeover costs. In the deep white-collar recession of the early 1990s office construction screeched to a halt. Competitors closed in from all quarters. Anderson knew he needed fresh leadership and recruited a hard-charging competitor named Charlie Eitel to help lead the company. To Anderson's everlasting gratitude Eitel helped to staunch the decline. But the company's brush with failure had rattled Anderson deeply, and watching his number two bring the company back from the brink made him feel like an outsider in the company he had created. Anderson's emotional travails are relevant because they drew him into a period of soul-searching and vulnerability that ripened him for what was to happen next.

In 1994 a number of the company's marketing people noted that some pesky customers were bugging the company with a persistent question: How much recycled material did Interface's products contain? The people who buy commercial carpeting would be apt to pose such a question; designers and architects tend to have a green streak, and their buildings are conspicuous statements about man's place in the environment. Nor was it an idle question. Some 3.5 billion pounds of used carpeting hit the landfills of America every year. Popular household recycling programs represent a drop in the bucket next to what commercial carpeting recycling alone could accomplish. The Interface marketing people hemmed and hawed, unsure what to tell their customers. In search of guidance, one of them asked Ray Anderson to appear before a major sales meeting to enunciate Interface's environmental vision. Anderson hemmed and hawed himself. Environmental vision? A carpet company? His vision was complying with the law, what else? "To be quite frank, I did not have a vision," Anderson would recall. "I sweated for three weeks over what I would say to that group."

Just then, serendipitously, Joyce LaValle, the manager of an Interface factory near Atlanta, received a book from her daughter called *The Ecology of Commerce*. LaValle walked into Anderson's office one day and left a copy on his desk. Anderson picked up the book in hopes he might glean something for the speech he was dreading. Instead, the next few hours changed his life.

The author of the fateful book, Paul Hawken, is not only a writer and environmentalist but an entrepreneur—mail-order businesses, among a few others—with a deep sense of systems thinking. His book explores the interconnectedness of all systems on the planet, human and nonhuman alike, the delicate feedback loops by which the lily blossoms of the Amazon basin, for instance, affect the weather in New York, and how the actions of man (not just business, but government) can tip these delicate balances into dysfunction. But far from being your typical anti-industrial screed, the book is mostly inviting to a business reader. Hawken calls for "honoring market principles." He is wary of regulation and of fashionable, soccer-mom solutions. ("Recycling aluminum cans in the company cafeteria and ceremonial tree plantings," the book notes, "are about as effective as bailing out the *Titanic* with teaspoons.")

Ray Anderson recognized this common-sense approach as something he could use in preparing for his speech. But as he read on, he grew disturbed. Hawken described at length the ever-deepening effects of man's industrial footprint—of toxins inexorably accumulating in mother's milk and animal tissue, and of species disappearing at the rate of 27,000 a year, the latter "tantamount to marching backward through the Cenozoic Age," a phenomenon he called "the death of birth." Our technologies permit us to create new substances overnight, but the rest of nature has not yet evolved to provide a place for their storage or a method for their degradation. The obliteration of habitats, particularly the teeming tropics, causes even more extinction. Species spend millions of years adapting to a state as close to perfect as anything the world has ever known, but nothing prepares them for bulldozers or dioxin, which may vanquish them in an instant.

"The death of birth"—the phrase drove Anderson to weeping. Reading along he could not stop thinking of his five grandchildren. "It was a spear in my chest," he later told me. He could see his own face on every page, the creator and builder of a company that sucked oil from the ground and spewed toxins into the air and water. He asked a staffer named Jim Hartzfeld to conduct some quick calculations and learned that for every dollar of its nearly $1 billion in sales Interface drew 1.5 pounds of material from the earth. "That just blew my mind," Anderson would recall.

Overnight he became a man on a mission, vowing to settle for nothing less than the eventual conversion of his company into a 100 percent "sustainable" enterprise. This meant turning Interface into a "closed loop" of resources, a system that not only turned raw materials into products but products back into raw materials. Nothing would escape—no toxic waste, no waste of any kind. Ultimately there would be no smokestacks, no wastewater outfalls. At present, "we use this stuff once and it's gone forever," he lamented. "We have to figure out how to use it over and over and over again and make that quantum change in efficiency." Anderson was convinced the company could make huge strides right off the bat simply by changing its mode of thinking. There was plenty of low-hanging fruit to grab right now, and the success of the earliest initiatives would create knowledge and momentum on which the company could rally employees around a shared vision. But Anderson also realized fulfilling his goal would require technologies that either hadn't been invented or that remained prohibitively expensive. "We could put solar power on all our plants today and go broke," he lamented. For all the emotion driving him, Anderson remained acutely aware that Interface could not throw away money in the name of sustainability. How sustainable was a company that drove itself into bankruptcy?

Anderson was not dismayed by this conundrum. On the contrary, he realized that concern for the environment was not only compatible with profitability, it would actually enhance profitability. Reusing materials would cut costs! Eliminating toxic waste would eliminate disposal costs! Wall Street would be delighted! And as Anderson had already learned, customers would like it, too. Respect for the environment, it seemed, was a value that could serve as a new principle of organizing and economizing. "Literally," he would write at one point, "our company will grow by cleaning up the world."

In yet another irony (or so it seemed at first) Anderson saw that Interface could do the least harm to the natural world by emulating the natural world itself. Over the eons what survived in nature was what worked and what worked was what survived. It was no coincidence that a business should most serve nature by acting like nature since a business, Anderson came to see, was part of nature. The business of the future, he believed, would build itself around that essential fact. "It will recognize the interconnectedness of everything. It will eliminate the inefficiency that ignores this interconnectedness. Evolution gets rid of the superfluous. If our enterprise emulates nature, it will not have any superfluous pieces. . . ." He went on: "We'll have to be smart enough to figure out how nature would design a company if nature had a chance."

Anderson began evangelizing within his own company. His initial speech on the subject aroused a mixture of skepticism and joy; some people thought he was nuts, others wept at Anderson's own display of emotion. He began evaluating his managers for compensation purposes on their effectiveness in reducing waste and insisted that they evaluate their subordinates accordingly. He also began sharing his ideas outside the company. One of his major suppliers, Monsanto Corporation, then a major chemical company, immediately grasped the significance of his views and set out to create its own program in sustainability, which quickly became one of the most significant in the world. Many other corporate chieftains thought Anderson was off his rocker, looking at him, as he later described it, as if he were an exhibit in a freak show.

The operating principle for the conversion was simple: "Eliminate any cost that does not produce value to our customers." Notably, this didn't specifically mention reducing waste or emissions, though that was precisely the effect. Interface was consuming more petrochemical feedstock than necessary under the latest tufting methods; adopting them immediately cut nylon use 10 percent. The company began "combing" used fibers back to new instead of melting them, which added to cost, consumed unnecessary energy, created emissions, and added nothing for the customer. Certain yarns were substituted with hemp and flax, a step toward what the company began calling "harvestable" carpeting. New sizing methods reduced the amount of carpeting trimmed at installation. Processing water was used for local golf-course irrigation; organic waste was composted for use as lawn topsoil. Local landfill refuse was combined with an asphalt material to pave a company parking lot. Employees figured out how to jump-start massive electrical motors with gravity-feed systems rather than huge jolts of electricity. Millions of gallons of water consumption, millions of pounds of waste, millions of dollars in oil and chemicals—all quietly vanished for no reason except that people were motivated to think up ways of eliminating them.

Another innovation was leasing carpet tiles instead of selling them. Interface had periodically attempted to lease carpeting for twenty years to no avail. Then, under the new vision, it launched what it called an "evergreen" lease, in which the company regularly inspected, replaced, and recycled worn carpet tiles one by one instead of trying to sell the customer more than he needed.

People are also nature. They, too, should be "sustained." Ray Anderson's number-two executive, Charlie Eitel, launched a program to inspire teamwork and self-confidence in production workers through wall-climbing and rope-pulling events. This kind of stuff sounds corny, until you realize the effect it can have on someone who makes her living in a carpet mill. With her fellow workers cheering her on, an over-weight, fifty-five-year-old production worker named Maria Luquin, a Mexican immigrant, scaled a fifteen-foot obstacle as part of her personal development training. "You can do it!" her colleagues screamed. Luquin later credited the experience with the confidence she needed to get through the naturalization process.

What about the workplace itself? Shortly after Anderson's conversion, an Interface division called Prince Street Technologies, which makes broadloom carpeting, broke ground for a new $5.6 million factory in Cartersville, Georgia. I have been in a lot of factories and never seen another quite like it. For one thing, everyone enters the plant through the same entrance and uses the same bathrooms—no special treatment for managers, as in most manufacturing locations. Workers entered the product floor by walking through a showroom of elegant product samples and a corridor with photos depicting employees hard at work. Kiosks around the plant provided workers information about orders and customers as well as access to the Internet.

The physical boundaries of the factory were also permeable. The design lab, administration, and the company showroom were integral to the plant, separated by see-through walls. The design studio looked out on the shop floor, enabling visiting customers to watch the workers making the product and the workers to watch the customers buying it. The back wall of the manufacturing area was a window eighty feet long and three stories tall, a height that inspired one to look up; the view, a perpetually sunny Georgia sky and acres of black-eyed susans and other wildflowers, was meant to inspire. Said Joyce LaValle, the division president who had once left *The Ecology of Commerce* on Anderson's desk, "All beauty starts with nature." In an area of Georgia known for perfectly manicured and chemically treated lawns, the grounds in front of the building were landscaped with wild grasses, occasionally causing competitors to ask if the project ran out of money before the landscaping went in.

This kind of stuff also makes an impression on customers, one thousand of whom went through the plant in its first year. Known for wild, custom-pattern designs, the division sold broadloom carpet to such trendy, image-conscious customers as MTV and the Gap. "If they come into this building I've got them hands down," LaValle said, "especially if they've been to other plants." The Gap, for its part, told me it hired Interface to outfit a new headquarters building because it was the low bidder—but only environmentally friendly companies had been invited to bid. Notably, "environmentally friendly" and "low bidder" were one and the same.

"These are very powerful feedback loops," Anderson told me. Wall Street, too, was every bit as endorsing. Though mutual fund managers and other big investors are usually blind to the long-term effects of short-term spending, Interface's success in chalking up immediate results had won the company favor among investors. By closely tracking the effects of every move in the sustainability effort, Interface has documented tens of millions of dollars in savings flowing straight to the bottom line. In time those benefits will magnify if any of its competitors fail to match the cost savings. "The resource-efficient companies will win," Anderson says, "and they will win big at the expense of their inefficient competitors."

He goes on:

> I'll be treated as a kook by most, but there will be a few who get it, and then every day I hope someone else will get it. . . . Today I'm just a tiny individual, one of six billion on this planet. But

Interface is bigger. Interface is 1/25,000th of the world's gross global product. That sounds pretty small, but it's bigger than one in six billion, and our influence can be greater than that if we get it right and demonstrate to the business world—these hard-headed, hard-assed people—that there's another way.

In this high-tech age, people worry about the gulf between the haves and the have-nots; they are wise to worry. Others say that technology and affluence lift all boats through higher overall standards of living; they, too, are correct. Blinded by politics or point of view, most people see only one side of the issue. They fail to grasp the paradox inherent in technology economics: Inequality is worsening, yet everyone is better off. The same was true with the advent of steam power. As the diversity of incomes grows, so, too, does median income, at least early in the cycle of progression. As technology creates a more efficient society, education and opportunity both rise.

What distinguishes the current technology cycle is that education and opportunity come in the same package. It's called the personal computer. The PC is the first classroom in a box. It is teacher, coach, and inspiration all in one, not just because the appliance can instruct but because it connects the user to a network of human and literary resources so vast as to be limited only by the individual imagination. Computers alone are no panacea, of course. People need access to them (fortunately, they are cheap and getting cheaper). They need to know how to use them (this is also very easily done). The big challenge in linking computers with economic development is conquering the culture of dependency created by massive government interventions. In a chicken-and-egg problem, businesses must come into the city in order to inspire the kind of motivation and personal accountability necessary for businesses to come in the first place. The city needs a catalyst to spark renewal. That catalyst is entrepreneurialism.

Meet Nick Gleason. His is not your typical do-gooder story, although social awareness is part of it. Gleason is an entrepreneur who is deferring personal gratification to seize on incentives that exist today, knowing that the payoff, financial as well as psychic, might be spectacular.

Gleason, I should note at the outset, is white. He grew up with his father's tales of working as an organizer in the Mississippi Freedom Summer of 1964 and watched his mother teach literacy with a social-service agency, inspiring him to an activist career of his own. After college he worked full-time for Habitat for Humanity and other nonprofit urban redevelopment programs in San Francisco and Oakland. But in time he grew frustrated to see well-intentioned programs organizing, training, educating, and motivating people in the city, only to leave no jobs at the end of the process.

Gleason experienced firsthand the need to bootstrap when he was thrown out of a full-time social-service job. So he became a one-man consulting firm to nonprofits and to local governments, setting up sites on the then-new World Wide Web. Owning his own business was an enthralling experience. "Starting a business from scratch was like being shot out of a cannon," he later said. "The process of creating an organization, of having ownership, of waking up in the morning realizing that success or failure was primarily on my shoulders—it was exciting and motivating."[6] Still in his twenties, he decided to study business seriously.

Going deeply into debt, he enrolled in Harvard Business School, which he selected not just for the reputation of its M.B.A. program but because of its proximity to the Roxbury section of Boston. In Roxbury white flight occurred so abruptly in the 1960s that many simply abandoned homes and businesses, which became nearly worthless. This touched off an epidemic of arson that pockmarked Roxbury with vacant lots. The lots, in turn, became favorite dumping sites for contractors (many of them looking for a cheap place to dispose of the debris from suburban construction). An organization called the Dudley Street Neighborhood Initiative, or DSNI, sprang up to clean up the lots, chase away the dumpers, and begin planting the seeds for small-scale economic development. Enrolled at Harvard Business School, Gleason lived in a ramshackle house in Roxbury to qualify for membership in DSNI and learn from the masters of neighborhood activism. "Community organizers," as he later told me, "are a lot like entrepreneurs."

Because he already had some experience with Hypertext Markup Language—HTML, the programming code of the World Wide Web—Gleason also found himself in hot demand to set up Web pages for nonprofit outfits and student organizations at Harvard. He was too busy to do the tedious programming himself, but thought it might prove interesting to turn over the work to some talented inner-city youth. He accepted a job from a business-school club and turned it over to a couple of kids who had been discovered in a technology talent search held on the nearby campus of Massachusetts Institute of Technology.

At the time Gleason was taking a class called "Managing Product Development," in which he was required to develop a product. Early in the semester he offhandedly mentioned his work with the young programmers to his professor, Marco Iansiti. "That's it!" the teacher cried. "That's what you should do for the class!" Unfortunately, the project quickly turned to disaster. Though the teenagers were killer programmers, they did not coordinate their efforts, leaving Gleason with two sets of mismatched code. Gleason learned there was a reason that people usually don't start serious work until their adult years. He also realized that he had fallen victim to the stereotypical view holding that the problems of the inner city are the problems of "inner-city youth." In fact, the inner city was full of people of all ages who needed work and who could use an entrepreneurial spark.

Professor Iansiti had an assistant named Jim Picariello who, as it turned out, was a whiz with HTML. Picariello not only helped Gleason rescue the disastrous project but encouraged him to conduct another. Soon the two men, both still in their twenties, had launched a new business they called CitySoft Incorporated. When Gleason graduated some months later, he turned down a high-paying job managing a bottle-cap plant for Alcoa, becoming instead the only member of the Harvard Business School Class of '97 to design a job for himself paying about $400 a week.

Part of his mission was proving the misguidedness of typical urban social missions. Too many well-intentioned people, especially whites who never go there, see the inner city as a charity case. This fosters a self-fulfilling prophecy on the part of the benefactor and benefacted. People get so accustomed to making handouts they don't think of making investments. People become so accustomed to receiving handouts they don't think of looking for work, much less starting businesses of their own. Setting up yet another nonprofit, Gleason decided, simply wouldn't do. He wanted to create a self-sustaining business, something with legs. Nonprofits by definition were not self-sustaining.

He also knew he had a good story and that telling the story would bring in revenue. Programming Web pages was pretty much rote work, sold as a commodity. With price and quality pretty much indistinguishable from one service to the next, Gleason figured the cachet of his concept would bring business CitySoft's way. In the identical way that Ray Anderson of Interface rallied customers, investors, and employees behind his environmental mission, Nick Gleason expected his social mission to be good for business. He resisted the trendy label "social entrepreneurship." All new businesses are socially beneficial, he believed. "To single out 'social' entrepreneurship might seem obnoxiously exclusive or self-righteous or imply that the work of other entrepreneurs isn't as valuable," he would remark in a case study he later presented at Harvard.

But at the same time he did not want to hide the fact that profit-making was compatible with a social mission. "We want to challenge the common perception in the business community that business can't have an explicit social vision or impact," Gleason told people. Comments like that make it hard to imagine it had been only a decade since John Akers of IBM declared, "We are not in business to conduct moral activity." What Nick Gleason understood, better than Akers or anyone else who wore a suit in a *Fortune* 500 boardroom, was that business has no choice in the matter. Business itself is a moral act, or an immoral one. It is never amoral.

When Gleason got CitySoft under way with Jim Picariello at his side, they received a quick and early dose of reality: inner-city Boston was not exactly brimming with programmers fluent in HTML. The skill was easily taught, but the last thing they wanted was turning CitySoft into a training operation. For one thing, training was no way to make money except by living on government subsidies. For another, as he had seen so many times himself, training meant nothing without a job at the other end, and CitySoft wanted to concentrate on bringing jobs to the city. The solution, he realized, was getting others to conduct the training for him.

Gleason and Picariello went to the Mandela Housing Projects, where a former Massachusetts state representative named Royal Bolling operated a training center for residents of the massive, monolithic structure. Sometime later, I dropped in there, too. Royal Bolling bowled me over. It was as if he had read this book while it was still being written. "The computer is instant feedback," he said. "That link is so vital, particularly to people who never made it in school. It all goes hand in hand. You see what you can do with the computer and you see that your attitudes and behavior need adjusting. People see themselves as part of a whole. They see how interconnected everything is."

The room full of PCs, Bolling went on, was an "oasis" of motivation. "Once the students get exposure they think differently not only about the whole technology wave but about themselves. There is no embarrassment when you get a wrong answer with the computer. . . . Once people get their feet wet," he said, "it's impossible to get them away from the computer." The Mandela Computing Center had a 60 percent job-placement rate and "a long waiting list to get in," Bolling said.

More to the point where CitySoft was concerned, the center added some HTML training and began training independent contractors to design Web pages at $10 to $15 an hour. One was Darlene Smith. "This is something you can do in your living room, on your job, practically in your car. All it depends on is the drive and the skill level of the individual. It's capitalism at its best."

Another early CitySoft recruit was Tony Alves, whom Gleason had met during his organizing days in Roxbury. "In my neighborhood there are no computers," Alves told me. "No computers means no good jobs for the future." Alves picked up HTML almost instantly and was soon working for $10 an hour under a CitySoft contract in the *Boston Globe* newsroom, cropping wirephotos and setting up pages for the *Globe*'s popular Web site.

By 1998 CitySoft had four full-time employees and a dozen part-time contractors. It had created Web pages for ITT Sheraton, Siemens, and more than a dozen clubs and associations at Harvard. Tony Alves had purchased his own personal computer. Gleason and Picariello were investigating whether they could duplicate the CitySoft concept in other cities. Every now and then Gleason thought wistfully about his own $20,000-a-year salary compared to the $110,000 that his classmates were averaging a year out of school, but his financial fulfillment would definitely come one day, he believed, and in the meantime the personal rewards were priceless. "If we make it, and I think we will, it will be that much more satisfying," he told his friends and associates in one of his periodic on-line newsletters. "If we make it, people won't so easily be able to rationalize poor performance of inner-city areas. A common attitude toward low-income areas is 'It can't be done' and so people don't even try—I mean, people inside and outside these areas.

"We want to take those excuses away and say, 'Yes, it can be done.' "

೦

In this book I've tried to talk about values as cornerstones of pioneering businesses. In a few businesses, the values themselves—not the product, not even the place of business—actually *are* the business. I learned this from Lorelei Anderson-Francis. A New Yorker with a master's in public administration, she had moved to Orlando for a finance job with Martin Marietta at the onset of the Reagan defense buildup. But after a decade, when the boom played out, she was downsized out of work with a child at home. Fortunately she and her husband, an electronics worker, had been frugal. With her savings, her severance, and her love of kids, she decided to open an ice cream store.

In scouting for locations she settled on a tiny town on the edge of Orlando called Eatonville, both because she thought there was a market there and because as an African-American she closely identified with the town's storied past: It was the first municipality in America chartered by blacks. It was also the birthplace of the writer and folklorist Zora Neale Hurston, an author Anderson-Francis loved, who chronicled her Eatonville upbringing in an acclaimed 1942 memoir called *Dust Tracks on a Road*. People in Hurston's time slept on sacks full of Spanish moss, and although sleeping conditions have progressed since then, the gnarly trees of Eatonville still remain draped in those delicate vines. For all its fame and charm, however, Eatonville of late had been depicted in the Orlando media as a crime center, causing Anderson-Francis to spend a few evenings hanging out in the town to assure herself she'd feel safe operating a retail business there. She knew she would often have her young son with her, and an ice cream store had to operate with evening hours in the summer.

She called the store Scoops, and she ran it like no other ice cream store of today. It became a gathering spot for Girl Scout troops, study groups, and a club called Teens Against Premarital Sex. (Unwed teens who already had children belonged to an auxiliary chapter.) There were movies and poetry readings during Black History Month and walking tours of the town. The walls were plastered with kids' paintings and portraits of role models, from Martin Luther King, Jr., to the pro-basketball demigod Shaquille O'Neal of the Orlando Magic. Scoops sponsored an Easter egg hunt. A black Santa (the owner's husband) visited at Christmas. Students who made the honor roll received a certificate for two free sundaes. "She was our ace in the hole," Ruthenia Moses, education director of the nearby Church of God, told me.

But eventually crime in Eatonville, always a distant fear, became a next-door neighbor. A group of boys on bicycles was gathering near the store to deal drugs. There were gunshots one night in the Scoops parking lot. On another occasion customers of a nearby hair-care salon were robbed at gunpoint. Then, when an elderly store owner in the neighborhood was shot, a news crew broadcast live from the parking lot in front of Scoops. Anderson-Francis saw her own pink awning in the background on her TV screen, a startling reminder of how easily it might have been her.

That was it, she decided. No more Scoops.

As she was packing up one day, a call came from a local school official who had scheduled an event at Scoops. The school was dismayed to learn of the store's closing. Hey, the school official said, why didn't she bring some ice cream to the school instead of having the school kids come to her? Why not work up a program—you know, talking to the kids the way she always did? Anderson-Francis agreed.

From then on Anderson-Francis served as a mobile point of sale for a small, local ice cream manufacturer, taking orders from schools, day-care operations, and vacation camps, and bringing along a live program with every delivery: music, an art project, a trivia game, or a dance contest, often involving friends recruited for the occasion. Scoops was a paying show, Anderson-Francis had taken the show on the road. The store had outlived its own storefront. It was now indistinguishable from the community itself.

I met up with Anderson-Francis on a sweltering afternoon at Winter Park Summer Fun Camp a few miles from Eatonville. Her entourage that day included a friend of hers named Juanita-Marie, who was a nightclub singer in Tampa, and a double-bass player named Kevin Stever. Eighty boisterous kids ages six to twelve were herded in an old cinder-block gymnasium. The bassist began slapping. The singer began scatting. "You know what the blues are?" the singer called out. Soon, the kids were doing three-part harmony.

And a minute later, to peals of delight, the singer yelled, "Ice cream is next!"

Finally, I would like to offer a brief postscript on progress.

In 1997 I found myself in the improbable position of sitting between two of the greatest minds on the planet, each the recipient of a MacArthur "genius" grant and each in his own way a candidate for Nobel celebrity. I was the "moderator" (I use the word advisedly) of a debate between the paleontologist Stephen Jay Gould of Harvard and the molecular biologist Stuart Kauffman of the Santa Fe Institute.

What burning question should pit these two great minds against one another? The issue, as unlikely as it seems, was whether progress exists. The answer is not so obvious as it might seem.

Kauffman took the affirmative. He had spent a career researching the origins of life and the dynamics of evolution, including technological evolution. Kauffman believed that life embodied an inherent tendency toward greater complexity, which he took as a sign of progress. He cited the work of the Mexico City economist Mark White, noting that the world was continually creating more and better ways of making a living. There was no disputing that humankind was also the first with the capability of committing species suicide. But that, by itself, was no proof that our race was terminal.

Gould took the negative. It was a terrible conceit, he said, to think of evolution as an inexorable path leading toward man when man is but a sliver of life on earth, both in terms of quantity (bacteria win hands down, not just in numbers but in total weight) and in terms of longevity (at less than one million years, scarcely a blink of the eye in the full day of life's existence). And by the way, man's ability to wipe himself from the face of the earth *was,* in Gould's view, pretty good proof that progress was more illusory than reality.

There sat I, vainly trying to moderate this debate, an ink-stained wretch of a business reporter. Week in and week out I visit people absorbed in the miseries of making a buck and, yes, trying to leave behind a slightly better world than the one into which they were born. But when I ask my interview subjects "How's business?," as I invariably do, it stuns me how regularly they answer by commenting on how things are going *that week*. Writing about business is a long way from studying the mass speciation of the Cambrian era or the death of the dinosaurs.

Acknowledging my own lack of expertise, I came down on Kauffman's side. Yes there was progress, of course. And this is my proof. A question so broad demands an answer in the form of a deep law, one whose properties are displayed universally, at all levels of scale. If progress exists anywhere, then it is possible everywhere. And for all the greed, stupidity, inefficiency, and sheer retrograde horror I have encountered in more than twenty years as a business reporter, my last several years on the front lines have persuaded me that progress at least in business is not only real, it is inevitable.

I think back on details so small I have neglected to include them in this book. The sheer giving: Bill Armstrong of Armstrong Ambulance donating one thousand smoke detectors to the residents of a small Boston suburb where a fatal fire had hit; Half Price Books in Dallas giving away a few million books every year; Bill Fulkerson of Deere & Company sharing with other companies the secret of the spectacular scheduling powers of genetic algorithms; Zildjian Corporation creating the cymbal market of the future by teaching young rappers in Roxbury the art of percussion; Geric Home Health Care of Cleveland producing a weekly radio show called *The Champions*, profiling patients who had conquered disabilities.

There were the innumerable acts of creation everywhere I turned: At LDS Hospital in Salt Lake City, technicians gluing together $15 worth of Plexiglas to build a housing for testing viruses that made a multi-million-dollar addition unnecessary; in Idaho Falls, Gary Schneider endowing his farm-planning tool with "stewardship" algorithms, so farmers could see how heavy use of fertilizers today might damage crop yields tomorrow; in Minneapolis, where Chank Diesel's latest font, called "Uncle Stinkey," was appearing, of all places, in a Jell-O ad.

There was stunning commitment and trust: Carol Latham and her sons at Thermagon in Cleveland, who happened to be working late one Friday when a customer in the Far East faxed in an emergency order— and working the weekend to have the order ready before the courier arrived from Asia on Monday morning; Joe Morabito, actively encouraging one of his best relocation vendors to offer her services to *his* competitors; the list goes on.

These are just a few impressions, just a few recollections, while contemplating whether progress exists. As the comic said, I got a million of 'em.

In 1962, while walking around the production factory at Non-Linear Systems with his tape recorder in his hand, Abraham Maslow dictated the following entry: "The most valuable one hundred people to bring into a deteriorating society . . . would not be one hundred chemists, or politicians, or professors, or engineers, but rather one hundred entrepreneurs."[7] In Maslow's time, entrepreneurs were much fewer in number, and almost none worked in major corporations. Today entrepreneurs abound, not just in small business but across the landscape of the corporate world. They have brought us this far, and they will take us further still.

Martin Luther King, Jr., who knew more than a bit about injustice, said, "The arc of the universe is long, but it tends toward justice."[8] The same might be said of economic progress. We, our tools, and the businesses by which we accomplish nearly everything are all products of the natural world. Wrong turns and backsliding will occur from time to time. But the arrow of evolution flies toward the pioneering.

Notes

Introduction: The Age of Adaptation

1. Jones, "Why Is There So Much Genetic Diversity?," in Brockman, ed., *The Third Culture,* page 1170.
2. I am indebted to Mark White for this turn of phrase.
3. This is a central theme of this book which I owe to the insights of several scholars, particularly William Frederick. His work and others are cited throughout.
4. Quoted in Senge, *The Fifth Discipline,* page 175.
5. Quoted in *The Declaration of Independence: A Study in the History of Political Ideas,* by Carl L. Becker (New York: Vintage Books, 1958), page 45.
6. Morgan, *Images of Organization,* page 16.
7. Mirowski, *More Heat Than Light,* page 3.
8. Quoted in "This View of Life," by Stephen Jay Gould, *Natural History,* October 1997.
9. The limitations of calculus are discussed in Goerner, *Chaos and the Evolving Ecological Universe,* pages 15–17.
10. Quoted in "Big Mistake," by Brink Lindsey, *Reason,* February 1996.

11. A brief revisionist account of Taylor's work appears in Drucker, *Post-Capitalist Society*, pages 34–36.

12. Quoted in "Disinvestment from South Africa," by Judith F. Posnikoff, *Contemporary Economic Policy*, January 1997.

13. Michael Lewis, "The Man Who Invented Management," *New York Times Book Review*, January 11, 1998.

14. Quoted in "Tales of the Eighties," by Kathleen A. Hughes, *Wall Street Journal*, December 22, 1989.

15. Lazard, Freres study, cited in *Strategy & Business*, Fourth Quarter 1997.

16. See study cited in "Making the Small/Green Connection," by Byron Kennard, *In Business*, May/June 1997.

17. "Common Ground," by Brent Staples, *New York Times Book Review*, March 8, 1998.

18. "Work & Family: Companies Are Finding It Really Pays to Be Nice to Employees," by Sue Shellenbarger, *Wall Street Journal*, July 22, 1998.

19. "New Work Habits for a Radically Changing World," article by Price Pritchett, Pritchett & Associates Inc., Dallas.

20. Quoted in "Deutsche Bank Gets Bankers Trust for $10 Billion," by Edmund L. Andrews, *New York Times*, December 1, 1998.

21. Quoted in Schumacher, *Small Is Beautiful*, page 35.

Chapter 1: Being in Business

1. Quoted in "Market Civilization," *Wall Street Journal*, June 11, 1990.

2. See, among other sources, Philip Lieberman, *Eve Spoke: Human Language and Human Evolution* (New York: W.W. Norton, 1998), and Ridley, *The Origins of Virtue*, pages 199 and 209.

3. Rothschild, *Bionomics*, page 7.

4. "The Merchant of Avon," by Frederick Turner, *Reason*, March 1997; "Overcoming Yuk," by Oliver Morton, *Wired*, January 1998.

5. Dawkins, *River Out of Eden*, passim.

6. Quoted in Hayek, *The Fatal Conceit*, page 15.

7. Frederick, *Values, Nature, and Culture in the American Corporation*, pages 37 and 173.

8. "Creatures, Corporations, Communities, Chaos, Complexity: A Naturological View of the Corporate Social Role," by William C. Frederick, *Business & Society*, December 1998.

9. Kauffman, *At Home in the Universe*, page 71.

10. Gleick, *Chaos*, page 304.

11. Volk, *Metapatterns*, page 84.

12. Kelly, *Out of Control,* page 125.
13. Prigogine, *The End of Certainty,* page 7.
14. Kauffman, *The Origins of Order,* page 404.
15. Fritz Dressler, letter to the author, November 3, 1997.
16. Dressler, letter to the author, December 3, 1997.
17. Goerner, *Chaos and the Evolving Ecological Universe,* page 130.
18. For a discussion of self-organization, see, among other sources listed in the complexity section of the bibliography, Kauffman, *At Home in the Universe;* Resnick, *Turtles, Termites, and Traffic Jams;* and Kelly, *Out of Control.*
19. Quoted in "The Trillion-Dollar Vision of Dee Hock," by M. Mitchell Waldrop, *Fast Company,* October–November 1996.
20. Garrett Hardin, "The Cybernetics of Competition," *Perspectives in Biology and Medicine* 7, August 1963, quoted in Jervis, *System Effects,* page 10.
21. Hawken, *The Ecology of Commerce,* page 136.
22. See A. Gabor, *The Man Who Discovered Quality* (Random House, 1990).
23. Polanyi, *The Tacit Dimension, passim.*
24. General Motors had an interest in the plant, owned by New United Motor Inc., although Toyota was the operator.
25. "Notes on Value Creation," Paul O'Malley Associates, Newtonville, Mass., October 1996.
26. Stewart, *Intellectual Capital,* page 16.
27. Volk, *Metapatterns,* page 76.
28. Frederick, *Values, Nature, and Culture in the American Corporation,* page 170.
29. McLuhan, *Understanding Media,* page 219.
30. For a detailed report on the development and use of genetic algorithms, see "Back to Darwin: In Sunlight and Cells, Science Seeks Answers to High-Tech Puzzles," by Gautam Naik, *Wall Street Journal,* January 16, 1996.
31. "The Big Picture," by Danny Hillis, *Wired,* January 1998.

Chapter 2: Everyone a Middleman

1. Smith, *The Wealth of Nations,* page 18.
2. These fragmentary quotes appear in Muller, *Adam Smith in His Time and Ours, passim,* and Coase, *The Firm, the Market, and the Law,* page 37.

3.   Quoted in Muller, *Adam Smith in His Time and Ours,* page 69.

4.   Smith's life and beliefs are described in Muller, *Adam Smith in His Time and Ours, passim.*

5.   Dunlap, *Mean Business,* page 47.

6.   Moskowitz, et al., eds., *Everybody's Business,* page 171.

7.   Frederick, *Values, Nature, and Culture in the American Corporation,* page 154.

8.   Margaret Wheatley, e-mail to the author, July 17, 1996.

9.   Goodwin, *How the Leopard Changed Its Spots,* page 181.

10.   Colinvaux, *Why Fierce Big Animals Are Rare,* page 144.

11.   Wilson, *Consilience,* page 105.

12.   Moore, *The Death of Competition.*

13.   Quoted in Csikszentmihalyi, *Flow,* page 50.

14.   Cited in Fukuyama, *Trust,* epigraph page.

15.   Lapham, *Money and Class in America,* page 55.

16.   "The Nature of the Firm," by Ronald H. Coase, *Economica* 4, 1937, in Coase, *The Firm, the Market, and the Law.*

17.   Lewis, *Babbitt,* page 6.

18.   Tapscott, *The Digital Economy,* pages 56–57.

19.   Patrick McGovern, "Circling Back to the Small and Simple," *Forbes ASAP,* December 2, 1996.

20.   Coase, *The Firm, the Market, and the Law,* page 14.

21.   Bar-Yam, *Dynamics of Complex Systems,* page 802.

22.   See Lynda Falkenstein, *Nichecraft: Using Your Specialness to Focus Your Business, Corner Your Market, and Make Customers Seek You Out* (New York, HarperBusiness, 1996.)

23.   Wilson, *The Diversity of Life,* page 165.

24.   Morgan, *Images of Organization,* page 64.

25.   Wilson, *The Diversity of Life,* page 403.

26.   Jacob, *The Possible and the Actual,* in Barlow, ed., *Evolution Extended,* pages 97–98.

27.   Borowski, *The Origins of Knowledge and Imagination,* page 109.

28.   Maslow, *Eupsychian Management,* page 185.

29.   "Researchers Go from A to B to Discovery," by Rick Weiss, *Washington Post,* January 26, 1998.

30.   Quoted in William A. Sherden, *The Fortune Sellers: The Big Business of Buying and Selling Predictions* (New York: Wiley, 1997).

31.   Hurst, *Crisis & Renewal,* pages 83–85.

32.   "Kauffman's Law," by Mark White, in publication.

33. Spinosa, Flores, and Dreyfus, *Disclosing New Worlds,* page 55. In this passage and a few others, I credit Flores with the authorship of the quoted words purely for simplicity; these passages derive from a section of the book dealing in particular with his philosophy and his business career.

34. Quoted in Nonaka and Takeuchi, *The Knowledge-Creating Company,* page 27.

35. "The Impact of Information Technology on Business," address by Fernando Flores to the 50th Anniversary Conference of the Association for Computing Machinery, San Jose, California, March 4, 1997.

36. Bernardo Huberman, "Collective Problem-Solving," presented to Ernst & Young Conference on Embracing Complexity, Cambridge, Mass., August 4, 1997.

37. Though not original with him, Stuart Kauffman's writings have impressed this point deeply on me.

38. Holland, "The Global Economy as a Complex Adaptive System," in *The Economy as a Complex Evolving System,* proceedings of the Santa Fe Institute, 1997, page 119.

39. Kauffman, *At Home in the Universe,* page 283.

40. Wilson, *Consilience,* page 294.

41. Mark White, e-mail to the author, July 22, 1997.

42. "Economic Growth," by Paul M. Romer, in the *Fortune Encyclopedia of Economics.*

43. "Facilitating the Formation of Flexible Manufacturing Networks in Rural, Southeastern Ohio: Five-Year Report," Appalachian Center for Economic Networks, Athens, Ohio, 1995.

44. *Burke and Paine on Revolution and the Rights of Man,* Robert B. Dishman, ed. (New York: Scribner's, 1971).

45. Smith, *The Wealth of Nations,* page 18.

Chapter 3: "Have It Your Way"

1. Galbraith, *The New Industrial State,* pages 6–7.

2. *HarperCollins Dictionary of Economics,* 1991.

3. Michael Rothschild uses the "consumer Perestroika" phrase in his book *Bionomics.*

4. Gleick, *Chaos,* page 108.

5. "The Future That Has Already Happened," by Peter F. Drucker, *Harvard Business Review,* September–October 1997.

6. Quoted in Khalil, ed., *Evolution, Order, and Complexity,* page 141.

7. Quoted in Kelly, *Out of Control,* page 74.

8. In addition to my own December 13, 1996, column on Cemex, an excellent account of the company's transformation appears in "Bordering on Chaos," by Peter Katel, *Wired,* July 1997.

9. A spokesman for Domino's told me that a snafu must have occurred, since Domino's regularly hosts visiting teams.

10. Chamberlain, *The Roots of Capitalism,* page 64.

11. Fernando Flores, "The Leaders of the Future," in Denning and Metcalfe, eds., *Beyond Calculation: The Next Fifty Years of Computing.*

12. Hebrews 11:1.

13. Scott Simmerman, posting to Learning Organization mail list, August 25, 1997.

14. Wilson, *Consilience,* pages 297–98.

15. Buber, *I and Thou.*

16. Quoted in "Keyword: Context," by Frank Rose, *Wired,* December 1996.

17. Steve Case, America Online, letter to members, October 4, 1996.

18. "Seeking the Limits of Growth: Don't Sell What You Can't Support," *Air Conditioning, Heating & Refrigeration News,* February 3, 1997.

19. Aaron Wildavsky, "If Planning Is Everything, Maybe It's Nothing," *Policy Sciences* 4, 1973.

20. Kelly, *Out of Control,* page 309.

21. Quoted in "A Natural Law, Stronger Than Gravity," by Don Taylor, in *Minding Your Own Business,* June 8, 1997.

Chapter 4: What Am I Bid?

1. "The Revolution Yet to Happen," by Gordon Bell and James N. Gray, in *Beyond Calculation,* Denning and Metcalfe, eds., page 17.

2. See Farrell, *How Hits Happen.*

3. "New Rules for the New Economy," by Kevin Kelly, *Wired,* September 1997.

4. E-mail to author from Ed Chuang, director of corporate marketing, SourceCraft Inc., August 16, 1996.

5. The concept of lock-in, as well as of increasing-return economics, has been detailed at length by the economist Brian Arthur.

6. Proverbs 11:24, cited in Hegel, *Net Gain.*

Chapter 5: From Planning to Playing

1.   Maslow, *Eupsychian Management,* pages 172, 176.
2.   Mintzberg, *The Rise and Fall of Strategic Planning,* page 6.
3.   Aaron Wildavsky, "If Planning Is Everything, Maybe It's Nothing," *Policy Sciences* 4, 1973.
4.   Gleick, *Chaos,* pages 11–17.
5.   Quoted in "New Work Habits for a Radically Changing World," Price Pritchett, Pritchett & Associates, Inc., Dallas.
6.   Wheatley and Kellner-Rogers, *a simpler way,* pages 13, 20.
7.   Kelly, *Out of Control,* page 340.
8.   Interview with Freeman Dyson, *Wired,* February 1998.
9.   Quoted in Goerner, *Chaos and the Evolving Ecological Universe,* page 128.
10. David Hurst, posting on complexity-in-management mail list, August 20, 1997.
11. Deming, *Out of the Crisis,* page 23.
12. From Barlow, ed., *Evolution Extended,* page 130.
13. Whyte, *The Organization Man,* page 6.
14. The Editors of *Fortune, The Executive Life,* page 76.
15. Wheatley and Kellner-Rogers, *a simpler way,* page 14.
16. Quoted in Mark Albion, *MBA News #36,* July 28, 1997, distributed by e-mail.
17. Spinosa et al., *Disclosing New Worlds,* page 19.
18. Bronowski, *The Origins of Knowledge and Imagination,* page 123.
19. Mintzberg, *The Rise and Fall of Strategic Planning,* page 26.

Chapter 6: Nobody's as Smart as Everybody

1.   "Adaptive Corporations," by Mark White, White & Associates, Mexico City, publication in progress.
2.   Some of Pete Wakeman's comments are taken from his personal writings and from notes he prepared for presentations to Great Harvest franchisees.
3.   Drucker, *Post-Capitalist Society,* page 20.
4.   *Ibid.,* page 64.
5.   Konosuke Matsushita, "The Secret Is Shared," *Manufacturing Economics,* February 1988.
6.   Drucker, *Post-Capitalist Society,* page 65.

7. Fritz Dressler, "Ethics or Else," unpublished monograph, 1997.
8. "Wild Minds," *New Scientist*, December 13, 1997.
9. Wilson, *Consilience*, page 110.
10. Davenport and Prusak, *Working Knowledge*, page xiv.
11. M.L.J. Abercrombie, *The Anatomy of Judgment* (Hammondsworth, England: Penguin, 1969).
12. "Collective Problem-Solving," speech by Bernardo A. Huberman, Ernst & Young Conference on Embracing Complexity, Cambridge, Mass., August 4, 1997.
13. Quoted in Wilson, *Consilience*, page 110.
14. Posting by Malcolm Brooks, Learning Organization mail list, September 11, 1997.
15. Baskin, *Corporate DNA*, page 96.
16. Quoted in "Fleet Improvement R&D Network," updated report by City of New York, Bureau of Sanitation, Bureau of Motor Equipment.
17. David Weinberger, "Upending the Org Chart," *Wired*, April 1997.
18. "The Leaders of the Future," by Fernando Flores, in Denning and Metcalfe, *Beyond Calculation*, page 179.
19. E-mail to the author, January 3, 1998.
20. The recording of *A Day in the Life* is described in *Paul McCartney: Many Years from Now*, by Barry Miles (New York: Henry Holt & Co., 1997), and in *A Day in the Life*, by Mark Hertsgaard (New York: Delacorte Press, 1995).
21. Michael McElwee, "Emergent Dynamics," posted on complexity-in-management mail list, July 24, 1997.
22. Morgan, *Images of Organization*, page 114.
23. Sowell, *Knowledge and Decisions*, page 26.
24. "The Importance of Market-Based Values to the Future of American Business," speech by Charles Koch, Hillsdale, Ill., March 10, 1996.
25. Quoted in "Koch and His Empire Grew Together," by Guy Boulton, *Wichita Eagle*, June 26, 1994.
26. Dunlap, *Mean Business*, page 161.
27. A delightful discussion of the ubiquitousness of binaries appears in Volk, *Metapatterns*, pages 74–97.
28. The "edge of chaos" concept is discussed in rich and revealing detail in, among other places, Lewin, *Complexity*; Waldrop, *Complexity*; Kauffman, *The Origins of Order* and *At Home in the Universe*; Bar-Yam, *Dynamics of Complexity*; and Levy, *Artificial Life*.
29. Quoted in Lewin, *Complexity*, page 51.

30. "Network Snags Imperil Sales of Motorola," by John J. Keller and Quentin Hardy, *Wall Street Journal,* February 24, 1998; "Wireless Goes Haywire at Motorola," by Roger O. Crockett, *Business Week,* March 9, 1998.

Chapter 7: All Together Now

1. Hal Croasmun described his father's preaching methods in a posting on the Learning Organization mail list, July 10, 1997.
2. Cited in "Thoroughly Modern: Mary Parker Follett," by David K. Hurst, *Business Quarterly,* Spring 1992.
3. Follett, *Freedom & Coordination: Lectures in Business Organization,* by Mary Parker Follett (Management Publications Trust, London, 1949), page 46.
4. *Everybody's Business* (Harper & Row, 1980), page 827.
5. *Chambers' Etymological Dictionary,* 1912, cited in McMaster, *The Intelligence Advantage,* page 68.
6. Cited in "Psychology and Corporations: A Complex Systems Perspective," by Jeffrey Goldstein, *Proceedings of the International Conference on Complex Systems,* Nashua, N.H., September 21–26, 1997.
7. "A Culture of Commitment," by Herb Kelleher, *Leader to Leader,* Spring 1997.
8. *Command and Control,* U.S. Marine Corps, October 1996, pages 46–47.
9. Warren Bennis, *On Becoming a Leader* (Addison-Wesley, 1989) page 39.
10. Cited in Karl E. Weick, *Sensemaking in Organizations* (Sage Publications, 1995), page 9.
11. McMaster, *The Intelligence Advantage,* page 69.
12. Richard Seel discussed "discussion" in a post to Complexity and Management Mail List on August 17, 1997.
13. Senge, *The Fifth Discipline,* page 10.
14. Cliff Hamilton detailed the Oregon fishing story in a series of e-mails to the author in March 1998. He also discussed these events in posting LO15943 to the Learning Organization Mail List, November 19, 1997.
15. The account of Richard Knowles's work at DuPont is based on an extended e-mail exchange with him in 1998. Additional facts were drawn from numerous postings by him on the Complexity and

Management Mail List, as well as from an interview with him appearing in *Vision/Action: The Journal of the Bay Area OD Network*, Summer 1997.

16. The concept of the attractor is discussed in most of the works listed in the "complexity" section of my bibliography. For the best technical discussion see Guastello, *Chaos, Catastrophe, and Human Affairs*, pages 12–21.

17. "Creatures, Corporations, Communities, Chaos, Complexity: A Naturological View of the Corporate Social Role," by William C. Frederick, *Business & Society*, December 1998.

Chapter 8: Money and Motivation

1. Quoted in "What a Steal," by Tom Verducci, *Sports Illustrated*, June 16, 1997.

2. Quoted in "Pirates' Martin Finds Happiness for Less Money," Scripps Howard News Service, May 17, 1997.

3. "Low-Paid Pirates Getting Most for Their Money," Associated Press, June 14, 1997. Figures are based on the first sixty-nine games of the season.

4. Dunlap, *Mean Business*, page 21.

5. Quoted in Kohn, *Punished by Rewards*, page 3.

6. James Baldwin, *Nobody Knows My Name* (Vintage, 1961), page 222.

7. Willie Sutton with Edward Linn, *Where the Money Was*, cited in Flannery et al., *People, Performance, & Pay*.

8. Quoted in Hoffman, *The Right to Be Human*, page 155.

9. Maslow, *Eupsychian Management*, page 5.

10. "A Chance for Everyone to Grow," by Vance Packard, *Reader's Digest*, November 1963.

11. Maslow, *Eupsychian Management*, page 188.

12. *Business Week*, January 20, 1973.

13. Maslow, *Eupsychian Management*, pages 208–209.

14. Polanyi, *Personal Knowledge*, page 59.

15. See Spinosa et al., *Disclosing New Worlds*.

16. Maslow, *Eupsychian Management*, page 11.

17. Quoted in Kohn, *Punished by Rewards*, page 189.

Chapter 9: At Home in the Economy

1. Quoted in "Perils of the Sphinx," by Alexander Stille, *The New Yorker*, February 10, 1997. This chapter title is inspired by Stuart Kauffman's *At Home in the Universe*.
2. Business's historical precedence over other social institutions is discussed in Ridley, *The Origins of Virtues, passim*. The family origins of the division of labor are discussed in "Work, the Division of Labour and Co-operation," by Sutti Ortiz, in the *Companion Encyclopedia of Anthropology*, pages 891–910.
3. Morgan, *Images of Organization*, page 121.
4. "Family Business as a Field of Study," Task Force of International Family Business Program Association, *Family Business Annual, Program Sessions*, 1995.
5. *Ibid.*
6. "In Praise of the Family Firm," *The Economist*, March 9, 1996.
7. "Homework Equals Happiness," by Carol Leonetti Dannhauser, *Home Office Computing*, August 1997.
8. See, among other sources, *Women-Owned Businesses: Breaking the Boundaries*, National Federation of Women Business Owners, April 1995.

Chapter 10: "All My Sons"

1. "Creatures, Corporations, Communities, Chaos, Complexity: A Naturological View of the Corporate Social Role," by William C. Frederick, *Business & Society*, December 1998.
2. Maslow, *Eupsychian Management*, page 103.
3. McLuhan, *Understanding Media*, page 223.
4. Quoted in "The Man Who Invented Management," by Michael Lewis, *New York Times Book Review*, January 11, 1998.
5. Quoted in "A Damning Moment," by Arianna Huffington, *U.S. News & World Report*, May 19, 1997.
6. Quoted in *CitySoft: Descriptive Institutional Materials*, case presentation to "Entrepreneurship in the Social Sector" class, Harvard Business School, Fall 1997.
7. Maslow, *Eupsychian Management*, page 186.
8. Quoted in Goerner, *Chaos and the Evolving Ecological Universe*, page 194.

Annotated Bibliography

Philosophy and History

Bohm, David. *Wholeness and the Implicate Order.* London: Routledge, 1980. The great quantum physicist delves into the holistic structure of everything. A powerful (if mathematically daunting, in parts) book.

Bronowski, Jacob. *The Origins of Knowledge and Imagination.* New Haven: Yale University Press, 1977. A mathematician's engaging account of how worldviews are shaped by our biology.

Polanyi, Michael. *The Tacit Dimension.* Gloucester, Mass.: Peter Smith, 1983. "We can know more than we can tell." These lectures are a cold shower for anyone advocating "knowledge management."

———. *Personal Knowledge: Toward a Post-Critical Understanding.* Chicago: University of Chicago Press, 1958. Deep philosophical discussion of how people play a role in creating their own realities, particularly in the sciences.

Sowell, Thomas. *Knowledge and Decisions.* New York: Basic Books, 1980. Philosophical explorations by a conservative scholar.

Spinosa, Charles, Fernando Flores, and Hubert L. Dreyfus. *Disclosing New Worlds: Entrepreneurship, Democratic Action and the Cultivation of*

Solidarity. Cambridge: MIT Press, 1997. The most original analysis of entrepreneurial action I have ever read, this book deeply influenced my thinking.

Wilson, Edward O. *Consilience: The Unity of Knowledge.* New York: Alfred A. Knopf, 1998. Brilliant attempt to bridge the gap between the physical sciences and social sciences, including, to a small degree, economics.

Biology

Barlow, Connie, ed. *From Gaia to Selfish Genes: Selected Writings in the Life Sciences.* Cambridge: MIT Press, 1991. A wonderful collection of essays and book fragments by leading neo-Darwinians and revisionists.

———. *Evolution Extended: Biological Debates on the Meaning of Life.* Cambridge: MIT Press, 1994. A sequel that equals, perhaps even exceeds, her earlier work, with selections from a century of leading thinkers.

Colinvaux, Paul. *Why Big Fierce Animals Are Rare.* Princeton, N.J.: Princeton University Press, 1978. Engaging study of ecosystems and interconnectedness.

Dawkins, Richard. *River Out of Eden: A Darwinian View of Life.* New York: Basic Books, 1995. A highly approachable and most absorbing account of Darwinism, despite the stridency of the atheism.

Magulis, Lynn, and Dorion Sagan. *What Is Life?* New York: Simon & Schuster, 1995. Magisterial coffee-table book on where it came from and how it persists, told mostly from the fungal and cellular point of view.

Volk, Tyler. *Metapatterns: Across Space, Time, and Mind.* New York: Columbia University Press, 1995. A biologist looks at binaries, spheres, boundaries, and other patterns across nature and society. Amusing and informative.

General Business

Brandenburger, Adam M., and Barry J. Nalebuff. *Competition.* New York: Currency Doubleday, 1996. Pathbreaking look at the integration of everything in business.

Davenport, Thomas H., and Laurence Prusak. *Working Knowledge: How Organizations Manage What They Know.* Boston: Harvard Business School Press, 1998. Good overview by two of the top figures in the field, even if it suffers from the misconception that knowledge can be "managed."

Deming, W. Edwards. *Out of the Crisis.* Cambridge: MIT Press, 1982. The definitive work by the high priest of TQM. Despite many pithy comments, he did know more about quality in manufacturing than quality in writing.

Denning, Peter J., and Robert M. Metcalfe. *Beyond Calculation: The Next Fifty Years of Computing*. New York: Springer-Verlag. Essays on the future by the titans in computing's past.

Dunlap, Albert J., with Bob Andelman. *Mean Business: How I Save Bad Companies and Make Good Companies Great*. New York: Times Business, 1996. The now-disgraced turnaround artist's screed against humanism. At once laughable and horrible.

The Editors of *Fortune*. *The Executive Life*. New York: Time Inc., 1956. A startling piece of anachronism that feels like the work of *Fortune* editor William H. Whyte, who also wrote *The Organization Man*.

Flannery, Thomas P., David A. Hofrichter, and Paul E. Platten. *People, Performance, and Pay: Dynamic Compensation for Changing Organizations*. New York: Free Press, 1996. A far more thoughtful treatment of this subject than you usually see from compensation consultants.

Hagel, John III, and Arthur G. Anderson. *Net Gain: Expanding Markets Through Virtual Communities*. Cambridge: Harvard Business School Press, 1997. Intelligent if slightly credulous speculations on the future of commercial communities in on-line marketing.

Mintzberg, Henry. *The Rise and Fall of Strategic Planning*. New York: Free Press, 1994. Already a classic, debunking the powers of central planning and arguing instead for the advent of "emergent strategy."

Moore, James F. *The Death of Competition: Leadership and Strategy in the Age of Business Ecosystems*. New York: HarperBusiness, 1996. Despite a misleading (and inaccurate) title, a fine popularization of biological metaphors through an analysis of cooperation among large firms.

Moskowitz, Milton, Michael Katz, and Robert Levering. *Everybody's Business: An Almanac*. San Francisco: Harper & Row, 1980. The irreverent guide to corporate America, one of my most prized and dog-eared reference books.

Nonaka, Ikujiro, and Hirotaka Takeuchi. *The Knowledge-Creating Company: How Japanese Companies Create the Dynamics of Innovation*. New York: Oxford University Press, 1995. A deep investigation, brimming with case studies.

Senge, Peter M. *The Fifth Discipline: The Art and Practice of the Learning Organization*. New York: Currency Doubleday, 1990. The powerful, classic popularization of systems thinking, team learning, shared vision, and other "disciplines" by one of the most important business theorists of the age.

Silver, A. David. *Entrepreneurial Megabucks: The 100 Greatest Entrepreneurs of the Last Twenty-five Years.* New York: Wiley, 1985. Despite the off-putting title, a well-done compilation of case studies.

Tedlow, Richard S. *New and Improved: The Story of Mass Marketing in America.* New York: Basic Books, 1990. Case studies of cola wars and other epic marketing battles, and what they say about Americans.

Whyte, William H., Jr. *The Organization Man.* Garden City, N.Y.: Doubleday, 1956. A deep, rich—and frightening—study of business at the high point of command and control.

Economics

Arthur, W. Brian. *Increasing Returns and Path Dependence in the Economy.* Ann Arbor: University of Michigan Press, 1994. Collection of articles by the popularizer of "increasing return" economics, including his fabled 1990 *Scientific American* article, "Positive Feedbacks in the Economy."

Coase, R. H. *The Firm, the Market, and the Law.* 1937, 1946, and 1960. Reprint, Chicago: University of Chicago Press, 1988. Classic essays by the economist who in 1937 created transaction-cost theory, a concept of sustained relevance.

Galbraith, John Kenneth. *The New Industrial State.* Boston: Houghton Mifflin, 1967. A thoughtful if ideological treatise on corporate dominance, produced at the apogee of the multinational firm.

Hayek, F. A. *The Fatal Conceit: The Errors of Socialism.* Chicago: University of Chicago Press, 1988. Despite a few ideological blind spots, a brilliant survey of economics, history, biology, and philosophy.

Kiekhofer, William H. *Economic Principles, Problems and Policies,* 3rd edition. New York: D. Appleton-Century, 1946. My father's college economics textbook—appallingly similar to those in use today.

Mirowski, Philip. *More Heat Than Light: Economics as Social Physics, Physics as Nature's Economics.* New York: Cambridge University Press, 1989. How discoveries in physics shaped thinking in economics.

Muller, Jerry Z. *Adam Smith in His Time and Ours: Designing the Decent Society.* New York: Free Press, 1993. Outstanding analysis of Smith's economics in the context of his moral philosophy.

Schumacher, E. F. *Small Is Beautiful: Economics as if People Mattered.* New York: Harper & Row, 1973. Hard to swallow much of the anti-industrial rantings, but otherwise an informative look at the virtues of the small and the role of business in the natural order of things. Highly influential in its time and still widely cited.

Smith, Adam. *Inquiry into the Nature and Causes of the Wealth of Nations.*
   1776. Reprint, Chicago: University of Chicago Press, 1976. The most
   important work of economics ever written, though described by J. K.
   Galbraith as one that people could freely cite without reading to conclu-
   sion. Worth dabbling in, but not devouring.

Ethics

Chamberlain, John. *The Roots of Capitalism.* Princeton: Van Nostrand, 1959.
   An ethical justification of capitalism, written from the right.
Epstein, Joseph. *Ambition: The Secret Passion.* New York: E.P. Dutton, 1980.
   Delightful accounts of historical, literary, and business figures who were
   driven to succeed, written by a modern master of the essay form.
Frederick, William C. *Values, Nature, and Culture in the American
   Corporation.* New York: Oxford University Press, 1995. Landmark study
   of business as a bulwark against the forces of entropy, with major reper-
   cussions for the study of business ethics. One of the important influences in
   my own quest to understand what makes business work.
Hill, Ivan, ed. *The Ethical Basis of Economic Freedom.* Chapel Hill, N.C.:
   American Viewpoint Inc., 1976. Essays on the moral underpinnings of
   business with an extensive treatment of codes of ethics.
Ridley, Matt. *The Origins of Virtue: Human Instincts and the Evolution of
   Cooperation.* New York: Penguin Group, 1996. Fascinating anthropology
   for the lay reader, although diminished somewhat by rightist political ideology.

Psychology, Sociology, and Culture

Capra, Fritjof. *The Turning Point: Science, Society, and the Rising Culture.*
   New York: Bantam, 1982. Pioneering look at the post-Newtonian sciences,
   although diminished somewhat by leftist political ideology.
Csikszentmihalyi, Mihaly. *Flow: The Psychology of Optimal Experience.* New
   York: HarperCollins, 1990. A wondrous examination of how control over
   consciousness generates happiness and personal growth, based on extensive research by the University of Chicago psychologist. The only self-help
   book I recommend.
Fukuyama, Francis. *Trust: The Social Virtues and the Creation of Prosperity.*
   New York: Free Press, 1995. A bold, convincing review of the merits of
   "social capital," arguing that cultures with high trust levels produce
   stronger growth.

Hawken, Paul. *The Ecology of Commerce: A Declaration of Sustainability.* New York: HarperCollins, 1993. Though excessively gloomy and judgmental in spots, this is a mightily important book about creating a sustainable free-market economy.

Hoffman, Edward. *The Right to Be Human: A Biography of Abraham Maslow.* Los Angeles: Jeremy P. Tarcher, Inc., 1988. A readable and insightful account of the great psychologist's life and thinking.

Ingold, Tim, ed. *Companion Encyclopedia of Anthropology.* London: Routledge, 1994. Massive anthology of essays on humanity, culture, and social life.

Kohn, Alfie. *Punished by Rewards: The Trouble with Gold Stars, Incentive Plans, A's, Praise, and Other Bribes.* New York: Houghton Mifflin, 1993. Powerful debunking of traditional motivation tools.

Lapham, Lewis. *Money and Class in America.* New York: Weidenfeld & Nicolson, 1988. An erudite and sardonic screed against them, by the editor of *Harper's.*

Maslow, Abraham H. *Eupsychian Management: A Journal.* New York: Irwin, 1964. Long-forgotten masterwork, at least forty years ahead of its time despite the ghastly title. Recently republished (in slightly altered form) as *Maslow on Management.* New York: Wiley, 1998.

McLuhan, Marshall. *Understanding Media: The Extensions of Man.* New York: Signet, 1964. Frighteningly foresighted look at a future arriving today.

Complexity

Bak, Per. *How Nature Works: The Science of Self-Organized Criticality.* New York: Springer-Verlag, 1996. A physicist discerns patterns in the structure of nature.

Bar-Yam, Yaneer. *Dynamics of Complex Systems.* Reading, Mass.: Addison-Wesley, 1997. Heavily mathematical; an ambitious synthesis of complexity, from protein-folding to economics.

Baskin, Ken. *Corporate DNA: Learning from Life.* Woburn, Mass.: Butterworth-Heinemann, 1998. Deep investigations of identity and organization at 3M and other exemplary practitioners.

Brockman, John. *The Third Culture.* New York: Touchstone, 1996. An oral history featuring complexity and "new science" intellectuals in their own words: Stuart Kauffman, Chris Langton, Stephen Jay Gould, Steven Pinker, Richard Dawkins, and others.

Capra, Fritjof. *The Web of Life: A New Scientific Understanding of Living Systems.* New York: Doubleday, 1996. Excellent layman's overview, with much less anti-industrial ideology than in Capra's earlier *The Turning Point.*

Farrell, Winslow. *How Hits Happen: Forecasting Predictably in a Chaotic Marketplace.* New York: HarperBusiness, 1998. Network effects in fads and fashions, by a consultant who studies consumers as self-organizing agents.

Gleick, James. *Chaos: Making a New Science.* New York: Penguin, 1987. The granddaddy of popular works on this subject. Elegantly written, told as a tale. Still perhaps the best primer out there.

Goerner, Sally J. *Chaos and the Evolving Ecological Universe.* Amsterdam: Overseas Publishers Association, 1994. A highly ambitious attempt, mostly successful, at debunking Newtonian science and synthesizing chaos with psychology, economics, and other sciences. An excellent overview for the layman.

Goodwin, Brian. *How the Leopard Changed Its Spots: The Evolution of Complexity.* New York: Touchstone, 1994. How complexity science may explain the forms and structures of life.

Hall, Nina, ed. *Exploring Chaos: A Guide to the New Science of Disorder.* New York: W.W. Norton, 1991. A collection of essays originally appearing in *New Scientist* magazine, each investigation a specific application—chaos in engineering, chaos on the trading floor, etc.

Holland, John. *Hidden Order: How Adaptation Builds Complexity.* Reading, Mass.: Helix Books, 1995. A short, mostly readable investigation of complex adaptive systems by the father of the genetic algorithm.

Hurst, David K. *Crisis and Renewal: Meeting the Challenge of Organizational Change.* Boston: Harvard Business School Press, 1995. Fresh and insightful look at corporate change through the lens of complexity, enriched with revealing historical research.

Jervis, Robert. *System Effects: Complexity in Political and Social Life.* Princeton: Princeton University Press, 1997. How unintended consequences afflict the military, diplomacy, and governance. Highly detailed, richly anecdotal, clearly written.

Kauffman, Stuart. *At Home in the Universe: The Search for the Laws of Self-Organization and Complexity.* New York: Oxford University Press, 1995. A bit daunting in places, it goes further than many other books in exploring what complexity theory might mean for the future of economics and organizations. Kauffman's speculations on the origins of life are thrilling.

———. *The Origins of Order: Self-Organization and Selection in Evolution.* New York: Oxford University Press, 1993. Most goes way over my head, but if you want the unexpurgated science behind *At Home in the Universe,* it's all here.

Kelly, Kevin. *Out of Control: The New Biology of Machines, Social Systems, and the Economic World.* Reading, Mass.: Addison-Wesley, 1994. Great writing, great thinking from the executive editor of *Wired.* Every page a delight.

Khalil, Elias L., and Kenneth E. Boulting, eds. *Evolution, Order, and Complexity.* New York: Routledge, 1996. Fascinating collection of essays linking social and biological systems.

Krugman, Paul. *The Self-Organizing Economy.* Cambridge: Blackwell, 1996. Though the tone is pompous and the math gratuitously dense, this book provides a nice, brief overview of the potential relevance of complexity theory to a few macroeconomic issues.

Legge, John M. *Chaos Theory and Business Planning: How Great Effects Come from Small Causes.* Melbourne: Schwartz & Wilkinson, 1990. A rollicking and irreverent book, despite its businesslike title.

Levy, Steven. *Artificial Life.* New York: Pantheon, 1992. Engaging account of the work of John von Neumann, Chris Langton, and others in creating software that emulates the living.

Lewin, Roger. *Complexity: Life at the Edge of Chaos.* Macmillan, 1992. Has the virtue of being extremely basic, a great testament to the writer. Readers interested in the relevance of complexity theory to history and anthropology might consider starting here.

McMaster, Michael D. *The Intelligence Advantage: Organizing for Complexity.* Boston: Butterworth-Heinemann, 1996. Complexity applied to knowledge management by a veteran consultant who has seen a lot and knows a lot.

Merry, Uri. *Coping with Uncertainty: Insights from the New Sciences of Chaos, Self-Organization, and Complexity.* Westport, Conn.: Praeger Publishing, 1995. Extremely approachable overview.

Morgan, Gareth. *Images of Organization.* Thousand Oaks, Calif.: Sage Publications, 1997. Second edition of a work that was years ahead of its time. Explores the value of metaphor in viewing organizations, with emphasis on self-organization and biological systems.

Prigogine, Ilya. *The End of Certainty: Time, Chaos, and the New Laws of Nature.* New York: Free Press, 1996. Challenging math in spots but otherwise a short and rather elegant treatise on self-organization and the "arrow of time."

Prigogine, Ilya, and Isabelle Stengers. *Order Out of Chaos: Man's New Dialogue with Nature.* New York: Bantam Books, 1984. A compelling historical account of the limitations of Newtonian science and the dynamics of complexity by a Nobel laureate in chemistry, with an emphasis on thermodynamics and dissipative structures.

Rothschild, Michael. *Bionomics: Economy as Ecosystem.* New York: Henry Holt, 1990. Exceptional treatment of the metaphor, rich in history and layman's science.

Resnick, Mitchel. *Turtle, Termites, and Traffic Jams: Explorations in Massively Parallel Microworlds.* Cambridge: MIT Press, 1995. A concise look at how software simulates life.

Stacey, Ralph D. *Complexity and Creativity in Organizations.* San Francisco: Berrett-Koehler, 1996. A book that seems to take great pains in describing the obvious—until you realize that most organizations fail to pursue the obvious. Academic but thoughtful throughout.

Stewart, Ian. *Does God Play Dice? The Mathematics of Chaos.* Cambridge: Blackwell Publishers, 1989. It helps to bring some math to this book—I didn't, unfortunately—but it is a worthy overview mostly suitable for the layman.

Wheatley, Margaret J. *Leadership and the New Science: Learning About Organization from an Orderly Universe.* San Francisco: Berrett-Koehler, 1994. A very approachable if somewhat loose introduction to quantum mechanics and complexity theory with speculations about the relevance for organizations.

Wheatley, Margaret J., and Myron Kellner-Rogers. *a simpler way.* San Francisco: Berrett-Koehler, 1996. A prose poem describing the virtues of self-organization in social and economic life. Delightful photos.

von Bertalanffy, Ludwig. *General System Theory.* New York: George Braziller, 1968. Master tome by one of the fathers of cybernetics.

Waldrop, Mitchell. *Complexity: The Emerging Science at the Edge of Order and Chaos.* New York: Touchstone, 1992. A clear, cogent, and well-written overview of the origins of complexity theory through the eyes of the explorers.

Acknowledgments

I researched and wrote this book while working as a full-time weekly columnist for the *Wall Street Journal*. The book and the column each benefited greatly as a result, but I also know that these arrangements required some forbearance on the part of my newspaper editors. So I would like to express my most heartfelt gratitude to Mike Miller, Stephanie Capparell, Cathy Panagoulias, Barney Calame, Dan Hertzberg, and Jim Pensiero. I'd especially like to thank Paul Steiger, our managing editor, who was the first *Journal* editor to grasp the "Front Lines" concept, who played a huge role in shaping it, and who has been unstinting in his support of it. At a time of growing concern about the ethics and truthfulness of American journalism, it is comforting indeed to work in a news department that defines the epitome of integrity, a standard that begins with Paul.

Several of my *Journal* colleagues provided invaluable help and encouragement. They include Kevin Salwen, Guatam Naik, David Wessel, Patty Davis, Carol Hymowitz, Walt Mossberg, Gregg Zachary, Hal Lancaster, Sue Shellenbarger, and Cynthia Crossen. I would also like to thank the mentors who taught me most of what I know about journalism: George Getschow and Norman Pearlstine, formerly of the *Wall Street Journal*, and Tim Yovich of the *Youngstown Vindicator*.

Although it was my *Journal* reporting that first exposed me to the new ethos of business, I relied on the work of many great thinkers to make sense of what I was seeing. Michael Thomas of Ohio State University helped me understand the meaning of dialogue. Christopher Meyer of the Ernst & Young Center for Business Innovation invited my participation in his annual conference on Embracing Complexity. Curt Lindberg of VHA Incorporated drew me into a vibrant discussion about creating better organizations. The consultant Helen Harte helped me understand the problems in health care. Mildred Myers of Carnegie-Mellon University shared resources and ideas. The author David Hurst contributed much wisdom on leadership and planning.

I also owe a deep debt to many scientists, writers, and management thinkers whose originality and creativity vastly exceed anything I could ever hope to accomplish. They include Peter Senge of M.I.T., Kevin Kelly of *Wired* magazine, the author and consultant Margaret Wheatley, Yaneer Bar-Yam of the New England Complex Systems Institute, Matt Ridley of *The Economist,* Mihaly Csikszentmihalyi of the University of Chicago, the writing partnership of Roger Lewin and Birute Regine, the author and *New York Times Magazine* columnist James Gleick, Jeffrey Goldstein of Adelphi University, professors Gareth Morgan and Brenda Zimmerman of York University, the author Connie Barlow, the author Mitchell Waldrop, Robin Wood of Genesys Ltd., Michael Rothschild of the Bionomics Institute, Tim Fohl of Technology Integration Group, Michael McMaster of Knowledge-Based Development, and the consultants Mike Greene and Mike Hollister.

Four thinkers in particular—my personal Mount Rushmore—played an especially heavy role in helping to formulate my views. They are the ethicist and economist William Frederick, professor emeritus and former dean of the University of Pittsburgh School of Business; the molecular biologist Stuart Kauffman of Bios Group and the Santa Fe Institute; Fritz Dressler, a consultant in Alameda, California; and the financial economist Mark White of White & Associates in Mexico City.

For most of the time I was writing this book I used two Internet mail lists as sources of knowledge and as testing grounds for my own ideas. The operators of these lists contribute an incredible amount of time and energy while receiving nothing in return but the awareness that they are helping others learn. Many thanks to Michael Lissack of the Complexity-in-Management list and Rick Karash of the Learning Organization list, as well as to the members of each who give so freely of their ideas and opinions.

Although I have learned something from every business person named in this book, a few had an especially important role in helping me understand the new world of business. They include Bill Fulkerson of Deere & Co., June Holley of ACEnet, David Isenberg of isen.com, Charles Koch of Koch Industries,

Fernando Flores and Ken Massey of Business Design Associates, Gary Schneider of AgDecision Resources, the Year 2000 consultant David Eddy, Saul Pilnick and Jo Ellen Gabel of Human Systems Inc., and Ray Anderson of Interface Incorporated.

No one played a bigger role in helping me shape this book than Frederic Hills of Simon & Schuster, one of the great deans of book editing. Indeed this book was his idea. Fred recognized that the changes sweeping business were far more fundamental than most business books had captured; I am humbled that he called on me to document the revolution. Fred is a demanding and exacting editor. He is also a great humanist and gentleman. In addition, I thank Victoria Meyer, Marie Florio, and Priscilla Holmes of Simon & Schuster, as well as Hilary Black, formerly of the company, and copyeditor Anne T. Keene.

Many friends and colleagues donated precious time to read all or part of this manuscript, offering suggestions and improvements too numerous to count. (Let the record also show that a couple of my readers disagreed with some of my arguments and analysis.) My deepest appreciation to Bill Frederick of Pitt, Ken Baskin of Life Design Partners, Mark White of White & Associates, George Anders and David Wessel of the *Wall Street Journal*, Ben Rafoth of Indiana University of Pennsylvania, T.J. McCue of Innovative Marketing, Chris Long of United Press International, Harry Van Buren of Pitt and Steve Cabana of Whole Systems Associates. My wife, Paulette Thomas, suffered through all of the earliest and ugliest drafts, while my mother, Jean M. Petzinger, the toughest copyeditor I know, found lapses that no one else would have discovered.

Speaking of family, mine contributed to this book in another vital way. Most of my kin are entrepreneurs. My father, Thomas Petzinger Sr., and my brother, Charles Petzinger, operate a successful travel agency. My sister, Elizabeth Holter, and her husband, Stephen Holter, run a private education business. My in-laws have long succeeded in a couple of the toughest businesses anywhere— Debra and Joe Millard in the restaurant industry and Brian Thomas in professional music. Each of them has shown me over and over, for years and years, that a commitment to quality and integrity always, in the end, pays off. Thanks too to my father and my mother-in-law, Betty Thomas, for creating havens from distraction as deadline pressures loomed.

My agent, Alice Fried Martell, has been with me for fourteen years. I honestly can't imagine writing a book without her handling the business details and providing the encouragement. She is also a model of integrity and a wonderful friend besides.

I thank my children, Beatrice, Eva, and Janis, for their inspiration and understanding. And I thank Paulette for more than I could ever put into words.

Index

DATE DUE			
JUL 5 2000			
JUN 2 2 2010			